ALL AT SEA

And Ticked Off with a God Who Went

IN

AWOL When I Need Him the Most

TALLAHASSEE

<< >>

Joséphine Christel

<< >>

www.bookstandpublishing.com

Published by
Bookstand Publishing
Morgan Hill, CA 95037
4322_7

ISBN 978-1-63498-196-5

For AMR, OWW, SNW, and
"JMag," as well as the yet-to-come
children that my daughter and my son will, I presume,
bring into this world. And the ones that
they will hopefully adopt.

<< >>

May you be blessed with the gifts of
brainpower, determination, and foresight. The
brainpower to learn to solve your own problems, the
determination to overcome the inner and outer obstacles
that will try to impede your ability to reach your
potential, and the foresight to not repeat
the avoidable mistakes of those
who came before you.

This book
is also dedicated to
all the street children of Haiti.

<< >>

May you be blessed with the
desire, the acumen, and the means
to ultimately turn your dismal conditions
into a catalyst that will set in motion the birth of a
functional, self-sufficient, and more benevolent society.

<< >>

AUTHOR'S MEA CULPA

<< >>

To all the hypocrites who will no doubt reprehend me for some of the controversial statements that are embedded throughout this book (yet view themselves as nice and non-judgmental), it would be fair to read the entire book before you go on vilifying me. It is also my hope that you won't waste any of your precious time waiting for the phony apology that is nowadays required from those of us who dare to say in public while most of you say in private.

To the hordes of religion experts who will surely be offended by this book, please bear in mind that I am merely expressing my opinions about the divine and the not-so-divine, not my facts. After all, only God has the facts. And to all the gramar police who had the missfortune to to pick up this book, Please be a-ware that youre going to grind your teeth—a lot.

Needless to say that in an attempt to protect myself from a group of people who are always on the lookout for a buck that they didn't earn, most names, many specifying characteristics and some dates have been altered. I deliberately chose to stand by the naked truth, though, by not going out of my way to conceal the identity of the baldheaded monster.

<< >>

AUTHOR'S NOTE

<< >>

In light of the sexual harassment scandal that erupted at The Shelter in February 2013, it's worth pointing out that this book was essentially completed in the early months of 2012, and had, therefore, not been influenced, much less inspired, by any of the accusations (real and imagined) that brought down the curtain on the Mel era.

For readers outside of Tallahassee who are clueless on this highly engrossing saga, please see the Tallahassee Democrat's March 30, 2013 front-page article headlined "Former Shelter director Mel Eby felt forced into retirement."

<< >>

ACKNOWLEDGMENTS

<< >>

Without access to at least one of the following libraries approximately 355 days a year, and the 7 a.m. Mass at the nearest Catholic Church, I would have assuredly gone insane my first few years at The Shelter.

(1) LEROY COLLINS LEON COUNTY PUBLIC LIBRARY where I printed tons of newspaper articles on a daily basis, flagrantly violating the "PLEASE LIMIT PRINTING TO 10 PAGES" policy, and where this book was printed in its entirety more than a few times. (Yes, I do plan to make a sizable donation in due time.) I would also like to thank my two favorite librarians, Sally and Susie, for treating me with kindness and respect the whole time—even when I was caught printing more than ten pages.

(2) STROZIER LIBRARY where the first draft of this book (more than six-hundred pages) was meticulously written between December 2007 and July 2008, and where this book was rewritten over a dozen times in 2009 and 2010. A special thanks to Ashley, Nicole, and Will (William Salkin) for making my formerly-dreaded-but-always-awkward morning experience at the entrance desk so pleasant.

(3) COLEMAN LIBRARY where this book literally went through weight loss surgery in the fall of 2008. The first rounds of edits were also done at Coleman in 2011 and 2012. Hello, Anthony Brunson. Hello, Angel Logan . . . of course, you did look familiar. Too familiar. (I met Angel when she came to volunteer at The Shelter one evening, but denied knowing her when I later saw her on campus.)

(4) TCC LIBRARY, which provided me with a great place to hide during my first year at The Shelter until word got around that a school ID, known in Shelter parlance as a free bus pass for an entire semester, is given to anyone who registers for GED classes, even if you only show up for class a handful of times.

(5) CO-CATHEDRAL OF ST. THOMAS MORE for giving me a sanctuary to escape to every morning. I wish that I didn't remain a mere spectator from start to finish, but I've never been good at pretending to be who I am not, in spite of my great fascination with the lives of the saints.

I am also grateful (sort of) to have crossed paths with many of "The Shameless." They have taught me more about certain issues than I could have ever learned in a classroom, or on a job.

Spring 2012
Tallahassee, Florida

<< >>

ACKNOWLEDGMENTS (2)

<< >>

Some appreciation goes to Peter, Tommy, Sammy, Jake (Jacob Reiter) and Mr. Hightower, five current Shelter staff, for not showing me any blatant disrespect over the years. Deepest appreciation to my favorite culinary artist, Rashad Amin, for bringing me much joy at least twice a week through his cooking. And to the megalomaniac Shelter staff who once ordered me to "Go get your stuff and get out of the building!" because of my reluctance to go wait for breakfast in the dining room from hell in the company of *The Loud & The Shameless,* I have this to say:

- I apologize for my unwillingness and inability to shower you with the kind of absolute obedience that you seem to expect from the homeless, but stroking overblown egos has never been one of my fortes.

- You may want to improve your people skills if you intend to stay in this line of work.

- At the risk of knocking you off your high horse all over again, I do feel obligated to add that someday, when you eventually grow up, you will have to agree with me that SHELTER POWER IS NO POWER.

Fall 2012
Tallahassee, Florida

<< >>

ACKNOWLEDGMENTS (3)

<< >>

Warmhearted thanks to Deacon Jeannie from Grace Mission Episcopal Church for not flinching when I told her that God's actions mean more to me than God's words, for offering to pray on my behalf when I did eventually lose faith in the power of prayers, and for understanding why seven years at The Shelter literally feels like an eternity in hell. Thanks are also due to a certain "Mr. Professor" I met in the spring of 2012 for being such an effective antidepressant during the most disillusioned year of my life, in spite of his own issues. And for being the first person to read (and hate) this book.

Spring 2013
Tallahassee, Florida

<< >>

ACKNOWLEDGMENTS (4)

<< >>

I also owe a debt of gratitude to the Glenarden Branch Library where the last major changes in this book were made, to Prince George's Community College where I was able to print for free, even though I haven't been a PGCC student in what now seems like a lifetime ago, and to the two guardian angels at the *House of Terror* who put a smile on my face and gave me a reason to get up in the morning for an entire year post-Shelter.

Spring 2014
P.G. County, Maryland

<< >>

ACKNOWLEDGMENTS (5)

<< >>

I will forever be grateful to the following women, whom I met at the Rescue Mission in Santa Barbara, California, for providing me with the opportunity to earn the income that permitted me to self-publish this book.

Shannon (Sarah) Townsend
Jill Wallerstedt

Summer 2015
Harpers Ferry, West Virginia

<< >>

FINAL ACKNOWLEDGMENT/AFFIRMATION

<< >>

My deepest gratitude undoubtedly goes to the omnipotent Creator of all for delivering me from my everlasting living hell, albeit dilatorily, and for giving me a credible leg to stand on when glorifying His name.

Date & Place TBD as of October 6, 2015

12:04 p.m. – She just got off the phone and the music in the living room is blaring at full volume once again, worsening my headache. The caller must have inquired about me at some point, I suppose, which prompted her to scathingly reply, "The woman is so weird." As she went on to elaborate on her plan to walk away from the apartment if I don't leave, she then made it perfectly clear that she didn't have an iota of respect for the child that I had become, that she should not be responsible for my poor choices, and that she couldn't wait to see me go. Who knew that a lifelong pursuit of emotional healing and spiritual fulfillment could turn out to be such a soul-crushing adventure?

2:16 p.m. – Sitting on the second floor balcony of apartment 6 after I had to go down to the parking lot to retrieve some of my belongings, and wondering if the few neighbors who are seemingly home at the moment have heard anything or, worse, seen anything. Cannot believe that I've become such a failure in all areas of my life, a burden to my children, an embarrassment to my mother, and surely the laughingstock of my former circle of friends. In truth, I can't even believe that I am in Tallahassee, a city I've never heard of until a few years ago, in a state I never wanted to be a resident of for a variety of reasons. Dear God, do you have any idea how utterly exhausted I am? Do you even care?

2:27 p.m. – "You might need this," I was just told after she threw open the apartment door to hand me my cell phone, which must have fallen off my backpack during the fracas. Supremely aware of her newly acquired power, she then added, "I would hurry to find a place to go if I were you. Today you're officially homeless." It took every ounce of self-control I could muster not to burst into hysterical laughter. Didn't I become officially homeless shortly before noon on May 27, 2003 when a P.G. County sheriff had knocked on my front door at 2900 Upshur Street and kindly asked me: "Do you know what today is?" I should have killed myself in New York City two years ago when I had the momentum.

10:06 p.m. – She just drove away, in all likelihood on her way to the nearest convenience store. The old adage about the apple and the tree turned out to be much more than a cliché, that's for sure. "Please don't let me come back and find you inside my apartment," she warned without a glance in my direction while double-locking the door. "I have nowhere to go," I mumbled, almost involuntarily. "That sounds to me like a person with a problem," she came back with calmly, chillingly, as she swaggered toward her car. Do I need to add that I've been back on the balcony since before 6 o'clock, waiting for JP to come home, and that I am itching all over from mosquito bites? Life is a gift, all right. A gift from hell.

Grateful that my eyes remained relatively dry while I underwent the registration process at The Shelter, 480 West Tennessee Street, Tallahassee, Florida, even though my heart was broken beyond repair and my spirit was on its knees and weeping. Grateful that the homeless men and women at The Shelter have separate quarters and even use different entrances because I got the jitters just from glancing at the two bums who were standing at the foot of the driveway when I arrived at 4:30 for the 5 p.m. check-in. Grateful that I didn't get physically ill at the thought of sleeping in a homeless shelter. Still, my stomach has been queasy all day and my chest can't stop cramping.

Grateful for the $23 a discombobulated JP practically threw at me around 12:30 this morning when his roommate ordered him to get inside the apartment because she needed to make sure that the security chain was on before going to bed. Grateful that the LeRoy Collins Leon County Public Library, simply known as the main library, and The Park Avenue Chain of Parks are located just a few blocks away from The Shelter, which is where I ended up spending the day. Grateful I was able to spend the night in the back seat of JP's roommate's car since she had left her doors unlocked, again, and I was fairly confident that she wouldn't come out of the apartment until 8 a.m. Grateful that I didn't have to drag behind me all day a carry-on filled with journals and books because JP did agree to take my possessions back into his bedroom, in spite of his roommate's objections.

Grateful that bed 6, the top bunk I was assigned to in the "front room," is positioned near a lighted stairwell, which allows me to keep writing even after the lights went out after 9 p.m. Grateful that there are no double-bunks on my right, only one on my left, and that the other two bunks are placed several feet away across the room. Grateful that Louvern, the green-eyed brunette from Georgia who sleeps in bed 8, the top bunk two feet away, seems quite nice even though I already formed an opinion of her after I heard her say that smoking pot and drinking beers are what her family and friends do for fun (and at funerals), and that her plan is to get high until she pees on herself the day she leaves The Shelter. Grateful that the private bathroom inside the women's dining room is about fifteen feet on my right because I can't picture myself using what the women call "the big bathroom," despite its entrance being just a few feet on my left. Grateful that the homeless shelter experience hasn't been as traumatic as I anticipated so far. The sleeping area is tolerably clean, and while the women appear to be rambunctious at first sight they do not smell.

Grateful that just for this moment, my desire to do your will, God, is much bigger than my overly bruised ego.

Today is JP's birthday. It hurts that I am so ashamed of who I have become that I debated with myself whether I should even call him. It hurts that when I did finally call him, he did not propose to get together for lunch with the woman who had brought him into this world. Partly because he has been behaving somewhat strangely around me even before his roommate threw me out, but mostly because he's so wrapped up around the little finger of a girl he only met five months ago. It hurts that he's on his feet six to eight hours five days a week earning a living as a waiter when he should be in college full-time preparing for a better future. It hurts that he's only taking one class at TCC (Tallahassee Community College) because he's not eligible for financial aid since I wasn't able to provide TCC with my tax information and the state of Florida doesn't grant independent status to a student unless he or she is twenty-four, married, a ward of the court or an orphan. In plain English, I would have been a more valuable asset to my son if I were dead.

Cannot believe that I forgot to stop at CVS to buy a pack of earplugs considering that I barely got a total of ten hours of sleep the past three nights. As per schedule, a Shelter staff came up to turn off the TV in the dining room around 11:30, yet I am wide awake twenty minutes later because I've simply been unable to fall asleep in this anxiety-provoking place until I literally pass out from sheer exhaustion. Louvern, for one, snores so loudly that it boggles the mind that a fellow human being could emit such monstrous sounds, much less a member of my own gender. And who could have thought that Lavermine, the older black woman who sleeps below me in bed 5, can be as malefic in her sleep as she is in her waking hours. In the meantime, bathroom doors are being slammed, toilets are being flushed and loud conversations are still taking place in the big bathroom, which turns out to be the women's second favorite hangout outside of the dining room. What on earth did I get myself into in my determination to remain faithful to God in good times and bad times?

Cannot believe that I got reprimanded by Mr. Jejune, the most capricious Shelter staff I've met so far, perhaps because he is as indiscriminate in his bantering as he is in his belittlement, for being on the phone with Lulu. I tried to explain that no one told me that the use of cell phones was prohibited inside The Shelter, but he wasn't willing to listen. Do I regret having taken the call? No. As expected, Lulu was aghast when I told her that I was staying in a homeless shelter. As I also expected, she unhesitatingly asked me to "come back home" and even took it for granted that her husband would not mind sharing their two-bedroom apartment with me and that their daughter, Patoutou, would be thrilled to have me around. I politely declined because I've learned from experience that the quickest way to damage a good relationship with family and friends is to lose one's home and move in with them. Besides, it's too painful to go back to the Washington, D.C., area the same way I left three years ago.

Cannot believe that Patoutou's birthday is coming up and I can't afford to mail her a gift. I do not understand why this child and her mother were placed on my path soon after her birth just so I could become an encumbrance to them four years later. I think I need to start considering the possibility that my expectations of God may indeed be too high and that I may have to adjust them for my own sanity, if nothing else. Do I need to add that I feel like a fool for expecting so much from a being who has been ignoring me most of my life?

And I definitely cannot believe that Mr. HornyBoy, the Shelter staff who filled out my registration card the day I came in, woke me up around 5 a.m. so that he could compliment me on my good looks, query about my marital status and express his desire to get to know me better, preferably with my clothes off. I actually like the guy, though knowing what I know now I can't help but wonder if he's simply a lonely young man looking for a mother figure, or a smooth-talking sexual predator in search of a new prey.

In bed 6 with a sheet over my head in a desperate attempt to create a semblance of privacy while most of the women are in the dining room doing what they do best as they wait for dinner: alternately cussing out each other, laughing out loud, and reflecting on the glorious day they had drinking, drugging, arguing, visiting friends in jail, reporting to their probation officers, and hanging out with their "husbands" in The Shelter's back yard. Meanwhile, I have so much on my mind I don't quite know where to start.

(1) Nightmare and resentment – This morning's nightmare was to find my blue notebook on the floor between the two bunks when I woke up around 3 a.m. to use the bathroom. I still shudder at the thought of what Lavermine, otherwise known as Shelterqueen, would have done if she was the one who found it. Still, I managed to go back to sleep and even woke up two hours later with a speck of serenity until I showed up in apartment 6 around 10 o'clock and found out that JP's girlfriend has, in essence, moved in. The memory of JP saying nothing to his roommate the day she kicked me out rushed back to mind at once, and I instantly convinced myself that the only reason he didn't insist that the apartment was half his and that I had the right to be there as his guest is because he, too, wanted me out. He later told me that Angie was only staying with

him temporarily because she had to move out of her dorm and opted to stay in Tallahassee until she leaves for her summer internship, but I still feel as if I've been thrown out of his apartment twice.

(2) Hope and nothingness – Watching the story on the 12 o'clock news of a ninety-year-old Florida woman who is retiring after sixty-nine years of teaching rekindled the hope that I too will have plenty of opportunities to be of use to society in the future. Yet all it took for me to feel completely useless a few hours later was for Caren, a friend of Louvern, to ask if I had a job and for me to be reminded that DOING NOTHING has become a chief characteristic of mine since I arrived in Florida last October, and the main reason I was asked to move out of apartment 6 (in conjunction with my suppositional point blank refusal to stop cleaning the living room.) Anyhow, Caren then suggested that I leave The Shelter with her at 5:15 tomorrow morning to go apply for a job since the company she works for is looking for more people. I told her that I'll think about it because I didn't have the nerve to blurt out that I had no interest in doing day labor now or ever. Yet, Dear God, how much longer can I continue to do nothing while I wait to be remunerated for work that I have already done for you?

Have more to say, but I am too dispirited to go on. Someone from the adjacent family section just yelled, "Smoke break. Smoke them if you got them!" Lavermine stepped out of the dining room in a flash, stopped long enough at her bed to grab her purse and turning to Louvern, she gushed, "Girl, let's go get cancer!" Dana Reeve immediately came to mind, as they exploded with laughter and made a dash for the back door. How is it possible that a woman who had everything to live for, contributed so much to the world and accepted her fate with such grace died of lung cancer at the age of 44 when she wasn't even a smoker while Shelterqueen and her kind are enjoying carefree living at the expense of others?

The walking definition of parental failure is how I felt this morning after I noticed a large number of cars on the streets of Tallahassee packed with boxes, suitcases, computers, ironing boards, comforters, pillows and everything in between. Spent the remaining of the day wishing that my children, too, were full-time students with a home to go to during school breaks, and fuming over their father's perplexing disinclination to help finance their college education, despite his six-figure income. And speaking of income, Louvern, who works at one of the fast food restaurants around The Shelter, spent the past few minutes praising her friend Jaklyn for all the money Jaklyn made today picking up trash from a pond ($60). How will they ever be able to pull themselves out of poverty working minimum-wage jobs, I automatically wondered. My life would have been so much happier if I only knew how to mind my own business. Can hear a woman shit in the big bathroom as I write this. Going to put the earplugs on and call it a day.

PS: I just reread the text message JP sent, promising to part ways with his roommate at the end of their lease. Am I counting on my twenty-year-old son to support me financially? No. But, it's good to know that he cares.

Delusion du jour: To win the $12 million Florida Lotto jackpot tonight and use the first annuity payment to send JP to film school (notwithstanding my hope that he will change his mind and become a schoolteacher given his potential to be a good role model for underprivileged boys), pay for my daughter's tuition for the next school year, give Lulu the down payment for a house, and, most important, pay off my debts and regain my dignity in the eyes of society. The reality is that I've been feeling so hopeless that I didn't even bother to waste another dollar on false hope.

Delight du jour: Spending nearly two hours at the Barnes & Noble in Tallahassee Mall, browsing through books and magazines. To my great surprise, *The Gospel of Judas* is already on the best-seller list. And while a part of me is highly amused at the thought that Judas Iscariot could have been a hero who actually helped Christ fulfill his destiny, another part of me can't help thinking that the whole thing is just another wild tale whose objective is to add more confusion to a bewildered world.

Aggravation du jour: Having to explain to Caren that I can't work as a flagger because I get dizzy if I spend too much time under the sun. She snidely replied that she didn't think she could do it either, but that it was "the only game in town." In other words, I am a good-for-nothing leech even from the standpoint of a shameless woman who does, in fact, wake up every morning to go to work, but only because she must support her addiction to hard liquor, nicotine, and thrift stores.

Discomfort du jour: Hearing Louvern tell Jaklyn that I was a writer. I don't know how they got on the subject since I wasn't paying attention to them until my name came up, but I still feel unreasonably exposed hours later because (a) I never told Louvern I was a writer and (b) being a writer is not exactly something that I am proud to be.

Ordeal du jour: Standing in line with a group of evil-smelling homeless men to get breakfast at the Haven of Rest Rescue Mission, a second homeless shelter almost right next to The Shelter where the all-male residents pay a small fee to spend the night.

Anxiety du jour: No control over what and when I eat. Dear God, do I need to remind you that I have some serious issues with food, which require me to plan my meals in advance and to avoid eating certain things?

On my way back to The Shelter from the main library and I am currently sitting on the front steps of Bethel Missionary Baptist Church, one of the churches I visited this morning since the buses don't start running until noon on Sundays and the main library isn't open until 1 p.m. Cried on and off all day, and I am still crying. I just cannot accept that the life I turned over to God when I joined OA (Overeaters Anonymous) on January 31, 1995 is going from bad to worse and there isn't a thing I can do about it. And a $6 an hour job on Tallahassee's streets is not going to solve my problems, nor will any other job that I am qualified to do in the eyes of man. While suicide is no longer an option, there is no denying that I would have been better off dead.

Exhausted beyond words and no desire to write, but I will not be able to fall asleep if I don't force myself to record the following:

- Had another too-close-for-comfort encounter with Mr. HornyBoy while I walked through The Shelter's kitchen around 6:30 this morning after another sleepless night. (I can still hear them yap at all hours, in spite of the earplugs. I just don't hear their footsteps, the toilets being flushed, the constant creaking of mattresses and the snoring chorus.) In any case, I managed to avoid kissing Mr. HornyBoy or being kissed by him, as he requested, but he caught me off guard when he opened up his arms on a whim and pulled me in for a hug. And it definitely didn't help that after he asked if I was okay, and I sourly answered that I'll be okay once I leave The Shelter, he tried to soothe me by recommending that I make The Shelter my home because "at least it's free rent." I don't recall what I told him word for word, but it was something along the lines of, "We may not have much where I come from, but we do have pride. I don't want free rent."

- "I am drunk. I feel good. Don't hate!" Lavermine quipped when she sashayed into the dining room shortly after 7 p.m. Their reaction? Laughter. And more laughter. I've never been around a group of so many cheerful women my whole life, and I clearly had no idea that so much fun could be had in a homeless shelter. And when one of the women shared that she drank half a pint of whisky and two cans of beer all by herself this afternoon, Lavermine's smile grew even bigger, "Oh girl, you're good. You're really good!" Dear God, do you have any idea what it feels like to be locked up fifteen hours a day in a windowless room with these shameless women?

- I guess the best thing that happened to me today is that I finally joined The Shelter's elite group of "Reserved Beds," meaning that from now on I can stay out until the last check-in at 7 p.m. and not worry that bed 6 will be given to someone else, or that I will end up spending the night two feet away from a loony. Though to be fair, the women who are visibly insane in this hellhole behave much better than the ones who are not. Louvern said that I am lucky because people usually have to wait fifteen days to get a reserved bed and a locker. Whatever.

- Attended the 7 a.m. Mass at the Co-Cathedral of St. Thomas More (STM), rather than wait for Shelter breakfast at 7:30. The priest, coincidentally, encouraged the parishioners to avoid working "for food that perishes," and I sat there thinking that I did just that and ended up in a homeless shelter as a reward. Needless to say that I also felt very much out of place during the communion service when all the God-fearing people stood up one by one to go receive the body of Christ while I, the bald-faced sinner, remained on my knees in a back pew.

- And because the glutton in me is already on pins and needles over the odds of starving to death at The Shelter, I used the $8 that I had left to buy a jar of peanut butter and a box of crackers although sneaking food in The Shelter is against the rules and will get me "put out," if caught. "Put out," by the way, is the most popular verb in the vocabulary of Shelter staff. Perhaps because it's the only menace that is taken seriously by, let's call them by their proper name, The Shameless.

6:04 a.m. – I am so depressed I don't want to get out of bed, but since all "Shelter guests" must be out of The Shelter by 8:30 rain or shine, I might as well go to church again before the real insanity begins once the lights go back on at seven. In passing, eighteen-year-old Ninabelle has been shooting off her mouth since before 5:30, and is currently hashing over her plan to spend the upcoming weekend at a local motel. It's hard to believe that women living in a homeless shelter spend so much time talking about sex; it's harder to believe that they luxuriate in weekend getaways. Ninabelle is the youngest woman at The Shelter who, from what I gathered, left her parent's home in Mississipi a year ago to move in with a guy in Tallahassee and ended up at The Shelter after they both got in trouble for beating up on each other and some other stuff. "Get the hell out of my fucking face," Ninabelle just barked after a woman who was coming out of the big bathroom told her that it was much too early for all that commotion. Time to hit the road. The madness has already begun.

2:46 p.m. – I forgot to record this morning that the main reason I woke up feeling so disoriented is because I had the usual recurring dreams about my failed relationships and my lousy credit report. Moreover, I just came from apartment 6 and JP seemed so tormented by my presence that for the first time in my life I didn't know how to comport myself around him so I didn't stay long, even though I had gone there initially with the intention to get my laundry done. And where am I at the moment? On a bench at the E. Peck Greene Park, the little park right behind the main library, part of The Chain of Parks, pretending to be thoroughly absorbed in the book on my lap when my head is so full of doubts I can hardly process my thoughts, much less comprehend the message Og Mandino is trying to convey in *The Greatest Salesman in the World*. Dear God, I know you know that I have great faith in you. I hope you also know that to keep trusting you when I have no confirming evidence to back me up is downright torturous.

7:17 p.m. – "If I don't get to take my pills, I am not going to be able to do my work," a grumpy Louvern just whined to herself for the second time. She's not feeling well and was alarmed at the thought that the nurse may have left while she took a pre-dinner nap. "Lavermine, I ain't in the mood for you tonight. Take a pill! No, take a swing of your bottle," another woman hollered as I wrote the above after Shelterqueen launched a verbal attack on her for standing too close to bed 5 while the woman waits to see the nurse. (The nurse's office is located in a walk-in closet by the entrance of the dining room.) "I take two nut pills but the rest is medical," Kichelle, the morbidly obese blonde in bed 1, said almost proudly earlier as she discussed her health issues with another woman. The bottom line: The Shameless are in love with their pills just like everyone else, and *Out of the Trenches* (OOTT) painfully comes to mind every time they deem it necessary to express that love, which is basically every night since most of them swear that they cannot fall asleep without their sleeping aids. I wish I could accept that I wasted four years of my life on a book that wasn't going to be of use to anyone, but I can't.

Cake was not only served with dinner, cake is being served, again. "Would you like a piece of cake?" one of the church ladies just asked on her way back downstairs. (Cooked meals are donated to The Shelter mostly by local churches.) "No thank you," I said. The truth? I not only want a piece of cake, I want an entire cake. Recovering drug addicts and alcoholics have it so much easier; at least they don't have to come in contact with their drug of choice daily. Incidentally, I made the mistake to check in early and ended up wasting over an hour talking to Louvern after she caught me staring when I heard her ask Jaklyn, "Why would you want to look like a black woman?" Jaklyn, a cute chubby blonde from San Diego, got her hair braided to titillate the black degenerate that she's dating while she waits for the white degenerate she's about to marry to come out of jail. Louvern later avowed that her concerns over sleeping next to me have been assuaged now that she knows that we can discuss race relations without me getting offended. I told her that I am exceptionally thankful for my inherent ability to easily tackle topics that most people are too afraid to contemplate. I chose not to tell her that the main reason I am able to remain unperturbed and unscarred in the presence of racism, overt or covert, is because on the basis of my personal relationship with you, God, I am deep inside more resilient and more self-assured than she'll ever be on the basis of her skin color alone.

Grateful that Chaim Potok's 1967 novel, *The Chosen*, which I found on a small bookshelf next to the emergency door across from bed 6, managed to keep my mind off my gloominess all day. Also grateful to have received a letter from Lulu. The $25 she sent will enable me to buy another weekly bus pass since the one JP gave me is about to expire, and more peanut butter and crackers. But I must decline the invitation to move in with her once again even though it is very much appreciated.

Grateful that Tallahassee is a college town with two major universities, Florida State University (FSU) and Florida A&M University (FAMU), in addition to the community college, which means that I don't have to be stuck at the main library or at The Chain of Parks all day. Though I don't plan to spend any time on FAMU campus since Lavermine claims that she used to socialize with very educated people in her heydays and that she often goes to FAMU to visit old friends. (I later found out that she merely rides one of the city buses that goes through FAMU campus on her way "across town" every morning, but I am getting ahead of myself.) Meanwhile, I spent this morning on a bench in front of FSU's newly built College of Medicine, and this afternoon at the main library since I am determined to stick with the decision to wean myself from apartment 6.

Grateful I was able to hand wash the dress I wore today and found a way to let it dry right on bed 6 without attracting the attention of anyone, a major accomplishment considering that the hand washing of clothes is also a no-no. Another rule no one told me about, but that didn't stop Shelterqueen from reporting me to Mr. ShelterDrillSergeant, The Shelter's manager, after she caught me hanging a wet dress on the front rail of bed 6 the other night. Mr. ShelterDrillSergeant was quick to point out that I can get my laundry done once a week if I put my name on the laundry list during the 5 p.m. check-in, and I didn't have the gall to tell him that the mere thought of turning my clothes over to Shelter staff to be washed along with everyone else's makes my stomach turn. Nor did I mention how Louvern recently scared the hell out of me when she forecasted that Lizzie Licehead, a mentally ill older woman from the back room whose scalp has started to bleed from a lice infestation, is going to spread lice to all of us sooner or later because the water in The Shelter's washing machine is probably not hot enough to kill lice. It later occurred to me that the lice from Lizzie Licehead's bedding and clothes could by no means survive thirty minutes in a hot dryer, but that still didn't stop me from itching all over.

Astonishment du jour: Learning that there are some people in this country whose primary pastime is to travel from one homeless shelter to the next while collecting government checks. And, no, they are not war veterans suffering from PTSD.

Observation du jour: That Mr. ShelterDrillSergeant speaks to all the women in the same tone of voice. It's not really what he says that riles me; it's the way he says it. But then again, if you think like trash, talk like trash, and behave like trash, maybe you shouldn't be too surprised if you're mistaken for trash.

Discovery du jour: That *The Chosen* belongs to Sabine, bed 3, not to The Shelter. Sabine, a Buddhist who later converted to Christianity through marriage, sleeps on the bottom bunk next to Kichelle's and is the third Asian woman in the room. She is also one of the most knowledgeable human beings I've ever met, and speaks fluent French to my delight.

Gratitude du jour: For a fairly quiet atmosphere at The Shelter this evening. I didn't even think it was possible not to be buried in an avalanche of chaos in this place at all times. Louvern told me to enjoy it while I can because it's the first weekend of the month and many of "the natives," go spend their "crazy checks" on motel rooms, but that they will all be back on Sunday.

Enjoyment du jour: The ability to watch *20/20*, in spite of learning nothing new from their special on real estate, since the women who usually stay in the dining room to watch BET or Lifetime either didn't check in, or went to bed right after the 9:30 smoke break. And because I had never spent time in The Shelter's dining room before, I felt compelled to place a folded sheet on the chair before I sat down. God, please help me be humble. Though with the benefit of hindsight, maybe it was you who gave me the wisdom not to sit on Shelter chairs without any protection.

Joke du jour: Being told by Lavermine who is noticeably in a better mood, perhaps because she's not high or drunk, that I should write a book after she heard me discuss a few current issues with Louvern. I was so stunned I don't recall what I said in reply. She also apologized for giving me "an attitude" since I got here because she now knows that I am a nice person who doesn't deserve any attitude from anyone. "I am not as bad as people make me out to be," she confided, adding that the women at The Shelter are so mean that she had to make some radical changes to her personality in order to survive. I was told by Louvern that most Shelter guests don't last a week in bed 6 because of Lavermine, and that a woman once cried her eyes out and begged Shelter staff to let her sleep on a rollaway in the dining room when she was assigned to bed 6. Her true nature will come to light in the course of time, I surmise.

Woke up with Mother Teresa in mind and a sincere desire to get acquainted with the virtue of humility after I spent several hours yesterday reading *Mother Teresa: Her Essential Wisdom*, and recording some of her most uplifting quotes in my notebook. My desire to ultimately become one of the most humble beings who ever walked the face of the earth began to waver when I was asked to smile for the camera by Pastor Eric whose church sponsors the "Frenchtown Breakfast in the Park" at the Haven of Rest on

Saturdays, and my first thought was: *Just one more reminder that there is no such thing as a free breakfast.* Followed by: *I don't recall reading any account of the Son of God smiling while carrying his cross, then why do his followers expect lesser mortals to be joyous on their own Golgotha walk?* And any trace of humility I may have acquired through osmosis totally vanished after I decided to give humility another shot by attempting to confront my fear of homeless men through making eye contact with some of them on my way out of the Haven of Rest. The three or four men I locked eyes with erroneously assumed that I was trying to pick them up. One even got out of line, walked up to me and said, "We really need to talk. Wait for me at the gate!" And it was crystal clear that Jesus is not what he had in mind. Dear God, please help me remember that Mother Teresa was shielded by a nun habit, and by the huge umbrella of the Catholic Church, which made it easier for her to deal with the vultures of this world. Besides, I have no business chasing virtues. Especially the ones I apparently was not destined to have.

7:19 a.m. – Sitting in a pew at Bethel with nerves so raw my hands are shaking. To sum up, I didn't fall asleep until after 1 a.m., then came very close from having a full-blown panic attack when I woke up around 3:30 with heart racing and the horrifying feeling that I was going to be trapped at The Shelter till the end of time. And for what seemed like an eternity, though it could not have been more than two minutes, I just wanted to scream bloody murder while I told myself that I had unmistakably lapsed into psychosis. I did eventually calm down through drumming into my head that I needed to get a grip before my fear of being homeless forever literally sends me over the edge, and even went back to sleep. Only to be jolted awake at 6:52 by Mr. Grouch, the Shelter staff who usually works the overnight weekend shifts, yelling, "Rise and shine, ladies, rise and shine!" The madness inevitably began the moment the lights went back on, and to save my sanity I just about fled The Shelter four minutes later and ended up brushing my hair on my way to Bethel and washing up in their restroom. Did I mention that my ears constantly itch because of the earplugs? And, yes, I already immersed myself into the vortex of fretfulness over the likelihood of another panic attack.

9:23 p.m. – Spent the last hour chatting with Louvern, a great distraction from the unrelenting despair that kept my spirit hostage all day. What a story teller that Louvern, and what a colorful life she has lived. She said she once had a very lucrative career in real estate until she "got stupid and wild" eight years ago, divorced her husband and went searching for a more exciting life. And, of course, I just had to tell her about my fondness for real estate, all the free real estate seminars I attended in Manhattan when I found myself living in New York after the eviction, and my hopes that my deliverance day will coincide with the burst of the real estate bubble so that owning rental properties can become one of my multiple sources of income while I pursue my non-monetary passions. We also spent quite a long time talking about our children since she too has "daughter issues," and is hoping that her three daughters will someday forgive her for her unfettered midlife crisis. Rachelle came to mind several times during the conversation. It pains me that she never wrote or inquired about me since my last phone call four months ago. And it vexes me that I've become such a persona non grata that even an orphan in Haiti does not wish to be adopted by me.

Nervousness du jour: Noticing a letter from the I.R.S. addressed to one of The Shameless on The Shelter's kitchen counter on my way in this evening and having all the fears, guilt, and shame over my money troubles reignited all at once. Most specifically, the fear that the I.R.S. is just waiting for me to go back into the workforce so they can pounce on me for the $30,000+ of back taxes that I accumulated while working at the bank because I was too undisciplined in money matters to pay those quarterly taxes like I was instructed to do when I got hired.

Awkwardness du jour: Forcing myself to go speak to Kelly Kearns, the social worker from the Big Bend Homeless Coalition/HOPE (Housing Opportunities and Personal Empowerment), about possible job openings because even Lavermine who has been living at The Shelter longer than everyone else is beginning to pick on me for not having a job. "I don't know what you all do all day, but you two need to shut the hell up. Some of us work for a living and need to get our rest," she spat out the night before last when Jaklyn came to ask me about Louvern's whereabouts a few minutes after lights out. (Louvern was working late.)

Accomplishment du jour: I got more than a little bored with all the talk about the Talmud in the last chapters, but I did finish reading *The Chosen* and what a great ending that was. I found myself over-identifying with the characters of the Hasidic rabbi and his son Danny because just like Danny I, too, struggled all my life to stay outside of the ready-made box the world had waiting for me even before I was born on account of my gender, my skin color and my birthplace. And just like Reb Saunders, I, too, have shed many tears over the suffering of not only my people, but of all people. Though the big difference between us is that I am not waiting for any messiah to come and change the world because it is my firm belief that the responsibility to change the world resides with each and every one of us.

Bitterness du jour: The memory of taking Jeremiah and JP to the Newseum in Northern Virginia shortly before they closed down to get ready for their new location in the District. Unbeknownst to the boys, I had bought two tapes of them playing anchormen with the intention to give a tape to each of them as a surprise years later. I lost both tapes (and countless family keepsakes) during the eviction. Also got more bitter than I thought I would be when I saw a young woman reading *Confessions of a Video Vixen* at a bus stop this morning. Am I envious of Karrine Steffans's authorial success? No. But it infuriates me that a jezebel who built a career through degrading herself got the book deal that I banked on and I got evicted. And I still can't believe that she had the audacity to say on *Oprah* that she felt no shame. Though retrospectively, what I really could not believe was Oprah Winfrey telling Karrine Steffans that it was a good thing that Karrine Steffans felt no shame.

Woke up with a calm spirit until I got caught into the mire of emotional distress all over again after I had to wait two interminable hours in The Shelter's Day Center for Kelly Kearns. The Day Center, located next door to The Shelter, is where The Shameless and their male counterparts go during the day to watch TV, drink coffee, use the restroom or simply cool off when they're not having a ball in The Shelter's backyard smoking and drinking (cigarettes and non-alcoholic beverages only—officially), philandering, playing cards, eating junk food, cutting and braiding each other's hair, listening to music, and all the good stuff. And there I was sitting in that godawful room in virtual darkness because someone had dimmed the lights so that the dozen or so older male Shelter guests present could watch a movie. I was already a nervous wreck when another woman arrived. Another woman who turned out to be one of the prostitutes I saw on the news during a prostitution bust a week or two ago. I recognized her because she was wearing the same outfit. The very polite Shelter staff at the desk, Mr. SoonToBeFired (for fooling around with one of The Shameless), told me around 10 o'clock that Kelly was on the premises but was busy taking care of an emergency that just came up. I could have left, I should have left, but I was too numb to move a muscle. Kaycee Boneheaded, the No. 1 happy-go-lucky member of the Black Shameless Club, showed up with two of her sidekicks a few minutes later, settled on the row of folding chairs right behind me and nearly drove me nuts with her boisterous bursts of laughter and trashtalking, as if I didn't get enough of that every evening. I arrived at the Day Center around 9:15 since Kelly had asked me to meet her at 9:30 and it was 11:23 when she was finally able to give me less than five minutes of her time only to tell me . . . I can't even remember what she told me. Something about forgetting to send my application for a free bus pass to Taltran (now StarMetro), but that she was going to do it ASAP. (The city of Tallahassee offers one free 31-day bus pass to anyone looking for a job, I was told.) She also gave me two single-ride bus tickets and the address of a place on North Monroe Street where I could go apply for jobs. Mother Teresa came back to mind on my way out of the Day Center through The Shelter's backyard since Shelter residents are not allowed to use the front door of the Day Center. And as much as I admire her, I will never understand her take on the liberating aspect of poverty. The way I see it, poverty is one of the worst misfortunes that a human being can be plagued with. More precisely, poverty is only a gift to the people who chose it, not the ones who were chosen by it.

Grateful I was able to spend the entire day in apartment 6 because JP, his girlfriend, and his roommate left for New York to attend the graduation of my oldest goddaughter. I am very happy for Claire, extremely proud of her determination to earn her degree right on schedule, and do wish her the very best, but a part of me feels like the remnant of a shipwreck because my own daughter is two years older than Claire and has yet to graduate. Also grateful that JP left me his cell phone and I was able to speak to Mama and Patoutou for as long as I wanted without having to worry about the minutes on my prepaid phone. "When are you coming to see me?" my Patoutou wanted to know, and thank God I can still satisfy her with the standard reply: "Soon." I also called Lucy, the woman who used to be a pillar of spiritual strength in my life until I began my own relationship with the God of my personal experience, and was hardly taken aback when she asked me to come back to North Carolina. But I already stayed with Lucy for two weeks post-eviction, and living in a home where a religious radio station is on all day all night to ward off evil, and in a neighborhood where godly women don't go for walks alone is not exactly an experience that I would like to replicate.

Grateful to have learned about the Marshmallow Experiment (children with the ability to delay gratification at age four grow up to be better adjusted adults) through reading *The Five Lessons a Millionaire Taught Me about Life and Wealth*. And how the true measure of a person's intelligence is not his or her IQ, but how well that person deals with his or her emotions. I guess that would explain why some very intelligent women behave so stupidly when they choose to make decisions based on their fleeting emotions, rather than their common sense.

Not grateful that Mama finally found out that I no longer live in apartment 6. My mother actually cried when she heard my voice. She said JP simply told her that I left the apartment, but that he didn't know where I moved to. She also reminded me, again, that I made the biggest mistake of my life when I walked away from my day job to go write a book. Who knew that my decision to do the will of God would end up causing so much pain to so many people?

Quite an interesting evening at The Shelter.

(1) Asian foolishness – The two Asian women sleeping on the top bunks across the room still behave as if they

don't see me or each other, but, Mi-Kum, a fourth Asian woman from the back room who wears a ton of makeup 24/7 and whose heavily penciled eyebrows are shaped like the Golden Arches, already has a serious problem with me because I am always speaking to Sabine, as she sees it, but never to her. She insinuated that maybe I just don't like Koreans, but of course it didn't occur to her that maybe I just don't like idiots.

(2) Black foolishness – The black Shameless are either laughing hysterically with Shameless Extraordinaire Kaycee Boneheaded as their ringmaster, or at each other's throats because that's just what they do when there is nothing good enough on TV to keep them entertained. "If I have to beat somebody's ass tonight, this shit is stopping," the pregnant black girl who showed up a few nights ago shouted after she went on and on about being tired with Shelter bitches talking behind her back, and how she would rather sleep in the bushes tonight than stay at The Shelter. "Fuck this shit, I ain't trying to feel sorry for nofuckingbody," another black Shameless who just got out of prison piped up in response. "Ain't nobody going no damn where, man," Darla, one of the bisexual prostitutes then chimed in. "Stop stirring up shit all the fucking time and grow up!" And they all laughed some more.

(3) White foolishness – It hasn't been a good day for the members of the White Shameless Club either because too many of them have been playing "musical beds" with each other's boyfriends, to quote Sabine. "If I catch you looking at my old man one more time, I am going to tear your ass up," was the warning one white Shameless gave to another a minute ago. The white Shameless are also in turmoil because blacks and immigrants appear to get better treatments than they do from the various social service agencies in Tallahassee. Louvern even swears that black women at The Shelter receive their food stamp

cards faster. "Maybe I am the wrong race," Kichelle concluded in mocked despondency after she told the cluster of white Shameless hanging around her bed that Sabine was getting more food stamps than she was. Then turning to Sabine, she added, "At least I was born in this country and didn't have to marry someone to get in here. I am tired of you getting everything you want around here while I get shit done, and I will find a way to get even."

I had no idea that such people even existed in the most powerful nation in the world, honest to God.

1:08 a.m. – Still awake, in spite of acute mental and physical fatigue. Partly because I have a very bad cold and my nose can't stop running, partly because a roach was crawling on the bed just when I was getting ready to lie down around midnight and partly thanks to Lissa, an innocent looking blonde in her early sixties, who has been standing in front the double sink in the big bathroom the past half-hour, justifying her hatred for The Shelter's "fucking nigger bastards." I was debating whether I should go downstairs (a different level, really) to go alert a Shelter staff when Mr. HornyBoy came up for one of his rounds, found me sitting up in bed and asked why I wasn't sleeping. "Because it's not my home," I groused. To which he answered, "It is now. You can make it your home." His feckless attempts to make me feel welcomed are beginning to incense me even more than his sexual advances.

3:31 p.m. – Sitting on the futon in the living room of apartment 6 where I spent the past few hours catching up with some much-needed sleep. Still tired, but feel much better only because I just hung up with Lulu and she confirmed that Mama did express some relief when she heard that I had a job. Grateful that Lulu was willing to lie for me, but, Dear God, do I need to remind you that unmitigated misery is not exactly what I signed up for when I decided to turn my will and my life over to you? For the record, I stopped at the terminal this morning to pick up my free 31-day bus pass and I am sorry to say that I feel more trapped by it than anything else because (a) I don't like free stuff and (b) I have no desire to go apply for any of those menial jobs they have all over Tallahassee for the poor. I left the World Bank to finish writing a novel that you, God, asked me to write, not to go flip burgers or work as a cleaning lady at some sleazy motel and you know it. I can feel the tears cascading down my cheeks, in spite of myself. Crying over being abandoned by God. Crying over robbing my children out of their home. Crying just for the sake of crying.

11:22 p.m. – "Are you afraid they'll make you feel better?" was the question a sarcastic Louvern, who spent most of the evening raising hell over the fact that Lizzie Licehead's scalp is still bleeding and no one seems to care, threw at me after she suggested that I go see the nurse to get some pills for my headache and I replied that I don't take pills. Louvern, of course, is snoring her head off by now while I am still seething. This is Louvern's last night at The Shelter, by the way, and while I won't miss her snoring I will no doubt miss her sense of humor. She said that she was already fretting over the probability that she will resume her drug use as soon as she gets comfortable in her new home, and I virtually exhorted her to develop a stronger relationship with you, God, and to ask you daily for strength to stay away from her weaknesses. But I don't think she even heard me because Louvern doesn't see herself as a drug addict, just someone who likes to have fun. Oddly enough, Louvern even believes that she doesn't have to worry about getting into heaven because she has not only been saved through the blood of Jesus, even her stepmother, a stony-hearted former madam, is presumably saved through her own salvation since the Lord is so good and merciful. The thought that Jesus is almost certainly not pleased with the deluded using his good name as an excuse to avoid facing and mastering their inner demons came to mind as she spoke, but I kept my mouth shut.

Spent my morning at the main library reading two of my three favorite newspapers (they don't have the *Washington Post*), went to sleep when I arrived at apartment 6 around 1 p.m., but spent my late afternoon watching *Coach Carter*. And my heart goes out to the real Ken Carter because his story illustrates so well the uphill battle that must be fought by anyone who tries to go against the grain, even if it is for the betterment of society. (Perhaps because the people who need to change the most are usually the ones who are temperamentally predisposed to hold on to their dysfunctions with a tight fist.) I then came to the madhouse and . . . lost my train of thoughts because Caren briefly stopped by the bunk to ask if I had a good day and a comment she made out of the blue last night sprang back to mind. "If anyone ever hit the lotto," she had said, almost pleadingly, "I would be really mad if they don't buy a house and put all of us poor women in it." I actually spent a great deal of time thinking about her *cri de coeur*, and it later came to me that I don't owe any material thing to the women at The Shelter if I ever win the lottery. (I should have said "when I win the lottery," but my confidence in my own dreams—or delusions—is a bit shaky today.) At any rate, what I owe these women, especially the ones who are not severely crippled by any physical or mental illnesses, is not a private house where they could continue to go on with their shamelessness without any responsibility of any kind. What I owe them is a few pointers:

Give up the drugs. Give up the booze. Give up the promiscuity. Give up the barbaric behaviors that keep taking you back to jail. Give up the addiction to negative excitement. And the aversion to being a responsible adult.

Give up the mindset that leads you to believe that being the best parasite that you can be is a token of brainpower. (Many of The Shameless think that it's okay to act dumb if that qualifies you for a check. Or to snatch up anything that is being offered for free even if you don't want or need it.)

Ask the Creator to clean you up body and mind, seek and follow His guidance in all aspects of your life, and one day, you too will be set free from the shackles of recklessness, thoughtlessness, slothfulness and all the other moral infirmities that usually go hand in hand with chronic homelessness, at least from what I've seen at The Shelter.

Cannot believe that no money miracle came to pass while JP and company were out of town, and that I will be back on the streets of Tallahassee again tomorrow morning. This cannot be my life. It just can't be.

Cannot believe that I spent my Mother's Day in a homeless shelter in the company of women whose children are either in foster care or completely estranged from them as a result of their repulsive conducts or mental illnesses.

Cannot believe that ExHusband who has never called me me on Mother's Day, even when I was raising his two oldest children and his only involvement in their lives was a measly child support check (he took great pride in being an "absent father"), decided to not only call me today but to also put his 14-year-old wife on the phone to say hello.

Cannot believe that FourteenYearOldWifey, who has been enjoying the privilege of being a stay-at-home mom, is now back in school while my children scramble monthly to make ends meet. She said she's studying "politics." Another great idea of ExHusband, I am sure, whose list of hobbies entails a propensity to marry women he thinks he can recreate in his image. Still wondering whether she was being sarcastic when she wished me good luck in publishing the novel since *her* husband once told me that my writing skills are so subpar that I should go back to secretarial work rather than waste more time working on *Out of the Trenches*. And when FourteenYearOldWifey hinted that maybe we should have a family get-together before they leave the country for his next assignment, ExHusband quickly got back on the phone and very diplomatically told me that he didn't think it was a good idea—as if I was even remotely interested—because he never knows when I will lose my temper and start talking ugly. It goes without saying that there wasn't a soupçon of diplomacy in my voice when I saucily replied that I didn't start talking ugly until I married ugly.

Wish du jour: That I could write another book. Was at my best while I wrote *Out of the Trenches*, even when the rejection letters from practically every agent who represent fiction dealing with women's issues began to pile up. I was frankly in a much better frame of mind even after I started contacting potential agents on my B-list, C-list, and D-list until there was no one else to query.

Gratitude du jour: That Deanna, the only female staff at The Shelter and definitely the nicest, agreed that Shelter dinner was big enough to fill up Patoutou's belly and gave seconds to all who wanted more even though she had to bend the truth a little by telling Rashad, The Shelter's cook, that she needed the extra plates because more women had showed up in the dining room at the last minute.

Resentment du jour: Listening to Lucy Pride, the other social worker (I think that's what they are) who visits The Shelter on Monday evenings, tell a young woman that she must believe in herself because "If you believe in yourself, you can do anything." *Another load of crap*, I thought, *I can't even get God to validate my existence and I did much more than believe. I sought. I listened. I trusted. I obeyed.*

Insult du jour: Being offered money, while I waited in The Shelter's driveway to check in, by a Hispanic delinquent who has been begging for my attention since he laid eyes on me a week ago. (I would rather spend my time counting rocks.) And being told by a black delinquent who appears to be very popular among his peers—so popular that The Shameless dubbed him Sweet Sexy—that he's willing to share his next check with me if I become his woman. (I would rather spend my time eating rocks.)

Disgust du jour: Sharing the double-shower in the big bathroom with the swinish creature known as Big [body part] Vilda because the dining room bathroom is out of order, then spotting her standing in the shower in all her glory because she didn't have the decency to close the damn shower curtain. Whoever had the idea to install a double-shower with one drain in a homeless shelter where things like staph infections and scabies, one can assume, run rampant is a moron. Had to wash my feet all over again after I walked out of the stall because water from her side was gravitating toward my side as we both showered. This is the same woman, mind you, I saw rummaging through a trash can at The Chain of Parks over the weekend. Cannot stand it, God. Cannot stand it at all.

12:21 a.m. – Planned to go to sleep soon after the TV went off (they were playing it so loudly I could hear it more than twenty feet away with the earplugs on.) But a roach was crawling on the bed again, prompting Jaklyn who saw me hunt it down to speculate that bed 6 is most likely infested with roaches because one of the women who last used it ate cookies in bed every night and didn't clean after herself. Do I need to add that, compounding my misery, I now expect roaches to start crawling all over me the moment I close my eyes?

7:29 a.m. – Mass just ended. I couldn't understand a word that came out of the mouth of the visiting priest, but the faithful know the routine so well that they would have responded in kind even if the priest had said Mass in Spanish. Though my main problem right now is not the English-challenged priest, but the reality that the day has barely begun and all I have to look forward to is another morning on a bench in front of FSU's College of Medicine. Dear God, do you have any idea how tired I am of you pretending to be blind and deaf?

7:28 p.m. – SonyaBette, another friend of Louvern, just offered me a pair of pants and seemed nonplussed when I told her that I didn't need any clothes. She must have noticed that I've been wearing the same three dresses again and again. Why would anyone want to amass a bunch of stuff while living in a homeless shelter is beyond me. Besides, I don't wear used clothes. SonyaBette also wanted to know if I did fill out the online application for food stamps like she has been urging me to do. I told her that I didn't need the extra food rather than divulge that I did apply for food stamps once after I had left my clerk typist job at the Fairfax County Police Department in the early '90s to attend Prince George's Community College full-time, and that I would gladly die of hunger before I go through that humiliation again. "Don't start no shit, and there won't be no shit," Lavermine just said to someone on her way out of the dining room where she spent the past few minutes chatting with Kaycee Boneheaded about a woman who recently left The Shelter. According to Lavermine, the woman's boyfriend once told her, "She's not my girlfriend. I just like to fuck her. I can fuck her in her ass and shit." And Kaycee Boneheaded, a thirty-four-year-old mother of one and soon-to-be grandmother, could not stop laughing her frenzied laugh even though she was in the same dining room minutes earlier reading her Bible out loud and testifying about the goodness of the Lord, and how nine years ago he gave her a new lease on life by blessing her with the gift of abstinence from smoking, drinking, and the use of profanities.

8:17 p.m. – Dinner wasn't served until 7:54. Four tiny strips of processed ham, one slice of cheap white bread, a mouthful of green beans, two mouthfuls of salad, a minuscule brownie, and grits. Cheeseless grits. Cheeseless and watery grits. I hate to put it this way, but some people do not deserve the praise they get for feeding the homeless. (A donor soon after told me that the not-worthy-of-an-American-dog rice and chicken dish that her church brings to The Shelter once a month is actually cooked by prisoners, and she seemed quite chesty about it.)

9:29 p.m. – Already worrying about breakfast, and the lights are not even out yet. Never, ever, thought that the day would come when I would cringe at the thought of eating more sugar and flour. Dante's Third Circle of Hell just came to mind. Perhaps because I am so keenly aware that metaphorically speaking, I am eating my own excrement at The Shelter. As if to prove the point, Shelterqueen just sneezed, and in a brilliant display of swellheadedness, she said to herself: "Bless you, baby, and I love you!" Where is a vomit bag when I need one?

Did so much reading today that I didn't create any time to write, and don't quite know where to begin. I guess I can always begin with JP.

- We met at the main library and he looked so uptight that I soon wished that he had called to cancel. He asked if The Shelter could find me a job, and I told him that I had a job interview on Friday. He gave me his word, again, that he was looking for an apartment so that I can come and live with him on August 1st, and I restated that I didn't want him to take my burden upon himself. "I don't like the thought of my mother living in a homeless shelter," he emphasized. And I did my best to persuade him (and myself) that God will deliver our family from this hell before long since I am where I am only because I chose to remain obedient to Him. He smiled but kept quiet when I commented that it was nice to see him alone for a change. (Angie showed up with him at the main library before they left for New York, acted quite strange when I said that I needed a half-hour to speak to JP privately, then texted him a hundred times during the time we were together.) He later took me to lunch, gave me forty dollars as we got ready to leave, then went to order another meal to bring home to Angie. And I sat there thinking that I had failed him almost as much as my parents failed me because he would not be shacking up at his age if I had money to educate him. (I truthfully did not see the fallacy in this line of thought until two years later while talking to another malcontent mother.)

- As painful as it was, being with JP was a cake walk compared to the mixture of emotions that surged through me an hour later when I came across a special issue of *Time* with a daunting photo caption of Darfur refugees sinking deeper into hell right in the table of contents. In contrast, it was just a few days ago that I was reading a magazine interview with a certain Hollywood star whose toy collection includes more than two private planes and more than half a dozen motorcycles, despite his image of being a man quite in touch with his spirituality. It's a good thing that happiness is not one of my aspirations in life because I cannot be happy in a world where the lifestyle of an elite few is a straight-out study in sinful self-indulgence while millions of others lack the basic necessities.

- Found myself reading more of St. John of the Cross before lights out, in spite of a burgeoning headache and sore throat. On the one hand, it's a relief to be reminded that he too felt that the greatest suffering on earth is to feel abandoned by God. Yet while a small part of me is inclined to posit that I am merely going through something that could very well be a universal soul-molding experience for all seekers, a greater part of me can't help feeling that his theory is nothing more than a magnificently thought-out rationalization of his own spiritual abyss. After all, what's the point of God putting a soul through a dark night if his only son already died for our sins?

A veritable zoo at The Shelter, and my nerves are being pushed to their limit to say the least. Kichelle was already harassing Sabine when I got here and an intoxicated Sabine isn't taking it lying down. "Go to hell and stay there!" Sabine just yelled after Kichelle told her that she needed to take some "psych pills" to keep her from drinking. Sabine also told everyone who walked through the room that Kichelle got baptized in a nearby church last Sunday, but that didn't stop her from engaging in fornication all week. Caren who just spent two or three days at TMH (Tallahassee Memorial Hospital) is currently standing in front of her locker (the lockers are located against the wall next to the nurse's office), and is in the midst of rattling off a list of reasons why she keeps smoking, in spite of doctor's order. And speaking of TMH, Estelle, a very attractive dark-skinned woman in her late thirties who dresses like a B-list celebrity and keeps over twenty pairs of shoes in her locker (the remaining two-hundred pairs are in storage), was rushed to the emergency room earlier, as the story goes, and is reportedly on life support. An enraptured Lavermine is still gloating over the splendid day she had at St. George Island where she went to clean the beach house of a friend who is throwing a birthday bash over the weekend. (Lavermine is a house cleaner, but refers to her clients as friends in order to elevate her social standing at The Shelter.) "Girl, I drank and I cleaned," she boasted, and I swear I could smell the alcohol on her breath from the top bunk. Jazzmine, a hot-tempered but compassionate young woman who volunteered to shower and dress an older woman who had defecated on herself the other night, is back in jail. I've heard so many versions of the story that I am not sure which one to believe, but I think it has something to do with her assaulting her boyfriend and/or his other baby mama. The older white woman in bed 7, whose name I can't recall because she's very quiet and only speaks to Sabine every now and then, has been admonishing one of her teddy bears relentlessly over the teddy bear's leanings toward vanity (the teddy bear wants Botox.) Zhouli, Sabine's bunkmate in bed 4, whom I had suspected to be mentally ill, also departed from her usual muteness and has been arguing loudly with her invisible enemies—in Chinese. To make matters worse, I spent the entire day thinking about food, and felt nothing but dread as I reread the second part of *Dark Night of the Soul*, a sharp contrast from the elation I felt when I first read the book five years ago because I felt so close to God then, and he, in turn, treated me as if I were one of his favorites.

5:34 p.m. – Already settled in bed 6 because if I didn't force myself to check in early I would not have come in at all, but where else could I go? Sabine just told me "*Bonjour, ça va?*" for the fifth time, a clear indication that she is drunk, again. BigBodyPartVilda accused me of making a pass at her when my backpack brushed against her arm while we lined up to sign in. "I know she doesn't want to have sex with you because I don't want to have sex with you," Mr. Jejune sneered while I stared at the two of them, dumbstruck. BigBodyPartVilda, a woman who was raised in a stable, prayerful and upper-middle-class family, from what I was told, but made her parents so sick with her freakish proclivities that they don't even take her calls anymore, laughed in response. Dear God, what the hell am I doing among these people from whom I have nothing to learn and to whom I have nothing to teach?

9:58 p.m. – Boiling up with resentment because Shelter-queen went to change the channel seconds before I got off the bunk, which means that I won't be able to watch *20/20* again. It's actually against the rules to touch the TV without permission from a Shelter staff, but I keep forgetting that Shelter rules do not apply to Lavermine. I heard her say the other day that the quality of the services rendered by The Shelter was dwindling because the staff was too busy smoking dope, and I could not help thinking that she's privy to such knowledge because she is for all one knows The Shelter's dope distributor, which would explain why they let her get away with so much. Equally frustrating is the fact that Charline, The Shelter's one and only Jehovah's Witness, is in the dining room as well, fussing over the fucking bitches who don't know what fucking pain is about. I feel as if I've been excised from my life. I miss my home. I miss my kids. I miss my privacy. I miss my garden. I miss being a dignified member of society.

10:15 p.m. – An argument between the two teenage girls in the family section and their younger brother just died down. I guess I should be thankful that I didn't have to drag my own children to a homeless shelter since my daughter had already left home and JP, who had just turned seventeen when we got evicted, was able to stay with the family of his best friend, Jeremiah, until the school year was over, then with Claire in New York during the horrendous summer that followed, and finally with the family of my godson Vladimir when he had to come back to Maryland to finish his last year of high school. I guess I should also be grateful that Lulu who was staying with us at the time, and whom I consider to be a child of mine, was quickly able to find another place to move to when it was time to leave 2900

Upshur Street. In the intervening time, Charline, the latest blonde who landed at The Shelter under the pretext that she's running away from an abusive husband, yet already found herself a Shelter husband who promised to rent her a room at the end of the month, is letting off more steam after Lavermine crustily told her that she might as well stop whining because no one here cares about her problems. "I am a Jehovah's Witness. I do not gossip. I do not create trouble. I do not judge people. Yet everybody with their fucking bullshit wants to be in my fucking face." From what I know about them, Jehovah's Witnesses do not do drugs, do not sleep around, and do not practice vulgarism as a way of life. Maybe Charline needs to start judging at least one person on this planet: herself.

Acknowledgment du jour: That my all-consuming desire to be a useful citizen of this world is not nearly as altruistic as I would like it to be, given that a life with no meaning is simply not worth living in my book.

Sadness du jour: Calling my mother. She did not ask any personal questions, but it is clear that she's still worried about me. Hope my mother will live long enough to see me bounce back from the fires of hell on earth.

Wish du jour: That people, women in particular, would focus on developing a one-on-one relationship with you, God, rather than turn to their fellow human beings, whose recommendations are almost always rooted in self-interest, for emotional comfort and spiritual guidance.

Bewilderment du jour: Bed 8 has a new occupant, and it's almost impossible to tell her apart from Lavermine. Too startled to elaborate except to say that thank goodness I had the foresight to put up a fence around bed 6 after Louvern left (a fence made of paper grocery bags), and as a result I can't be seen by them once I lie down.

Paradox du jour: Wandering through the aisles of Michaels brought back memories of the many arts and crafts classes the children and I took over the years, and especially after I made the decision to leave the bank and began to engross myself in my new life as a full-time mom and future best-selling author. The most hopeful period of my life, no doubt. Yet here I am questioning the authenticity of the bliss I had experienced during that time. Was it merely a well-adorned chimera based on hope for a better tomorrow and not the reality of the day? The reality that I was a not-particularly-skilled divorced mother of two who had taken the biggest risk of her life, but didn't consider the possibility that things may not work out as projected.

Outrage du jour: There was no one in line and no volunteers serving grits or syrup after I collected the usual two pancakes and eggs at the Haven of Rest this morning and headed for the second set of tables. So I assumed it was okay to self-serve until Mr. FrenchtownCowboy, who usually hands out the bowls of grits, appeared from nowhere and yanked the bottle of syrup out of my hand without a word. "There was no one here," I stammered. "I am here now," he hissed. "You could have asked for the bottle back instead of snatching it from my hand," I protested, my voice rising. Ignoring me, he turned his attention to the new line that was already forming. My name is not ~~Marie~~ Joséphine Chrisnel Muller if I don't get that knucklehead back for his unearned insolence. ("Marie" was automatically added to my birth certificate just because I was a girl.)

The Shameless are so euphorically thankful tonight that they're not only laughing. They're singing. They're clapping. They're dancing. And they're praising the Lord. "This is one day I will never forget," Kichelle just told her new bunkmate in bed 2, a pretty black girl who categorically refuses to give her name to anyone. "He loves me and I love him back." Kichelle used to go to sleep right after dinner, but has been staying up lately because her pills don't work like they used to. Jaklyn went to visit her fiancé and he's being released next month and they're already making plans to go back to San Diego. The real excitement, however, is that she's getting ready to leave The Shelter because she has been there three and a half months too long and can't take it anymore. The heavyset Mexican woman is in seventh heaven because God told her that it's okay to keep eating a bag of chips every day since they're his favorite food, too. Ninabelle and her "husband" had such a good time honeymooning that they wanted to stay out one more night, but they ran out of money. Jazzmine is out on bail, must go back to court, but she's keeping herself occupied for now by sharing her pearls of wisdom with her cronies. The black pregnant girl has reconciled with her mom and only came in tonight to say goodbye to her friends. Caren finally got her laundry done in a Laundromat near The Shelter because Shelter staff keep losing her stuff (she only has thirteen pairs of jeans left.) Lavermine, too, has a lot to thank the Lord for. "I got screwed really good, and I am on cloud nine!" was her official proclamation this evening. "I can still crank it up when I have to." And Kaycee Boneheaded can't stop bragging about how she miraculously stopped smoking, drinking, and cussing when she accepted the Lord seven years ago.

On the contrary, I barely got any sleep, woke up in a terrible mood, spent my morning in church listening to preachers and priests dwell on how Jesus died and rose again just to give a free ride to heaven to all who believe, spent my afternoon at the main library feeling sorry for myself and reading more of *The Unofficial Guide to Managing Rental Property*, which left me even more depressed because it's another confirmation that the real estate business is not nearly as unburdensome as those gurus in New York advertised it to be, ate so much at dinner time that I got sick to my stomach (Sabine gave me her plate.) And I still can't relax nearly two hours after lights out because the two CS workers cleaning the bathrooms have been talking so much nonsense that they can hardly get any work done. (CS workers are lawbreakers who chose to do their court-ordered community services at The Shelter.)

Grateful that the food monster went back to its cage because I've been eating more pastries than I care to recall, and have put on a few pounds. But then again, maybe I am making a big deal out of nothing since I've managed to stay away so far from my former fixation: chocolate cake.

Grateful for my tendency to feel guilt and shame whenever I do transgress my own moral boundaries, though I was once told in OA that guilt and shame were "character defects" that I needed to shake off. The longer I stay at The Shelter, the more evident it becomes that the lack of guilt and shame in a human being is a personal and societal tragedy of enormous magnitude.

Grateful for a lovely afternoon at the main library in JP's company. Grateful he stopped looking so distraught about my situation. Grateful for the $20 he gave me. Grateful that he did not ask how my job interview went. Even more grateful that he did at last acknowledge that Angie was "a bit controlling," and that he was trying to let her know as gently as he could that he wasn't a pushover just because he didn't like to argue.

Grateful that Cardilac, my new neighbor in bed 8, is such a social butterfly that she spends her evenings in the dining room catching up with the latest gossips and comes to bed only after the 10:45 smoke break. Cardilac, too, is a Shelter veteran who has been coming and going for years—no questions asked. Likewise grateful for the decision to start sleeping with my head at the foot of bed 6 because while I am very good at acting as if I don't see Lavermine, Cardilac is the one that I can clearly see, hear and smell.

Grateful that I've become quite savvy on the topic of money management, thanks to all the books that I've read on the subject since I became homeless, and am now able to pinpoint the flaws in other people's relationship with money the same way others used to pinpoint my own. Yet I opted to keep my opinions to myself when Jaklyn came to say goodbye rather than tell her that it was plain stupid to go stay in a motel room at nearly $40 a night when she's saving money to go back home. Perhaps because I understand all too well why she feels that she will snap if she stays one more week at The Shelter. "I am sick of these white bitches," a rancorous Cardilac bellowed the other night when Jaklyn had asked if anyone had a cigarette to sell for a quarter (as opposed to two quarters). "You need to go sit your fat ass somewhere." Not to be outdone, Lavermine had followed suit a second later with: "Eat shit, suffocate and die! I hope something bad happen to your ass."

2:20 p.m. – At the drop-in center on East Tennessee Street, across from Leon High School, waiting for Lucy Pride with whom I had a 2 p.m. appointment, but was just told by the receptionist that she got delayed with another case and is on her way. I already know that Lucy Pride won't be able to help me, but felt pressured to schedule the appointment because Lavermine was listening last night when she had asked me, "What can I do for you? Do you need help with finding a job or an apartment?" I mean, I couldn't exactly answer, "Trust me, you have no job or apartment that I want." Or "I don't want help from the government because I wasn't created by the government, nor did I turn my will and my life over to the government eleven years ago." Dear God, my life is in a state of complete collapse and it's going to remain that way if you don't step in to fix it and it will be all your fault because I would still have a job and a home and a car and my self-respect if you didn't ask me to go write that stupid book.

4:25 p.m. – Sitting on the front steps of Bethel once again. "GIVE THANKS TO THE ONLY ONE WHO CAN DO GREAT MIRACLES," is the message in the marquee on the front lawn of the church this week. And my first thought was: *How can I honestly say that God is a great miracle maker when I have not been a recipient or even a witness of any miracle of his?* Suffice to say that Lucy Pride, just like Kelly Kearns before her, had nothing meaningful to tell me. But then again, it's not their fault if I do prefer to bleed to death rather than accept any of the band-aids that they're so good at dispensing to people who are usually more than satisfied with band-aids. Yet because she said that I could make a free call from the drop-in center and I didn't want to appear lazy, I did follow her advice and called ECHO (Emergency Care Help Organization) to inquire about their free employment assistance program, and was told that their next Jubilee Job-Link Seminar Orientation begins at 9 a.m. on June 5th and to get there early since they operate on a first-come first-served basis. And the nightmare on West Tennessee Street goes on.

8:08 p.m. – Dinner was so good I didn't think it was fair that The Shameless were eating such a fine meal while children die of malnutrition daily in some parts of the world. And because I don't eat red meat, I gave Sabine the nasty-looking meatloaf and she gave me her serving of the delicious pasta-mushroom-chicken casserole that was added to the usual mashed potato and salad. Sabine also gave me her slice of chocolate cake and I ended up eating both hers and mine, in spite of all the patting in the back I've been giving myself for being so good. On another front, Estelle, who was purportedly on her death bed, made another grand entrance an hour ago dressed to the T, her long and curly weave still glued to her head just like the last time I saw her. The excitement over her return didn't last long, alas, because minutes later she stormed out of the dining room and stepped toward Lavermine who was in bed listening to her Walkman and shrieked, "Fucking old bitch, what did I ever do to you for you to wish me death?" From the torrent of obscenities that followed, I learned that Lavermine is a drug addict who has been living at The Shelter "since Moses was a baby," as well as a thief who allegedly steals everything she can get her hands on to go buy crack. (Sabine later confirmed that Lavermine had stolen from her, too. And before you know it, I myself was gratified with Lavermine's theft record online, which I unabashedly devoured with gusto.) "You don't have to tell us your business," I heard a Shelter staff say to a young woman a few nights ago. "You can stay here for as long as you want." If I were a *sans-honte-ni-vergogne* kind of person, or one sufficiently zombified by prescription and non-prescription drugs, being homeless in Tallahassee would have truly been an oasis of complacency amid hellfire.

I completely forgot about yesterday's "anniversary" until I was about to fall asleep last night. Grateful that I didn't kill myself two years ago, but I would be lying if I were to say that I am grateful to be alive because I am not. What's the point of being alive when I have nothing meaningful to look forward to? "If you pray right, God can use you in spite of your limitations," one of the assistant pastors at Bethel confidently stated last Sunday. In retrospect, I should have gone to him after the service and begged for the correct prayer formula because I've never felt more useless.

On my mind at the moment:

- It's 9:18 a.m. and here I am sitting on a deserted sidewalk in the parking lot of the Walmart on West

Tennessee Street because I couldn't think of anywhere else to go and it's kind of quiet here and I can get some reading done. The problem is that I just saw a sign warning that security cameras are in use and taking a quick look around, I detected several cameras on the roof of the building and one seems to be pointed directly at me. Absolutely nerveracking considering how fanatical TPD (Tallahassee Police Department) is in issuing trespassing warrants, at least according to The Shameless.

- It was confirmed that I am not being entirely phobic when I use toilet tissue to open Shelter doors after Jazzmine found feces on the door handle of the big bathroom. And speaking of Jazzmine, what a shock it was to find out that she has six children under the age of ten, that she gave birth to her last child in jail, that four of her children are in foster care, and the other two with relatives. She told the whole sordid story to a new woman while they got ready for work in the big bathroom this morning, and there wasn't a smidgen of self-reproach in her voice. A brutal reminder that one's character shouldn't be determined by a few good deeds alone because even the devil does some good deeds sometimes.

- Still angry at Mr. ShelterDrillSergeant for forcing me to stand in the dining room after I got out of the shower last night just to watch him scold The Shameless for their flagrant display of Shelter love in The Shelter's driveway (a passing motorist called to complain) when he knows perfectly well that I don't engage in such behavior. Twenty minutes later, still on a power trip, he ordered Sabine and me and a handful of women who tend to avoid the beastlike ambience of the dining room to go sit in there because it was no longer acceptable to stand in the sleeping area to eat. I didn't have to eat at the fiendish table only because he went back downstairs shortly after the food was served and I walked out right behind him and went to eat in the stairwell, right next to the lidless garbage can, but I fumed about my powerlessness all night. And I am already wondering if I should be bracing myself for an encore performance since he looks like the type who thrives on power. Shelter power.

Too nervous about TPD to stay here. Going to catch the next bus back to the terminal and go to Borders from there for I am not about to show my homeless face at Barnes & Noble, again.

Realization du jour: That I too am being a hypocrite whenever I expect others to give up their vices in exchange of character growth while I keep indulging in mine. Cake or me is the question God seems to be asking me all day. So I ate what I hope to be my last three slices of cake. Do I need to add that I felt more sadness at the thought of never eating cake again than I felt when I was about to lose my house? A not-so-subtle reminder that chocolate cake and its many relatives are my booze, my crack, and my cigarettes, all rolled up into one. (I was eating cake again a week later. I just can't get away from the thing; it's all over The Shelter. At least, that's the story I told myself.)

Enjoyment du jour: Another wonderful day with JP in apartment 6 while his roommate was at work. This boy has remained loyal to me during some of the worst periods of our lives, and I hope that I will soon be given the opportunity to make it up to him for all the humiliations he was subjected to after the eviction. I also felt a sense of usefulness for a change while I did his laundry (and mine), washed the pile of dishes that has accumulated in the kitchen sink since my last visit, cleaned the living room and bathroom, which pretty much looked as if a tornado had gone through them. And I am glad that I resisted the temptation to give his roommate's bedroom the usual once-over, and for leaving his own bedroom untouched since the bulk of Angie's stuff is still there even though she left for her summer job.

Reality check du jour: Venturing into the infamous "back room" for the first time when I went outside during the 8:15 smoke break to return a call from my mother, and realizing that bed 6 is the best located bed I could possibly have under the circumstances. The back room is actually divided into three sections: two small rooms with two double-bunks placed <u>less</u> than two feet apart on each side of the room and one large rectangular room with six double-bunks lined up against the wall, dormitory-style. No windows, of course, though the larger room does have a door that leads to the back yard. I would have suffocated to death in any of the small rooms, which I instinctively christened Mental Torture Chambers No. 1 and 2. And I would have been a card-carrying resident of Chattahoochee by now if they had assigned me to the larger room with its concentration of malicious and malodorous women.

Wish that someone did remember the hell I went through on this day three years ago when I got kicked out of the home where I had raised my two biological children, as well as provided a second home for many neighborhood children for seventeen years, and offer me a pat in the back along with a few empty words about hope, faith, loyalty, long-suffering or whatever, but even JP and Lulu forgot. And what did I dream about last night? Of being homeless on the streets of D.C., and hiding from World Bank people.

And guess what I overheard Lavermine say to her best buddy Kaycee Boneheaded earlier? That I surround myself with bags every night so that I can masturbate in peace. If this isn't hell on earth, I don't know what is.

A day fraught with anguish from beginning to end. (a) Got more disturbed than I thought I would be when Darla revealed that she was raped a few days ago. Darla seemed so exuberant beforehand that Lavermine told her, "Honey, there is no need to keep looking at yourself in the mirror because you look exactly like who you are: a hooker." Yet she dissolved into tears after smoke break and dropped the bomb. And as much as I cannot stand these women, I wish there were something I could do to help the younger ones stop their downward spiral before it's too late. Not so surprisingly, Deceitful CJ, the double-crossing man of God I was madly in lust and in love with for over a decade, just came to mind. "You can't stop another person from drowning if you don't know how to swim," he often told me. There isn't much about Deceitful CJ that I want to remember, but I think it would do me good to keep this particular message in mind. (b) Spent another afternoon at the main library catching up with the usual newspapers and got angry all over again as I read a recent article on the cozy relationship between drug companies and psychiatrists, and how too many studies on psychiatric drugs are being funded by drug companies. When will women realize that they have been had and stop being a cash cow for the mental health industry? (c) Found myself holding back tears at Bethel this morning after the pastor of the church, Reverend Dr. R.B. Holmes, Jr., asked visitors to stand up so he could welcome them and this woman sitting a few pews in front of me got up to say that she was in Tallahassee visiting her daughter who was in medical school at Florida State. And that was more than enough for me to infer that the woman was a great mother who was financing her children's college education single-handedly while I had brought shame to mine. Adding salt to my wounds, mother and daughter then sat so close to each other that their body language alone said everything that needed to be said about their relationship, in my way of thinking. And as I watched the mother shake hands with church members after the service, I took one good look at her and asked myself, *What does she have that I don't have?* And, as always, any flicker of daughter envy instantly brings Robin back to the forefront of my mind. Was she fated to be the daughter who was going to love and cherish me? Robin would have turned thirteen this month. Would my life have turned out differently if hers wasn't terminated in order to help me keep my own moral deficiencies under wrap?

6:21 a.m. – Wish I could leave now, but have nowhere to go since it's Memorial Day and Mass at St. Thomas More doesn't start until 9 a.m. on holidays. Beyond grateful that Cardilac didn't come in last night, but the new white woman in bed 8 didn't shower, didn't change the sheets and went to sleep with her shoes on, which already told me more than I want to know about her. I think I need to start "acting as if" by telling myself daily that "this too shall pass" because I am going to lose my mind if I don't.

8:26 a.m. – Grateful the doors of the church were open when I got here because I could not stay one minute longer at The Shelter. Breakfast was served at 7:18: spaghetti and fried chicken. Even a glutton of my caliber doesn't want that kind of food in the morning, but I did wolf it down since I can't exactly afford to pass up on meals, not knowing if the next one will be edible. Don't recall the last time I felt so all at sea for lack of a better word. I am not feeling pain. I am not feeling fear. I am not feeling anything at all.

11:02 a.m. – Just arrived at Barnes & Noble and I am sitting on a bench in the magazine section, raging over the sorry state of public transportation in Tallahassee. Knowing that the buses would be running on a Sunday schedule, I decided to walk to the mall from STM only to end up back on West Tennessee Street after I mistakenly took a left on Alabama Street. I was on my way out of Albertsons' (now closed) where I had stopped to buy the usual two mango and peach yogurts when I spotted the No. 33 heading toward TCC, and was rather peeved when the bus driver told me that, yes, they're on a Sunday schedule, but that they were told to start working at 10 a.m. Well, had I known that, I would not have done all that walking in the first place, especially since it had just come to my attention that the soles of my only pair of shoes have gotten so thin that they won't be lasting much longer. Needless to say that the first thing I did when I got off the bus was to take a look at the Florida Lotto billboard across the street from the mall and my heart broke all over again.

9:03 p.m. – Joline just called and I didn't pick up because in addition to being unable to answer the phone once I enter the madhouse, I only have seven minutes left on it. Plus, I am too ashamed to tell a woman who has known me since childhood, has always stood by me through thick and thin, and whose faith in God is at least as strong as mine that things have gotten from bad to worse since we last spoke because while God can provide, he chose to sit idly by and watch me waste away.

10:40 p.m. – The term "rock bottom" just came to me for no reason that I can think of. "For someone who is at rock bottom, I can't believe how arrogant you are," JP's roommate had told me the day she put me out. She doesn't know this, but I already outlived my rock bottom. And if I survived living in a Brooklyn housing project where my spirit got assaulted nonstop for over a year, then sharing a rooming house in Queens with sex addicts and a suspected murderer, I suppose that I will survive The Shelter.

Heartbreak du jour: Being told by Lulu that she found a new job, a backbreaking, uninspiring, and barely-above minimum wage job, and that Patoutou will be staying with a babysitter nearly twelve hours a day since she will be working ten-hour shifts five days a week. "WHATEVER GOD TEACHES US THROUGH PAIN IS GAIN," was the message in front of the Anderson Chapel AME Church on Alabama Street yesterday. How much more pain will I have to go through before I can see any gain?

Flashback du jour: Being one of the ten speakers at the yearly OA Candlelight Promises Meeting in Northern Virginia in the late '90s. As fate would have it, I was asked to speak on the first of the twelve Promises, which happens to be my favorite. (OA also uses AA's Big Book.) What a great speech I gave that night—straight from the heart. I was so high on God back then that I literally felt like the poster child for freedom and happiness. Wish someone had told me that the honeymoon would not last forever, yet knowing me I would not have listened.

Revulsion du jour: Listening to the string of filth that spewed out of the mouth of the most coquettish Shelter guest I've seen so far—a twenty-six-year-old mother of three who just got out of jail for violating her probation, and who has been staying at The Shelter on and off since 2001—after one of the women suggested that she should look for a job and go visit her children who live with her brother in a nearby town, rather than vegetate around The Shelter all day with her new boyfriend, a thirty-year-old scumbag who is the exact opposite of what one would expect a young white man in America to be.

Annoyance du jour: Listening to Jazzmine, The Shelter's most distinguished relationship expert who is on her way back to jail and doesn't seem to care, offer more guidance to her fellow Shameless while they waited for dinner. "Those are the things you should know if you're going to spend your life with someone . . . really and truly, when it boils down to it, it's not about what you want. It's about what God wants for you and your children." She talks a good game, doesn't she? But what made my blood go cold was when she told a twentysomething white woman who is pregnant with baby number four while she's trying to get her oldest three out of foster care, "Focus on yourself and your children. Don't worry about what the world thinks of you because you'll go crazy if you do." Jazzmine is popping children left and right and asking the world to raise them while she goes in and out of jail for crimes committed while under the influence of her volatile temper. Jazzmine needs to start worrying about what the world thinks.

Cannot believe that May 2006 came and went, and I am still at The Shelter. Never in my life have I suffered so much and for so long over money, something that means so little to me, yet something that I desperately need if I am ever going to be a productive member of society in a world that is so money-obsessed even its Son of God spoke more frequently about money in his parables than he did about brotherly love.

Cannot believe that after I forced myself to pick up the phone when Joline called again this morning, her advice was that I need to cast my pride aside and go on welfare. And because I wasted all my minutes trying to explain myself to her, I had to spend $10.86 from the $20 that JP gave me to go buy a $10 phone card. I know Joline means well, yet I wonder if I should even take her calls in the future. I already feel like an overstretched rubber band as it is, and don't need anyone to help push me further to the breaking point.

Cannot believe that chili was served for breakfast (I got so little sleep I was too tired to go to church.) I walked away at the sight, but The Shameless had the TV on, and I was in the dining room long enough to hear a newscaster say that Angelina Jolie was now the biological mother of a baby girl whose birth has the potential to change an African nation. While I am not the least bit impressed by movie stars—an actor is someone who is very good at pretending to be someone else, and for the life of me I just can't see what the big deal is about—I do have some admiration for Angelina Jolie because she seems to be a woman with a newfound desire to put her past behind her and help make this world a better place. Yet the notion of a newborn being the savior of an entire country nauseated me even more than the prospect of eating chili for breakfast.

The fact that I didn't win last night's jackpot as I had hoped and prayed kept me teetering on the verge of despair all day. "You think God owes you!" was the sin that Bertha, a friend I met in D.C. several years ago, once accused me of during that staggering month I stayed with her in her Northern Virginia apartment right after the eviction. I still don't understand why Bertha could be so sure that my expectations of God were too extravagant when she readily believes that God parted a sea for her ancestors, gave them a land free of charge, got them out of a fish belly and a lion's den unscathed, and much more, but I have one question for you, God. If I had told you that you were going to write a novel and you dropped everything to accomplish the task and the book didn't get published, would not you at least want a compensatory check from me?

PS: I finally met someone in this hellhole that I can actually relate to. She's intelligent, she's articulate, and she's not an alcoholic, a drug addict, or a prostitute.

Well, friendship at first encounter proved to be just as disastrous as love at first kiss. "I am sorry I was rude to you this morning, but I was a bit agitated," Z'Laitah—she took great pains to spell out her name for me when she had introduced herself—walked up to me and said when I arrived in The Shelter's driveway for the 6:30 check-in. "It's okay," I murmured, still a bit shaken by her blatant hostility after the genial conversation we had last night about our wishes for our children, our hopes for ourselves, and our love of words. "I hate it when I get like that," she continued in the same apologetic tone. "It's okay," I repeated as I told myself that there was no need to let her know that she had, in effect, hurt my feelings, especially since I had gone to bed fantasizing about how I was going to rent her an apartment and pay all her expenses for a year when I win the jackpot. My bogus indifference must have incited her to make her true feelings known. "To be honest, I don't really trust you very much." I was too stunned to think of a riposte, but since she appeared to be waiting for me to say something, I took in a breath and held on to my new mantra: "It's okay. It's really okay." She stared at me for a moment as if she was expecting me to say more, and then walked away. And that was it. My great Shelter friendship was over even before it began, leaving me wondering what lesson, if any, I should be learning from this woman. As if I didn't have enough Shelter bagatelle to mull over.

Midnight quandary: full-blown period nineteen days late. And since I can't shower in the morning (showers are locked at 10 p.m. nightly), I had to worry about how I was going to wash up upon awakening. And I still worry about where I am going to shower this evening because I find myself using the double-shower in the big bathroom more and more and would not want my bloody water to travel to the other side. I heard that there was a second private bathroom in the back room, but I've never used it before and don't plan to start now . . . "All right, ladies, it's 8:15. It's time to go," Mr. Grouch just growled from the family section. Why is he forcing people out of the door at twelve past eight? Don't plan to walk out of the room until 8:29 just to spite him. I guess I have yet to get over his smart-mouthed reply at breakfast time when I had asked if I could have a plastic plate (he was serving grits on a flimsy paper plate when he had a pile of plastic plates right in front of him) and he answered, "Yes, you can. If there is some plastic in this paper plate," which, of course, prompted a hearty laugh from Lavermine. And why am I still at The Shelter at this hour on a Saturday morning? Because the Haven of Rest does not serve breakfast during the month of June and Shelter breakfast was served too late for me to make it to the 8 o'clock Mass. Dear God, in case you think that such a crappy life is worth living, I am here to tell you that it's not.

When I read some people's account of their Sunday morning experience in the church of their childhood a few weeks ago, I concluded that they were greatly exaggerating, but that was before I attended the 11 a.m. service at Bethel. Let's just say that the whole thing was much more entertaining than many Broadway shows I've paid big money to attend. The choir brought the house down with "He's so Excellent," and people sang along, shouted hallelujahs and amens, fanned themselves and each other, and so on. I also attended the much quieter early morning service at the Trinity United Methodist Church near the main library (actually, both churches are near the main library) where the pastor spoke about passion and power, the two things, he feels, that are necessary to achieve anything meaningful in life. And as you would expect, I felt deluged with an assortment of negative feelings while listening to him. I have passion galore, yet look at me. Lots more to record, but I don't see the point in all the writing that I do. A waste of time, at best. A mild case of hypergraphia, at worst.

"If you're eating dinner, get down so you can be seen," Mr. ShelterDrillSergeant just roared on his way to the back room to announce dinner (I am hiding under a sheet again.) Will get off the bunk when they start bringing up the trays for I refuse to allow this man to frighten me into submission. Meanwhile, he's already back in the stairwell and is now yelling at Pamelia, a humanlike talking thing that is so beastly she's not even qualified to be a member of the White Shameless Club. "I told you time and time again that I am not one to play with. If I catch you downstairs again, I will put you out." Pamelia's answer? "And they want to know why people want to jack them up. I am not a fucking child. He needs to learn how to respect people." Of course, she waited until Mr. ShelterDrillSergeant exited the family section to vent. It's kind of sad that these women, most of them middle-aged, have yet to realize that you do ultimately lose your right to complain about people who don't treat you with respect once you have demonstrated over and over that you have no self-respect.

"When I get to heaven, I am going to sing and dance all over heaven while I thank the Lord for all his blessings," the new woman from Hoboken, Georgia, who just picked up a pair of used sneakers from a Shelter staff just said to herself as she walked through the room. What do these women think heaven is, a 24-hour concert?

On a bench in front of FSU's Westcott Building. Lots of students nearby, walking to and from class, or just sitting around, enjoying the sun while using their cell phones or laptops. Hope I won't see anyone related to The Shelter here for they seem to be everywhere I go. (A Shelter staff told me yesterday that he saw me sitting in front of the College of Medicine and I just hope that he didn't mention it to anyone else.) In any event, I just left ECHO and I can barely contain my tears. "And you need to be dressed in business attire for your appointment tomorrow," Miss Edwards, the retention specialist I was assigned to—what the hell is a retention specialist?—told me as she handed me her business card. She must not have heard me when I told the entire class an hour earlier that I didn't own any business attire. And according to Miss Palmer, another retention specialist, poor personal appearance and lack of enthusiasm are the first two things employers notice in a job applicant, and I failed at both during the mock interview I had with her. The mock interview I refused to participate in at first, but relented at the last minute because . . . I am so stressed I can't recall why I agreed to go on with the charade. Yet I need to start rehearsing the very sad story I am going to tell Miss Edwards tomorrow about how I ended up homeless when my ex-fiancé basically left me at the altar after I quit my job to raise his small children. Upon contemplation, that's exactly what you did to me, God. You left me at the altar.

The white Shameless are quite in a frenzy tonight. "These women don't need another reason to bitch. They're already one spark away from explosion," Kaycee Sourpuss, also known as White Kaycee, just told a Shelter staff who had come up to collect towels, and to remind everyone that all used towels must be returned to the red basket next to the staff bathroom within twenty minutes after check-in. Caren got so excited that her new boyfriend found them a place to stay that she got drunk, peed on herself, and one of her friends had to help her out in the shower. Lizzie Licehead went to see her private doctor and he assured her that she has willow trees growing on her head, not lice. She also went to the golden palace to visit her sixteen children, and is now debating whether she should move in with them. (Lizzie Licehead left The Shelter many times over the years to go visit imaginary relatives, sometimes in the middle of the night, but thank goodness she always comes back.) Kichelle is so smitten by her new lover that she decided to give away her supply of condoms because it's awfully important for her to "feel it going in and out and a condom gets in the way." Kaycee Sourpuss is also in a pique because Shelter staff are not taking her complaints about her new bunkie seriously, and she knows it's because she's white (most Shelter staff are black.) An unhinged Pamelia got so cranky by the sound of two toddlers crying in the family section that she went downstairs and told the mother, "Hey, can you control them children?" Without skipping a beat, she then added, "If you can't shut your children up, you don't deserve to have them." Lissa spent quite a long time in the big bathroom, ranting about the fucking pieces of shit who refuse to leave her alone until Bekkie-Sue, a salacious black Shameless who usually stays at The Shelter when she's between jobs, threatened to beat her up. Topping it all off, I finally had the honor to meet April, the duly appointed chairperson of the White Shameless Club, a thirty-eight-year-old brunette with a boyish figure who presided at the dining room table before dinner where the main topic was "Do you spit or swallow while giving head?" And whose crowning achievement in life is the expensive bottle of wine that was awarded to her when she once won The Craziest Chick in Town Contest, a yearly event in her hometown in the Midwest.

Taking into account the many sleepless nights I've spent ruminating on the shortcomings of the black race, it gives me great comfort to know that the white race hasn't fully evolved. But, Dear God, why didn't you strip me of my mental faculties before you threw me in the pit of hell with America's Most Shameless?

5:11 a.m. – Woke up even more miserable than I went to sleep after I dreamed that I was living in a house where the utilities have been cut off and the children came home from school and there was no food to feed them. My mother who was still living with us in the dream then burst into tears when she realized what was going on. Do I need to add that I am feeling like the personification of failure as a daughter and as a mother? I've never felt so hurt. Shoot, hurt is not even the word. I've never felt so baffled.

9:00 p.m. – I've been doing such a good job ignoring Lavermine that she actually stopped singing "Baby, baby, baby, you are stupid, and you are suicidal" whenever she sees me. She must have heard me tell Sabine that I empathize greatly with people who are suicidal because I too used to be suicidal until God literally took the temptation away from me, and wrongly assumed that she could use the information to hassle me. I, however, refused to hold my tongue when I overheard Kaycee Boneheaded say that I am trying to pass myself off as a student, and that she knows for sure that I have no job and don't go to TCC. But I digress, because what propelled me to become uncorked was not Fibbing Jailbird Kaycee Boneheaded telling another Shameless that she saw me standing at a bus stop near White Drive twice, which means that I must have a man in one of the apartments nearby, but that she just found out that my son is as lazy as I am and has been living off his girlfriend since he got out of jail. I told her that she was an embarrassment to her family, to her country, and to her race, that she's wasting her time initiating those Bible studies in the dining room because they were obviously not helping her in any way, that she needs to spend less time fabricating stories and more time begging God to give her intelligence and character, but that's not enough. I need to get more dirt on her so I can be fully equipped to slaughter her the next time she attacks.

11:38 p.m. – Still too angry to fall asleep because the argument with Kaycee Boneheaded keeps replaying in my head. And being told by Sabine that she too is in pain because she's going through her "dark night experience" didn't sit well with me at all. I am suffering because I chose to remain obedient to God in good times and bad times and God went AWOL in my greatest hour of need. Sabine is suffering as a result of turning alcohol into her god. There is a difference. A stark one.

Paradox du jour: Seeing the $45 that Lulu sent both as a blessing and a curse. A blessing because I only had 48 cents left. A curse because it's a painful reminder that I need so much more.

Disturbance du jour: Watching the farewell roast for Meredith Vieira on *The View*. Hard to believe that people who call themselves civilized can behave so third-worldly in the name of entertainment.

Surprise du jour: Woke up pregnant with hope. Yet how can I sincerely thank God for the gift of hope when I know all too well that today's hope can easily be crushed by tomorrow leaving me even more beleaguered than before?

Wish du jour: That I was prepared to face life on life's terms right from the start. For example, I wish I were told of the crucial role that self-restraint ought to play in both romantic and platonic relationships, in view of the fact that love and friendship rarely last a decade, much less forever.

Discomfort du jour: Being told by Frances, a black lady who attends the 7 a.m. Mass, that I should come over and say hello to her and her husband sometimes. I smiled cordially, nodded vigorously, knowing full well that will never happen. Of course, I let her believe that I was a student. What else could I say? "No, I am not a student. I just carry a backpack wherever I go because I am homeless."

Highlight du jour: A few hours in JP's company. He said I should have asked Z'Laitah why she doesn't trust me. And when I told him that I think God placed me at The Shelter because he wants me to be trained for works he would like me to do for him in the future, he thoughtfully answered that it could be true since many superheroes routinely work with criminals with the goal of beating them at their own games. And when I rolled my eyes in reply, he said that he pitied me for being so narrow-minded because a lot can be learned from watching movies.

Conclusion du jour: That Lavermine is irrefutably the most depraved human being I've ever met, and a prime example of why my long-held belief that people always get better with age needs to be squashed. "It's going to be as hot as fuck tomorrow," she just said to herself. "Those jeans are going to burn my ass up." I think I forgot to mention that The Shelter has a rule against the use of profanities, and Lavermine is always reminding everyone about Shelter rules. Everyone but herself, that is. She also monopolizes the dining room bathroom for an average of forty minutes every morning, yet throws a hissy fit if anyone else dares to use it for more than five. I am not ready for a replay of yesterday's showdown with Kaycee Boneheaded any time soon, but it's almost impossible to keep ignoring Lavermine because her shamelessness knows no bounds. In other words, the more I ignore her, the more repugnant she gets.

At The Chain of Parks since the main library closes at five on Saturdays, and I am not in the mood to go lock myself up with The Shameless earlier than I have to. I am so tired. Tired of being anxious. Tired of being ashamed. Tired of feeling guilty. Tired of hurting senselessly. Tired of feeling that my tears do not matter to God. Tired of wondering whether I am being perseverant or delusional. Tired of wandering the streets of Tallahassee. Tired of sitting on benches. Tired of telling my children that God will provide while I watch my life devolve into a complete nightmare. ("Would you like to go over the list of broken promises?" my daughter once asked me.) Tired of looking like a fool in the eyes of people who knew me before the eviction. Tired of looking like a thief in the eyes of my creditors and the few friends who had offered to loan me money. Tired of hiding from the I.R.S. Tired of living in a homeless shelter with a group of women with whom I have nothing in common. Tired of taking orders from all Shelter staff, but especially the ones whose demeanor is almost as grotesque as the demeanor of the skunks they have been hired to boss around. "You need to keep moving," one of them told me last night when he heard me ask Rashad what we were having for dinner on my way in. "I am moving," I said. "You're not moving fast enough," he snapped. And let's not forget the one who tartly told me: "Don't do it again because I won't let you back in next time!" when I had rung the bell one morning—seconds after I had walked out of the building—to ask for his permission to go back inside to pick up a book. I would not have hired the dumbbells to mow my lawn, yet here they are giving me orders just because they can. In the meantime, it's 6:42 p.m. and I have to get going if I don't want to miss my 7 p.m. curfew. I feel like a prisoner of faith. I put my faith in man, I got hurt. I put my faith in God, I got hurt even more.

Talking about Jesus is an utter obsession at The Shelter, notably on Sunday mornings when most of them get their best clothes ready for church, and on Sunday evenings when they usually gather around the hellish table to go over the day's highlights. I quickly learned to tune them out whenever the J-word comes up, but the Lord seems to be in their midst for real tonight. April for one was so touched by the sermon at St. Mary this morning that she cried. And miracle of miracles, I haven't heard one foul word come out of her mouth yet. (St. Mary Primitive Baptist Church is located across the street from The Shelter, behind Popeye's, and it's where many of them go at 7:45 on Sunday mornings before they head over to the Haven of Rest or Grace Mission after 10.) Even Shelterqueen is sober tonight and on her best behavior. In fact, I even heard her say that she's learning to calm down her "storm" so that she can become "worthy of society."

As for me, I attended the early Mass at STM where the emphasis was on defending the Trinity against people like Dan Brown who is not evil in and of himself, but is undoubtedly an instrument of the devil. Then rushed over to the Trinity United Methodist Church again just to take a look at what their 9:45 contemporary SUN service was like. And while the choir wasn't as good as I expected, I very much enjoyed the sermon delivered by Rev. Wayne P. Cook, "This is my Story," in which he used incidents from his childhood to evince how pain has helped mold him into a better human being. *En passant,* I was the only black person at the SUN service, but thankfully no one seemed to care. And two hours later, I was similarly pleased by Rev. R.B. Holmes's sermon at Bethel's 11 o'clock service. Fear is the number one reason people are afraid to do God's will, he said. *And who can blame them?* I thought. But when he added that if you conquer your fears, you will in time find delight, I had to pay attention. Dear God, please help me keep my eyes on you, and not on my feelings, which are forever vacillating between hope and despair. Yet, deep down, I am sort of grateful for my fears because to not be afraid, I would have to be insane.

I guess the astonishment du jour was to find out that Goodwill is not nearly as cheap as I thought:

Dresses: $5.99

Skirts: $4.49

Shoes: $3.99 and up

Was even more surprised to find out that I wasn't going to do a whole lot of "shopping" with the two vouchers ($35) that Miss Edwards gave me since the 50 percent off sale the Goodwill off West Pensacola Street has on clothes on Mondays doesn't apply to purchases made with vouchers. Dear God, do I need to remind you that I am not an actress? How do you expect me to show up for a job interview with a smile on my face, wearing clothes and shoes that don't belong to me, and feigning interest in a job that I would not want to do for all the money in the world? On the other hand, The Shameless are out on smoke break again, in spite of the heavy rain, and Lavermine quickly jumped on the opportunity to denigrate all the stupid-ass bitches and nasty-ass whores who chose to go out, and is even wishing pneumonia on them. Too upset to go on.

8:44 a.m. – Sitting at a picnic table under the overhang of a classroom building next to Westcott, and all I can think of is: Thank God I found this place and let's just hope that FSUPD doesn't find me. And why did I skip Mass and walk straight here from The Shelter? Because I have an 11:30 appointment with Miss Edwards (ECHO is located four or five blocks away), and I couldn't bear the thought of doing all that walking in torrential rain. Do I need to add that my lower half is completely drenched, my feet are freezing, my backpack is soaked, and that I hate my life?

6:52 p.m. – Just arrived in The Shelter's driveway, and I am grateful to be here alone for once because I am not quite ready to see those women. Harold Kushner said that most people who pray for a miracle do not get one and that we need to . . . oh my God two police cars are here and three police officers are running toward the driveway . . . a third car just arrived and another cop headed for The Shelter's backyard though Macomb Street . . . four police cars in the parking lot altogether. More chest pain. Who could have guessed that I would end up sharing roofs with criminals while trying to grow along spiritual lines? This just can't be the life I turned over to God with the belief that he could manage it better than I could.

9:49 p.m. – Forgot to record this morning that I dreamed of JH for the first time in my life, and while I don't recall the details, seeing her in a dream brought back a particular misstep that I would rather forget, though I am probably being too hard on myself, considering that I wasn't the one who went after *her* boyfriend. While we're on the topic, I also dreamed of FirstBadChoice over the weekend. The same recurring dream in which he was looking at me with cold, accusing eyes because his ego was still bruised over my decision to marry ExHusband soon after he told me that he had no intention to ever get married to me or the two other girls he was dating simultaneously (JH was his favorite.) Another pitiful chapter in my long history of romantic blunders that is simply not worth revisiting.

11:27 p.m. – Back in bed 6 after watching the 11 o'clock news. Grateful that Alberto, the first tropical storm of the hurricane season, moved on, though more rain is expected tomorrow. Not grateful that I spent the afternoon reading *When Bad Things Happen to Good People,* a book I meant to read two decades ago, because I can't get Harold Kushner out of my head. See eye to eye with him on many of the questions he raised, perhaps because I've already wrestled with them myself, but cannot go along with the idea that you, God, is a being with limited power over the challenges that fate may throw at us. Wish I could believe that and move on, but something in me would not let me. So just for today, I am choosing to hold on to my high expectations of you, as unrealistic as they may seem to others, trusting that you will eventually correct my thinking if I am wrong, as you have done so many times before.

Sick as a dog and discouraged *à en mourir.* I've caught more colds at The Shelter than I have caught the past five years. Feel as if I am being hit from all sides. Homelessness is killing me *à petit feu,* and I don't see a way out. God, please deliver me from this hell. Please. Because I am going to die from a broken heart if you don't.

Relief du jour: April was put out of The Shelter for doing what she does best: acting ugly. And unsurprisingly, members of the White Shameless Club were frantic. Kaycee Sourpuss went so far as to insist that April didn't deserve to be banned because "she wasn't doing anything worse than anyone else in this fuckhole was doing."

Highlight du jour: A phone call to Lulu just to hear Patoutou's voice. Lulu said that someone recently asked Patoutou who she looks like and the answer was: "Like myself." My kind of girl. Lulu also said that Patoutou refuses to speak on the phone to anyone but me. Music to my ears bearing in mind that one of my greatest fears is that I am going to call one day and she won't know who I am.

Provocation du jour: Being shoved by Shelterqueen on my way back to the dining room bathroom to pick up a wet dress that I had inadvertently left on the shower rod. I told her that I just needed to retrieve something, but she replied that it was her turn to use the bathroom and when I nevertheless went in, she pushed me, to the overmerriment of her fellow Shameless who are always eager to fuel a fire. Something must be done with this woman, but what?

Shelter drama du jour: Pretty black girl in bed 2 who after some time had told The Shameless that they can call her "Secret" was kicked out tonight because, as Shelter staff told it, she remained in the back yard long after smoke break to flirt with the male Shelter guests on the other side of the fence. (All Shelter guests share the same back yard and Day Center during the day, but the women are not allowed to speak to the men once they check in.)

Plea du jour: Kaycee Boneheaded is actually thrilled to see April gone, even though she always laughs the loudest whenever April sits at the dining room table and proceeds to update everyone on her electrifying sex life (she has a husband, a boyfriend, and a girlfriend.) Kaycee Boneheaded even claims that she had prayed the night before last "that Jesus makes whoever don't belong here leave," but never thought that the Lord would answer her prayer so quickly. Jesus, help me. Help me carry my cross like you carried yours. Help me embrace my destiny like you embraced yours. Help me obey *our* Father like you have obeyed Him. And, above all, help me ignore all the credulous folks who take it for granted that they have earned a one-way ticket to heaven just for believing all the stories they've been told about you all their lives.

Grateful for all the attention I got after the 5:15 p.m. Mass (was so depressed I went to church twice) from the cutest little guy I've seen in a while: thirteen-month-old Stevie who was standing in front of the main entrance of St. Thomas More with his parents, along with some other wedding guests, and the boy just walked up to me and gave me the biggest hug—twice. Thank you, God, for the love of a child is always more trustworthy than the love of an adult.

Grateful to have heard a young woman remind her son to use his "library voice" as they entered the main library this afternoon because too many mothers simply plant themselves in front of a computer, Myspacing, and let their children run wild, expecting librarians to keep an eye on them. (I've seen five year olds going to the restrooms alone, and in the elevators. Even had to help a four-year-old boy find his nine-year-old sister the other day.)

Grateful for the spunk to tell Mr. ShelterDrillSergeant that he needs to speak to Shelter staff about the need to start implementing Shelter rules after he gave his acclaimed on-my-mama's-grave speech to a woman who was demanding that everyone be searched because her purse was missing. ("I swear on my mama's grave that I will put you out if there is one more complaint about you tonight.") I know Shelterqueen resents me even more for speaking up, but I couldn't help myself. Also grateful for the courage to tell the new blonde in bed 8 (The Shameless are infatuated with blondness, too) that I can't thank God for putting a roof over my head in a homeless shelter because The Shelter's roof is not my roof. And since she seems to be almost as drunk as she is thankful, maybe I need to take up beer drinking as a hobby in order to drum up more thankfulness.

Grateful I am no longer the woman I used to be. Heard the song *Listen to Your Heart* when I went to Publix this morning to buy a lottery ticket, and it automatically took me back to 1989, and I began to smile until I remembered all the unhappiness I created for myself while listening to my heart. Also grateful that I've always been the self-help type, not the type who relishes in my imperfections, and definetely not the type who let myself be defined by any labels. "You will always have a special place in my heart because you're the most messed up kid I have," a fifty-three-year-old redhead who just arrived from Alaska with the goal of starting over in Florida after a lifetime of drinking said a moment ago, recalling a conversation she once had with her dad. "He saw right through me. I've always been messed up when all I ever wanted was to be happy." I was tempted to tell her that some of us came into this world to overcome, not to be happy. But I don't speak to those women unless they speak to me first, especially since this one has already established herself as a devil's helper through her futile attempts to befriend Lavermine out of fear.

A pretty uneventful day, and thank God. Spent my morning on a bench at Tallahassee Mall, then at Barnes & Noble, and my afternoon at the movies. First went to see *Failure to Launch*, which turned out to be a good investment of a dollar since I walked out of the theater, smiling. *Just my Luck* wasn't as bad as I anticipated, but the plot did strike fear in my heart in terms of the kind of message those silly romantic comedies send to the myriad of women who have yet to realize that the mating game was never meant to be taken so seriously, something our male counterparts have long figured out. (And something that all preteen girls should be made aware of in order to better protect their mental and emotional health when the time comes.)

Ninabelle just asked if I have a pen. "I have one, but I am using it," I said. Of course I have an extra pen, but she's always coming to me for paper and pen to write to her friends in jail, and I am through enabling her, especially since she's already planning her next weekend getaway. Unadulterated selfishness is what I am being taught at The Shelter so far, in spite of myself.

"People say you're a witch but you're not even that," I just told Lavermine. "You're a beast. An evil beast."

> She can't wait to finish cleaning her purse so she could go lie down and listen to some good shit.

> She knows that someone is trying to get her kicked out of The Shelter, but she won't be leaving alone.

> She feels bad for all the haters who keep complaining about her just because they're jealous of her and want to steal her joy.

> She knows she's a bitch, but she ain't that bad a bitch. But then again, she doesn't give a flying fuck about what the motherfuckers think.

> She's tired of being at The Shelter because the stupid-ass bitches and nasty-ass whores worry about all the wrong things. Typical niggers. And that's why they're going to be homeless forever.

> She must thank Rashad for a nice dinner because her stomach is so full she can afford to skip her late-night snack and eat it for lunch tomorrow. (Dinner was lovely, indeed. I guess they're making up for all the nasty pasta, gummy rice, and straight-from-the-can green beans that the donors have been bringing all week.)

She and her man are going country next weekend. Way out. Far away from all the motherfuckers, and she needs to look her best. Her man has been showering her with so much attention that she feels more desirable today than she felt in her younger years. So desirable that she must strive to contain herself because she doesn't want her sexual prowess to go to her head.

I am 99 percent sure that the lowlife doesn't have a boyfriend. Who would want to kiss her? Yet, I had to listen to all the above and more since I returned to bed 6 after dinner because the baldheaded monster spent the whole evening sitting below me describing out loud everything that she's doing, and every thought that crossed her mind. Yet she had the nerve to accuse me of encouraging people to congregate by her bed when SonyaBette momentarily stood by the bunk to say that Louvern was at The Shelter this afternoon and asked her to tell me and two other women that she would be glad if we would come for a visit the Saturday after next.

Made an appointment with a temp agency today just so I can have something to tell Miss Edwards when I see her again for I don't want her to think that she wasted her time helping me update my résumé last week, or that I am misusing the 31-day bus pass she gave me to facilitate my job search. Used JP's phone to call the agency and the call went very well once I was told that they were located near a Books-A-Million and I replied that I wish I had known earlier that Tallahassee had a Books-A-Million because I used to be a habitué at the one on Dupont Circle in D.C. (I said nothing, of course, about the huge amount of time I spent daydreaming about seeing *Out of the Trenches* prominently displayed in the store's front windows.) At any rate, I have an interview tomorrow and I'll be wearing my Goodwill clothes and shoes for the first time, heaven help me. Incidentally, the latest guest in bed 8 is a forty-year-old white woman with barely an inch of hair, and I am embarrassed to say that my first thought was: *Is she another lesbian straight out of LCJ* (The Shameless affectionally refer to the Leon County Jail by its acronym), *or another loony who just got released from the Apalachee Center?* She turned out to be a cancer patient traveling through Tallahassee.

A rather interesting day:

    (1) Lustful Shelter staff – Mr. HornyBoy got himself fired because it turns out that I was not the only Shelter guest he had the hots for, and one of The Shameless denounced him just for fun. A part of me immediately felt that he would have changed his behavior if I had only impressed upon him the importance of keeping his pants zipped up on the job. Dear God, please remind me that I have more important issues to invest my time and energy on.

    (2) Multifaceted enigma – Lavermine apologized to me again for her bad attitude of late (as if she ever had a good one), and just about begged me to understand that she is not who people say she is. It's just hard for her to be at The Shelter, and she sometimes says the wrong thing out of self-preservation because the other women are always trying to intimidate her. "Intimidate," by the way, is one of Lavermine's favorite words, in addition to "typical niggers," "stupid-ass bitches" and "nasty-ass whores."

    (3) 21st century job search – I haven't been to a real job interview in years, and boy have things changed. To be brief, my potential employers were not interested to learn anything about me face to face, just what their computer said that I could do. And it didn't say a whole lot, given that I couldn't even pass their basic math test. During the few minutes I actually

spent speaking to a human being, I was nicely told that because I've spent the past six years being a stay-at-home mom, my computer skills were rusty at best and that the agency needed people who were up to par with technology (I still don't have a grasp of basic Power Point and Excel despite taking each class three times while at the bank), but that they will call me if an entry-level position comes up. (I am still waiting for their call with breathless anticipation two summers later as I write the first draft of this book.) It's worth pointing out that I felt completely lost when I was asked to list my three top accomplishments at my last job since I've always viewed myself as a *mal-dans-ma-peau* office helper who was so not a team player. But I had no problem coming up with my three top accomplishments in life once I left the building: the decision to turn my will and my life over to you, God. Raising my children. And writing OOTT.

Shelter quotes of the day:

I didn't call the heifer a bitch. I respect motherfuckers that I call bitches.

Somebody is going to get their ass whipped if I don't find my cigarettes.

Just because I have white skin doesn't mean that I am. I am blacker than you are. So, tread lightly.

I ain't the bitch to be fucking with, fucking cunt. You need to put a big fat cock in your mouth and shut the fuck up.

I know God don't like ugly, but she better shut up before I knock her motherfucking ass out. If I have to go to jail, I will make sure I go with a bang.

Shit, I need to wash my ass, too. What the fuck is she doing in the bathroom all this time, playing with herself?

> If I miss smoke break, I am going to be fucking mad. Jesusfuckingchrist!

> So what if I have two children and spend my money on weed and motel rooms? Do I tell all the wild-ass hoes around here how to spend their money? My kids are fine where they at. Worry about your own damn kids.

The brazenness of these women almost defies belief. And the more I listen to them, the more I understand why so many boys grow up to be fiends with such low regard for women. If you have no respect for yourself and for other women, solve all your problems with your fists and filthy language, what kind of role model can you be for your daughters and sons? The line about going to jail with a bang was actually uttered by a mother of four right in front of her children. No wonder going to jail has become a mere rite of passage in so many families. (I later met a woman whose boyfriend was a convicted rapist, yet she was surprised when her own son stood accused of a sex-related crime. The same son had already fathered two children with two different girls by the time he dropped out of high school, yet all she could talk about was how proud she is of him because he's so handsome.)

Surprise du jour: Both April and Mr. HornyBoy are back. According to April, she was only banned for one night, but decided to go spend some time with her two-year-old grandson whom she lovingly nicknames "My Cute Little Fucker." (April, I recently found out, does have a job and only comes to The Shelter when she doesn't have money for motel rooms.) And according to Lavermine, Mr. HornyBoy didn't get fired yet, to her dismay, but he got a slap on the wrist and he's being watched. She also knows without a doubt that his days at The Shelter are numbered because he's still carrying on a torrid affair with someone else and they think they're fooling everybody, but she's no fool. Why do I sense so strongly that I am that someone else?

Gratitude du jour: That Deanna gave me a big welcoming smile when I came in this evening. I told her how good it felt to see a friendly face because I get a knot in my stomach every afternoon at the thought of going back to The Shelter and she laughed. Unlike me, Deanna actually enjoys being around The Shameless. "I like being of service to the women," she had answered with a broad smile when I once asked her why she was working at The Shelter. I told her that she needed to be in college at her age, not being of service to a bunch of ingrates who were by and large taking the system for a ride. (Okay, I didn't exactly say it like that, but it was implied.)

Demoralization du jour: Coming across a September 28, 2005 *New York Times* article about obstetric fistula in which a Dutch doctor who travels to Nigeria several times a year to perform fistula surgeries all but said that to be born in Africa is one of the worst things that could happen to a woman. Dear God, I know I asked you this question before, but I am asking it again since you have yet to answer me: Forget about compassion and conscionable leadership, where is the racial pride of African leaders?

Admiration du jour: Read a small article about India.Arie in the current issue of *Essence*, and can't help feeling a bit proud of her tenacity to remain true to herself, in spite of all the pressure to conform. As gifted as she is, India.Arie would have been a superstar by now if she at least tried to downplay her blackness like all the other long-and-straight-hair wannabes in the black entertainment business

Hunch du jour: That young women in this country are being encouraged to reject the suggestions of the people who know them best—and care about them the most—in favor of high-priced discourse with so-called mental health experts who will tell them over the course of one year what their aunts, grandmothers, godmothers and mothers could have told them in one hour.

8:25 a.m. – Still at STM an hour after the end of Mass. Have been spending so much time here that I won't be thrown off balance if the groundkeeper walks up to me one day and say, "I think you got our church confused with The Shelter's Day Center." Not taking communion is also attracting more attention to me than I anticipated. "I come to Daily Mass because I enjoy being among seekers," was the answer I gave to a curious lady yesterday. Didn't think it was a good idea to unveil that I was born and raised Catholic, but was never a believer in the full sense of the word, and only started going to church in the year 2000 because I had to some extent hoped that Christianity would have the answer to some of the questions that were beyond the sphere of OA/AA. (I was officially in OA, but attended lots of AA meetings because they had more substance.) Should get ready to leave the church now, but I am too tired to head out. Woke up around 1:30, courtesy of Shelterqueen who created an uproar going through her bags before she went to hide in the dining room bathroom to eat fried chicken as she often does. (She leaves crumbs on the bathroom floor and chicken bones in the trashcan.) She went back to sleep right away but I did not, especially after seeing more roaches crawl on the rails of the bunk and on the nearby wall, despite all the spraying I've been doing. And when I did finally doze off, I dreamed that I was back working at the bank and even had my own private office, which was decorated even more charmingly than my old cubicle, yet I still hated the job and was as miserable as ever. I never imagined that my decision to focus on emotional stability, character building, and spiritual maturity could backfire so colossally. If I only knew what I was paying for.

9:20 a.m. – Sitting on the usual bench in front of the College of Medicine. Cannot believe the construction of the new psychology building next door is practically over and I am still in Tallahassee. Homeless, hopeless and purposeless in Tallahassee. The new FSU parking garage on West Tennessee and Macomb, almost right across the street from The Shelter, is standing tall, too, even though it was just an unpaved lot when I moved here from New York eight months ago. Enough to make me feel as if I am regressing while the rest of the world is progressing.

7:12 p.m. – In bed 6, at last, after spending a good twenty minutes cleaning the dining room bathroom just to be able to use it for ten minutes. (Water was spilling into the dining room, yet no one bothered to remove the long strands of hair that were clogging the shower drain, yet there they were at the ungodly table rhapsodizing about King David as if he were a living relative of theirs.) Dear God, why do I have this gut feeling that you care more about our current attitudes and behaviors than about us parroting tales from old books filled with inconsistencies and half-truths?

Andrelene, one of the few decent Shelter guests who does hang around the black Shameless but does not behave like them, and with whom I do exchange a few words from time to time, just asked how my day went and I said "bad." Since it was clear that she wanted me to say more, I told her that I had a sore throat and could hardly talk. How could I disclose to another soul that I spent the entire day fighting back tears because God broke my heart even more than all the assholes I've fallen in love with combined? And guess who came to apologize to me while I sat at The Chain of Parks this afternoon? Z'Laitah. Too depressed to elaborate on our interesting but bizarre conversation, which lasted over an hour, but boy do I love to hear her speak.

PS: April is here again tonight and she's mad as fuck and she's ready to burst her foot off someone's ass. Lavermine, too, is cussing up a storm. I wonder if they're cussing at each other. Now that would be something. The Shelter's whitest trash versus its blackest.

PPS: It's 8:54 and Lavermine just took it upon herself to "cut out the lights" because she's tired of "all the white whores with no place to stay" trying to intimidate her, and wants to go to sleep. And I am going to flip the switch right back on just to remind her that she's not staff.

The 8:30 Mass just ended and I am sitting on one of the three benches that were installed on the lawn between the church and the rectory a few days ago while the priest is at the main entrance shaking hands with the parishioners and making small talk. "Do you really believe that God had that silly talk with Satan pertaining to Job?" I want to ask him. But I am too exhausted to be alive, much less go expose my heretical self to a living disciple of the Lord. In truth, I am paralysed with so much anxiety and fear that if I were a member of a caring and well-to-do family, today would have been a good day to have a nervous breakdown and let my parents take over for a while. Must do my utmost to insulate myself from any situation that is likely to trigger more stress in the next few hours because I am going to go off the deep end if I don't. Is that how perfectly sane people wind up in the psych ward, and then become insane?

A much better day than yesterday. Spent a very pleasant afternoon with JP, mostly discussing current events. He thinks that the idea of China acquiring a fleet of "death vans" so that they can carry out capital punishment in a more efficient manner is quite original. He recoiled at the thought of his future wife being impregnated through DI (Donor Insemination) if he were infertile, and would rather they adopt a child. He agrees that the *Tallahassee Democrat* appears to go out of its way to splash every single bad news about FAMU on its front page just because FAMU is a historically black university. I am still not sure whether I should laugh or cry over him telling me that he has already been exposed to many of the issues I broach with him just from watching TV, and that *Law & Order*, for instance, has taught him a great deal about the law.

Meanwhile, it's barely 8 p.m. and I am getting ready to put on the dreadful earplugs in an effort to prevent another confrontation with Lavermine who's sitting below me at this moment in time singing, "I don't like you. Nobody here likes you. Find your own place and go away." And prior to that she was singing, "Hater, don't hate me because I have a hot dog to go with my hamburger and you don't because nobody wants your sorry ass." I finally understand why that homeless woman I once spoke to in New York said that she feels more comfortable living at the Port Authority than in a homeless shelter because it was the lesser of two evils.

Wide awake at 3 a.m. because Shelterqueen let out a stream of expletives when I woke up to go use the bathroom, and while I couldn't make out what she said (had the earplugs on in spite of the burning itch in my ears), and for all I know she could have been cussing in her sleep again, I still feel too jittery to go back to sleep. Do I need to add that Lissa is in the big bathroom stewing over her biggest problem in life? "I don't see them as black, but they do see me as white," she just said in the voice of an utterly defeated woman. I still don't feel sorry for her. She probably was a pampered and small-minded Southern belle in a previous life (if there is such a thing) who's just paying back for her sins by being forced to live among the most imbecilic and despicable group of black people I have ever stumbled upon. But then again, if that is the case, what does that say about me? Who was I in a past life?

An insouciant mother whose last priority in life was the well-being of the children she brought into the world as long as they were well-fed and well-dressed?

A bourgeois father who was well respected in his community yet refused to take financial and moral responsibility for his illegitimate children?

A bright but deep-down insecure husband who would move mountains to advance his career at the expense of everything else?

A greedy landlord with a malevolent predisposition to kick tenants out of her property just because she could?

A narcissistic boyfriend who needed a string of women at his arms just to feel good about himself?

Who was I, God? And who am I?

Sitting on a bench in front of Westcott with tears of frustration rolling down my face after my weekly meeting with Miss Edwards. Need to stop going to ECHO. I've been telling so many lies about how busy I am looking for a job that I can hardly keep up with my own stories. As helpful as she wants to be, Miss Edwards simply doesn't have any "job lead" that I have any interest in. I don't want to work as a customer service representative for Kelly Services. I don't want to work as a claims examiner for Capital Health Care Plan. And I definitely do not want to work as a custodial worker for the city of Tallahassee. God, I think it's time for me to be bluntly honest with you: I am too old for this shit.

Woke up with chest pain and frowning. Going to bed with chest pain and frowning. The only thing worth recording is that I did finish reading *House of Sand and Fog*, and I guess it's a good thing that I didn't shed any tears over the plights of the characters this time around considering that I went to sit at a table in Bryant Park and wept uncontrollably after I saw the movie at the AMC on Times Square a week or two after it came out. As shellshocked as I was on eviction day, part of me held on to the belief that the worst was over. Little did I know that the worst had yet to come.

Sadness du jour: Reading that Patsy Ramsey died of cancer. Another woman whose journey through hell on earth makes my own look like a walk in the park.

Wish du jour: That I could cook myself a meal in my own kitchen. I don't even like to cook, yet I miss cooking. Hell, I even miss paying bills. And going grocery shopping. And raking leaves. In a word, I miss being an adult.

Realization du jour: That writing *Out of the Trenches* has given me somewhat of a love for fiction, and for it benefits. As ornery as she can be (even when she's not stretching the truth), I bet Ann Coulter would have gotten away with all she said about the Jersey Girls if she had said it through fiction.

Faux pas du jour: Starting a conversation with Ninabelle after I heard her say that Shelter life is wearing her out, and she wants to go back home. To be sure, Ninabelle is unquestionably a proud member of the Black Shameless Club, but unlike most of them, she does seem remorseful every so often after behaving badly.

Humiliation du jour: I went to sit in the dining room during the 9:30 smoke break just to prevent Shelterqueen from changing the channel at 10 p.m. What did she do? She said that I must be a fool to think that I can "take over the TV every Friday night" and went downstairs. Next thing I know, Mr. Jejune came up and turned the TV off—as I watched it—without saying a word to me.

Satisfaction du jour: That I came out of the dining room bathroom right on time to watch Lavermine and her buddy Kaycee Boneheaded go at it. To hear Kaycee Boneheaded say it, Lavermine was in the back room gossiping about her new boyfriend, a white *fainéant* who spends hours online every day filling out 10-cent surveys, and she "ain't the one." (The one to pick a fight with, that is.) Kaycee Boneheaded is clearly not a woman to whom forgive and forget comes easily, but I have no doubt that she and Lavermine will be friends again in no time at all because the two of them sort of go well together, like maggots and rotten meat.

Disturbance du jour: A picture of Bill Gates on the cover of *The Economist*, holding an African baby. Didn't read the article since it is most likely related to the new gift his foundation just received from Warren Buffet, and I've already read more on the topic than I need to know. Dear God, when will Africans realize that only Africans can save Africans? Besides, Africa has problems that no amount of money can solve. Can money get through the heads of the African people that a continent divided in too many languages, too many tribes, and too many prehistoric customs (as opposed to America with one official language, two major tribes, and ever-changing mores) will never thrive until they, Africans, decide to do something about it?

"I am going back to bed. A fucking senile bitch is what she is!" Kaycee Sourpuss squealed two minutes ago, in reference to Lavermine, as she walked out of the dining room. "She ain't got but six teeth in her mouth and I'm going to knock them all out," the woman from Hoboken whose name I still don't know and don't care to know just cried, also in reference to Lavermine who is in the dining room making revolting comments about people with varicose veins. The good news, if you can call it that, is that

I am so perturbed by my afternoon visit to Louvern that their sickening disposition doesn't faze me one bit.

- It saddens me that the precariousness of Louvern's financial situation was worsened when her work hours were reduced, prompting her to go back to what I suspect has been a long-term on and off occupation just to pay the $365 a month rent on her studio apartment. (Rent is cheap in Tallahassee, but the shockingly-high utility cost is a major drain.)

- It stupefies me that she had no stab of conscience over going to The Shelter's backyard to recruit black associates to help her go spray more toxicity on the landscape of Frenchtown, a poor African-American neighborhood in the back of The Shelter. She even got mad at a male Shelter guest for being "too lazy to get off his ass to go make some good money," but Estelle, thankfully, needed to buy new hair and more than welcomed a chance to earn fifty dollars.

- It flusters me that I was so bowled over upon learning that Tallahassee, too, has its share of crack houses for I stupidly assumed that such realities only exit in big cities. I may be wrong, I hope I am wrong, but it seems to me that *generally speaking* poor black people try to excel at all the things that are either irrelevant to their integrity, individually or collectively, or the ones that only serve to perpetuate the negative stereotypes the world has of them. God, forgive us and help us.

Cannot believe that Z'Laitah who had been quite friendly with me all week (she even told me to be careful with Lavermine because she thinks that Lavermine may be a Shelter spy) acted as if she didn't know me when I said hello to her this evening, yet spent a good half hour talking to Ninabelle as if they were the best of friends.

Cannot believe that a 60-year-old black Shameless who hasn't seen her children in 17 years and don't even know the names of her grandchildren told me that God is going to punish me, my children, and my country for "mistreating" her after I knocked on the bathroom door to tell her that her 20 minutes in the shower were over 10 minutes ago.

Cannot believe that I ended up in line with male Shelter guests all over again around noontime after one of them saw me sitting at The Chain of Parks and asked if I wasn't going to get my "chicken box." Come to find out, a box of two-pieces fried chicken with biscuit and mashed potato is served at 12:30 p.m. on Sundays at the First Presbyterian Church a block away from the main library. I didn't know, then, that Food Not Bombs also serves vegetarian meals at the gazebo behind the main library at 3 p.m. on Sundays. (Things haven't been the same without you, Joselle.)

Cannot believe that "Sudhira is getting married to a blond and blue-eyed Anglo-Saxon," was the spine-tingling news an upbeat Sabine shared with me the moment she saw me this evening, as if having blond hair and blue eyes was all the introduction that Sudhira's future husband needed. "I wonder what kind of man would marry her," I deadpanned. My question was answered minutes later when I heard Sudhira, a mixed-race CS worker who is highly regarded among The Shameless because she acts just like them, say that her fiancé just got out of prison and is having trouble finding a job. And once again, I can't help but be in awe at the power of the white race to spark white envy in non-white people.

Cannot believe that the same Lavermine who was having a nice, grandmotherly conversation with a toddler when I came in was giving the following advice to Nicolitta, the young Latina who slept in bed 8 the past two nights, an hour later: "Girl, don't ever let drugs take the best of you. Take the best of it." Nicolitta was silent for a moment before she acquiescently replied, "I get it!" and Lavermine's lips stretched into a gratifying smile. "You're really fucked up, you know?" Kaycee Sourpuss who had witnessed the conversation frostily remarked. "What-the-hell-ever!" Lavermine retorted with a dismissive wave of her hand. (In the interest of fairness, it must be said that Lavermine is one of the few women at The Shelter who doesn't treat children like uninvited guests whenever they venture upstairs without their mothers. Children from the family section are told to stay downstairs at all times, but they don't. And most female Shelter guests expect better behaviors from three year olds than they do from each other.)

Grateful that I did not answer the phone when Miss Edwards called to ask for the name, address and phone number of my new employer so that she can close her case. (I had left her a message a few days ago, saying that I found a job through my church.)

Grateful for my ability to connect with people from all the major world religions as long as the conversation is based on you, God, not on Abraham or Jesus or Muhammad or Joseph Smith. (Spent about an hour this morning conversing with two lovely young ladies. Lovely young ladies who also happen to be missionaries from The Church of Jesus Christ of Latter-day Saints.)

Grateful for my determination to not accept the unacceptable from others, nor from myself. And for my tendency to keep my focus on quality, not quantity. It came to me on my way to Mass that I would rather spend the rest of my life being committed to one single cause, than to be involved in an eye-popping array of projects just to earn bragging rights about how powerful and indispensable I am.

Grateful I didn't feel overly miffed when I was told by Joline that I need to find myself a man because all aspects of my life, including my mood, would improve for the better if I do. (I told her that a man can give me a short-term solution, but that only God can provide me with a long-lasting one.) Equally grateful for the persistence to keep seeking you out, God. You are the last house on the block.

Grateful for a quiet afternoon spent reading excerpts from the writings of some great religious thinkers, such as Dallas Willard, in a book that Sabine loaned me last night. Also grateful for the guts to tell Sabine that I didn't come into the world to pray for evil when she told me that she doesn't pray for me because I don't need her prayers, but that she prays for Lavermine daily and that I should do the same.

Grateful that the suicidal thoughts that resurfaced soon after JP's roommate decided to come home for lunch, found me on her couch "looking mighty comfortable" (the futon I paid for when I had a job), and proceeded to kick me out of apartment 6 all over again, evaporated almost as quickly as they appeared. I know too much about you today, God, to kill myself. What's more, suicide is not only a waste of time since we can't possibly escape the plan that you have set out for our souls. Suicide is a lack of trust in your wisdom, and most specifically in your mercy.

A harrowing Fourth of July spent in church, at Barnes & Noble and on FSU campus. Saw FSUPD drive by twice while I sat in front of the College of Medicine, and have this creepy feeling that they're going to have a talk with me one of these days just to make it clear that the campus of Florida State University is not a hideaway for the homeless.

Realization du jour: That the widely-held perception that people cannot be changed is false. The fact of the matter is that people are being programmed and re-programmed daily through watching television alone, which explains why the nation's social engineers sometimes request popular

TV shows to address a specific topic whenever a fresh wave of national brainwashing is in order.

Exhilaration du jour: Reading an article about the declining population in Europe, a great concern for the European powers that be. In short, France and Russia are flat out begging women to have babies. I hope women on every continent follow the trend just to remind the masters of this universe of their limitations. On second thoughts, since the credit for birth control doesn't go to women, maybe I am the one who need to learn to accept my limitations.

Gratitude du jour: That Deanna is back because my life in this hellhole is more bearable when she's around. She said that she went to a family reunion in Texas. And speaking of Shelter staff, I chose not to apprise Mr. HornyBoy of our ongoing affair, but I did tell him to be careful because I heard that he was being watched. And I didn't blink an eye when he innocently replied that he doesn't understand why the women are making up stories about him because he's just being nice as part of his job description. Nice. A pretty little word that can harbor oodles of wickedness.

Question mark du jour: Felt a ridiculous twinge of pride as I stood across the street from FSU's new Department of Psychology in perfect contemplation, as if the building were a brainchild of mine, and found myself wondering what is it about the design and construction of homes and buildings and roads that fascinate me so much? To tell the truth, one of the reasons I remained so crazily in love with Deceitful CJ long after I should not have is because he could build houses from scratch. Yes, he was an unimaginative and sloppy builder. But I could always take charge of refining his work, I reasoned, once he divorces his wife and marries me. (He divorced his wife and married another woman two years later, right under my unsuspecting nose. And, yes, I did spend more than a brief moment plotting his murder, or at the very least his castration.)

3:46 p.m. – I just came across Juliet Dietrich's business card while cleaning out my backpack, and it inevitably brought me back to that day in late May 2004 when I broke down in tears while walking down Flatbush Avenue as I agonized over how I was going to get back to work after my one-week "suicide vacation" since I had sent my last paycheck to the kids thinking that I would not be needing it. Juliet Dietrich who is clearly a New Yorker who does mind other people's business somehow spotted me, double-parked her car, and honked unremittingly until she got my attention. I don't recall what I told her, but I do recall her giving me money to buy a 7-day MetroCard, and I am eternally grateful to you, God, for having placed that warmhearted woman on my path that horrific day.

7:05 p.m. – In bed 6 with a smile on my face. Lavermine started singing her latest tune "Silly girl, silly girl, silly, silly, silly girl," as I got ready to take a shower thirty minutes ago, and had switched to "Lord, make them go away because they're trying to steal my joy," by the time I came back. And I couldn't be more proud of myself for saying the following "prayer" out loud the moment she paused for breath: "Lord, please deliver me from evil and drunks and crackheads and jailbirds and prostitutes." What a riveting Shelter moment that was! I think I shocked her into silence. (Louvern told me on Saturday that Lavermine is a former prostitute who still blows her own horn about how good she used to be and can still be whenever she wants to bask in the adulation of the scelerats in The Shelter's backyard.)

8:00 p.m. – Marguerite, one of the nurses who cater to The Shameless every evening, just stopped by the bunk to tell me that she noticed that I try hard to maintain some kind of equilibrium amid madness. She went on to say that she does understand where I am coming from because she, too, is an introvert who does a lot of reading and writing. I thank you, God, for sending another like-minded soul my way, yet the reality is that I've never felt so alone. Or so trapped. Trapped in a hell that was tailored-made for me. If I were born in a war-ravaged country, I would not have lived long enough to tell the story because adaptation is not part of my character. Yet here I am stuck in a homeless shelter in the United States of America as a result of choosing to do your will. My mouth is perfectly shut, but I am screaming inside.

I am so angry I can't think straight, but the situation with Lavermine is not what's exactly pressing on my mind just now. Called my mother on my way back to The Shelter from the main library and according to her my daughter has given up on trying to finish school and is thinking about moving back to P.G. County to become a hairdresser. Dear God, you know and I know that I have great admiration for people who use their natural talents to earn a living as long as it's legal and ethical, but my brainy, bilingual little girl who spoke in full sentences before her first birthday, read her first book at the age of three, and scored in the 99th percentile for the gifted and talented program in kindergarten, was not raised to be an office helper, or a service worker.

"You better get it together and leave me alone," Lavermine is now singing. She not only sang a variety of obnoxious tunes since I got here, she came to stand right across from me at dinner time and stared me down until I went to finish the meal in the stairwell, again. "You're sitting with your foot on top of a rattlesnake," Kaycee Sourpuss later told me. "It's no time to turn the other cheek, it's time to have the bitch kicked out." Kaycee Sourpuss is right. Lavermine will not stop until she's forced to stop. If she wants a war, a war is what she's going to get.

Grateful that coveting over other people's material goods has never been one of my flaws. Dreamed about a relative of mine last night, perhaps because my mother couldn't stop talking about how well she and her husband are doing: Another trip to Europe, oldest son graduated from college and on his way to medical school, a bigger home in a better neighborhood. My mother has made it her mission to keep me updated on the monetary successes of family and friends since the eviction. She even told me about a family from her church who recently purchased a brand new home, even though I don't even know the people.

Grateful that my children are as leery as I am of the mental health industry. Wish I could have told the tall, well-built, handsome young man on FSU campus this afternoon who was talking to someone on his cell phone about his mood disorder that whatever is wrong with his mood is in all likelihood a natural byproduct of the society he lives in, and if something is intrinsically wrong with his mood, it's nothing that God can't fix, but he would have thought that something was wrong with my mood. The mental health savants did a fantastic job convincing women that we can't function without a shrink and at least one bottle of pills. I guess the time has come for them to start exploiting their own gender.

Grateful for the presence of mind to hand over the note I had written for Deanna to Mr. ShelterDrillSergeant when he told me that Deanna will be off the whole week. Why did I feel the need to write Deanna a note? Because my instinct tells me that I need to start keeping a paper trail on the hell that Lavermine is putting me through. (She went to stand in front of me this morning while I wait for breakfast and taunted me until I was forced to walk away.) "*. . . For whatever reason,*" I told Deanna in my note, "*this psychopath has carte blanche to terrorize whoever she wants in this shelter without any of the consequences that other guests are subjected to. I don't understand why she gets away with so much, but then again Shelter politics is not any of my business.*" I hope they didn't believe me because I am going to start making Shelter politics my business.

A fairly good day until I went to sit on a bench at The Chain of Parks after I left the main library (the main library closes at 6 p.m. on Fridays and Sundays), and was joined moments later by Sweet Sexy who decided to park himself right next to me, in spite of my attempts to shoo him away. He then spent the next fifteen minutes reiterating his desire to take me to the nearby Holiday Inn (now Four Points by Sheraton), to smilingly sign over to me his monthly $613 check (a small fortune in Shelter parlance), and to buy me a house since he doesn't plan to be at The Shelter forever (he has only been there three years.) He's also fascinated with my curves, though he strongly feels that I would look much better if I put on more weight since I am not as "thick" as he would like me to be. And when I stood up to leave thinking that the nightmare was finally over, he also stood up and walked side by side with me all the way to The Shelter. I was so afraid to be seen with the man that I could barely breathe. I ended up taking the longest shower of my life because I couldn't stop crying, and would have stayed in the dining room bathroom until lights out if The Shameless weren't knocking on the door every other minute. Cannot stand it, God. Cannot stand it at all.

Woke up with red and puffy eyes from crying so much, with a headache and chest cramps from feeling like the No. 1 loser in the world, and with a painful ache in my lower back from spending so much time on benches. Also woke up with my mind racing:

(1) Lavermine – Wonder if Mr. ShelterDrillSergeant gave her another warning for I've never seen her so docile. She didn't even look my way while she stood near the lockers to eat dinner last night. She usually

eats in the dining room, but all the chairs were taken by the time she was done upbraiding two women in the back room because she does not shower in the big bathroom and the door of the dining room bathroom was inexplicably locked, again, by the time she got in at seven. (The women were next in line for the private shower in the back bathroom and Lavermine had no intention to wait for her turn.)

(2) Rev. R.B. Holmes – Learning to wait was the topic of his sermon at the 11 a.m. service yesterday. To wait on God is to believe that he will deliver you from any bondage, he said. He also said that we should not worry about what others think of us or say to us while we wait because discouragement is a trick of the devil. Yet almost twenty-four hours later, I can't help thinking that the only reason his words resonated with me so strongly is because he was merely reaffirming my own beliefs, but that the fact remains that there is a vast difference between beliefs and truth.

(3) Deanna – I heard that the reason she had to take more time off is because one of her sisters was killed in a car accident. And it goes without saying that the first thing that came to mind was how cruel it was that Deanna's family had to regather a week later to bury one of their own—a young woman with a husband and a baby girl—while so many nefarious individuals are alive and thriving right here at The Shelter.

(4) Ellie Weisel – Finished reading *Night* in the dining room bathroom last night after the TV went off. Too disheartened to comment except to say that the more I read about other people's experiences of hell on earth, the more certain I am that we are, in fact, living in hell. The HELL we're so terrified of.

(5) FSUPD – Will have to spend my morning in front of the College of Medicine again since my feet hurt too much to walk to TCC. I've been seeing FSUPD more and more on and off campus. And in my mind, they're watching me, the trespasser.

(6) Z'Laitah and JP are also on my mind, but it's time to leave for church. Let's just say that I don't plan to contact JP any time soon just to see how long it will take him to get in touch with me.

7:42 p.m. – No shamelessness at the dining room table tonight. They pretty much ate as quickly as they could and hurried to bed, especially after Mr. ShelterDrillSergeant came up to give his I-don't-want-to-hear-no-gripe-from-any-of-you-tonight speech. Even Kaycee Boneheaded is sulking. "I know too many people in this town," she had said earlier, her voice quivering. "Too many important people. I just can't be seen at The Shelter." Kaycee Sourpuss isn't feeling any better. "I wonder where is our good fortune in all of that," she had exclaimed at dinnertime, adding that she would not mind talking to them if they were serious about improving the lives of the homeless, but they're not. "Go to sleep, Andrelene, and snore them away!" Sabine just proposed, perfectly echoing the sentiments of everyone else. And who are they? A reporter from the *Tallahassee Democrat* who should be here at any moment to interview The Shameless about an upcoming article regarding The Shelter's need for more funding. According to what is being said, the city is doling out a few millions to several local agencies that deal with the homeless, but not to The Shelter, and The Shelter wants its share.

8:30 p.m. – The reporter is finally here, camera in hand, but there is no takers. Well, maybe there is . . . . Lavermine just sprang out of bed with bright eyes and a dazzling smile. Mr. ShelterDirector solemnly introduces Lavermine to the reporter by saying "This is [her real name]!" as if Lavermine is truly the queen of The Shelter. Lavermine beams at the reporter some more. The reporter and Mr. ShelterDirector are looking around and making small talk as Shelterqueen looks on, beamingly. "You want your picture taken?" a smiling Mr. ShelterDirector walks up to Sabine and asks. "No, not today," Sabine answers in a small and ostensibly sleepy voice. Lavermine is still beaming. The reporter and Mr. ShelterDirector make their way to the back room and swinging into action, Lavermine makes a mad dash for the dining room, grabs a broom from the utility closet next to the bathroom and begins to sweep. Still, no one took her picture. It's going to be a hell of a night because somebody will have to pay for such a mammoth disappointment.

10:47 p.m. – I must have dozed off because I was rudely awakened a minute ago by Mr. Jejune yelling "Smoke break!" even though everyone in this room seems to be asleep. (Most Shelter staff shout out orders as unrestrainedly in the dead of night as they do in the evening hours.) Surprise, surprise, Lavermine didn't say a word to me or anyone else after she came to grips with the fact that her picture wasn't going to be in the paper any time soon, but the others had plenty to say. And in their version of events, the only person from the back room who spoke to the reporter was Didi, a redheaded character who spends her days at the main library working on her own business, a very lucrative enterprise that earns her thousands of dollars daily. (Didi also thinks that she and I are possibly related because we both share ancestors from another part of the world with the same last name.) Suffice to say that the madness was back in the dining room minutes after the reporter left. These women need so much more than what the city of Tallahassee can offer. They need mind cleansing, body cleansing and soul cleansing. Things that only you, God, can do. If they cooperate.

An unshakable dreariness permeated my heart and soul all through the day. JP and his roommate are due to leave apartment 6 at the end of the month, and JP still has no idea where he'll go because his work hours have also been cut, and he doesn't make enough money to move alone. "If you pray long enough, one day will be your day," is a refrain that I hear from Rev. Robert Powell almost every Sunday morning at Bethel. I am tired of praying. What if God really is who Christians conceptualized him to be before they got politically correct? An old white man with a long white beard who created black folks only to be at the service of his more worthy children, and I just need to get on with the program just like a good number of black people seem to have done the world over.

Grateful that Lavermine didn't pester me or anyone else today because she has a lot on her mind. To put it mildly, she just found out that her sister died and while most people cry when someone dies, she plans to get drunk because her sister, the dumb ass, should have died years ago. She also hated her sister because her sister's daddy stole from the family, unlike her own daddy who was an excellent provider until the day he died. And she plans to go to the funeral "just to make sure they put the bitch in the ground." (It came to me while rewriting this book that an apropros epitaph for Lavermine would be: *She was as bad as she could be, and the devil had nothing on her.*)

Grateful for the half-hour I spent speaking to Ninabelle about the need to create a more stable future for herself through making better choices since she changed her mind about going home, and about learning to protect herself by not giving TPD an excuse to put their hands on her. (She said she nearly got arrested a few days ago when she visited some friends whose house was under surveillance.) I know by now that her sporadic pledges to change can't be taken too seriously, but because she's so young I try to give her the benefit of the doubt in the hope that if she talks the talk long enough, you, God, will one day give her the willingness and ability to put her words into actions.

Grateful for the gumption to trust my own personal experience with you, God, rather than accept as unvarnished truth the experience of other people. "Can I have a picture of Jesus?" one of the black Shameless asked a white woman who was in The Shelter's driveway distributing religious leaflets and what-not. "You can't have a picture of Jesus because no one knows what Jesus looked like," I told her. She ignored me, of course. And once again, I tried to imagine just how the human race would react if it had a chance to take a peek at you, God, and it turns out that you do, indeed, bear a strong resemblance to Morgan Freeman. Or that you are *The Color of Water* for real.

Sitting on the floor in front of the big window in the romance section because it's the only place at the main library where I don't have to catch sight of all the homeless men who have virtually become LeRoy-Collins-Leon-County-Public-Library fixtures. (They eventually took over that area, too. The same way they eventually took over every single section of The Chain of Parks. Male Shelter guests are like cockroaches, unwelcome yet ubiquitous.) Anyway, I am here with the usual pile of newspapers in front of me, but the following book titles just caught my eye:

Lost without his Love

Transformed by his Love

Nothing Matters but his Love

Flirting with the Town's Bad Boy

Bedding the Town's Bad Boy

Taming the Town's Bad Boy

Okay, the above are not the exact titles of the books on the shelves, but they might as well be. I now know why I have yet to see a man in the romance section, unless he had been dragged there by a woman. Dear God, when will women realize that while romance novels do undeniably provide an ephemeral escape from reality, they are insidiously designed to help keep them in emotional bondage? (I actually saw a man in the romance section about a year later, and felt obligated to accost him only to find out that he was new in the country and was trying to improve his English so that he could increase his chance of finding a nice American lady.)

Puzzlement du jour: I was pleasantly surprised to find Z'Laitah in bed 8 after the plethora of weirdoes who have occupied that bed the past few weeks—including the one who proudly "served ten years in the pen for beating up a cop." Yet she gave me a blank look and simply said "I would rather not discuss it" when I asked why they moved her out of the back room, and once again I feel like a fool for trying to be friendly to this woman who's cold one day and hot the next. Is that what they call a mood disorder?

Indignation du jour: Lavermine rushing to the front desk, unbeknownst to me, to go fetch a Shelter staff after she saw me talking with Mr. HornyBoy. Thank goodness, Mr. HornyBoy walked toward the back room seconds before she came back with Mr. ShelterDrillSergeant in tow, and the look on her face fully mirrored the disappointment she must have felt when her long-awaited gotcha moment didn't come to pass. Though in restrospect, maybe Lavermine was just getting me back for the way I glared at her while she told a young woman who was inquiring about the atmosphere inside The Shelter at check-in time that the young woman must steel herself and get ready for a free-for-all because the place was packed with evil-ass bitches waiting to manipulate and intimidate newcomers. It's true that the average woman at The Shelter tends to be quarrelsome, hedonistic and uncultured, but only Lavermine deserves the evil-homeless-woman-of-the-year award.

Resolution du jour: Spent two hours at the main library this afternoon engaging in one of my much-loved pastime: thumbing through interior decorating magazines. Yet as pleased as I am with all the new ideas I now have for my future custom built home, I still have trouble digesting the concept of the kitchen being a family gathering place in a country with an obesity epidemic. In my dream home, my private library will take center stage, and the kitchen will be in the back of the house where it belongs.

4:15 a.m. – Dreamed that my house caught on fire, that no one answered the phone when I called 9-1-1 (a recurring dream since eviction day), that the house burned to the ground, and that my children and I were living on the streets. In many ways, I would have been better off if my home had burned down. At least I would not have to feel so much shame and guilt over being homeless and people would have felt sorry for me, not blame me.

7:24 a.m. – Maggie, the woman who usually sits in the pew in front of me at Bethel's early service, just asked if I was a student because she saw me writing again. I said yes. A graduate student. A Florida State graduate student. She smiled and congratulated me for being such a hard-working student. I smiled and gracefully thanked her while I winced inside. Let's just hope that she doesn't see me standing in The Shelter's driveway anytime soon.

7:20 p.m. – Labrina, another loud and vulgar member of the Black Shameless Club, is here again tonight. And where has she been? Out of town. In jail. But it's all good, and she's grateful to be back in Tally. She's also grateful that Jesus loves her no matter what because his love is unconditional. Though you would think that if Jesus really loves her, he would have warned her that agreeing to service an undercover cop for $10 was not a good idea.

8:12 p.m. – Lavermine is below me musing over the good old days when they use to eat fried chicken and pickled pigs feet almost every night because they were allowed to bring in their own food (as well as their boom box), and everybody got along so well. All the fun stopped seven years ago when Mr. ShelterDrillSergeant came on board because he's a very unhappy man and a joykiller, she somberly added. Two sides of the same coin, if you ask me.

10:08 p.m. – A young and pretty CS worker with long micro braids is in the big bathroom, sobbing. It's not fair that she has to clean fucking toilets in a fucking homeless shelter just because she had a fucking fight with that fucking girl who refused to stop talking about her. I hope it doesn't take her long to familiarize herself with the one word that seems to be largely foreign among The Shameless before she, too, ends up on a first-name basis with TPD: self-control.

Lavermine is in the dining room once again, wistfully paying homage to her daddy, the great provider. Interesting how she still refers to her father as "my daddy." Wonder if her depravity is innate or acquired, though, quite frankly, I don't really care. Before I forget, there was an article about The Shelter in today's *Democrat* and Mr. ShelterDirector was quoted as saying that The Shelter remains crowded throughout the year because it is a "revolving door" of new and returning guests. Indeed, it is. Pamelia who was reportedly banned for thirty days is back, and has been acting out since she got here. Pamelia also swears that she's sick and needs to go to TMH and Kaycee Sourpuss who is a tad smarter than the average white Shameless just told her that she's "under the fucking influence," not sick, and that she needs to learn the difference. (I later met an older woman who went on a drinking binge nearly every month, then conjures up an excuse to go spend a night or two in the hospital just to keep her reserved bed.)

PS: I'll be sleeping in a bright yellow room tonight. Not my favorite shade of yellow, but it's a big improvement from the grayish white walls I've been staring at so far. I wish some good Samaritans would also get together to give The Shameless a makeover. A character makeover.

Cannot believe that I made the mistake to prematurely conclude that Lavermine wasn't going to misbehave tonight just because she went to sleep right after the 9:30 smoke break. "Don't start up there, you dumb ass," she snarled after the mattress creaked (Shelter mattresses creak if one breathes too hard) when I sat up in bed around 11 o'clock with the intention to go turn off the light in the hallway leading to the back room that the CS workers had left on. I told myself to keep quiet, but my silence must have emboldened her. "Are you having an orgy up there?"

Cannot believe that Mr. ShelterDirector had the audacity to use my note to Deanna against me. "Lavermine, again?" he cautiously asked when I marched downstairs and told him that we had to talk. And when I insisted to know why Lavermine gets away with so much, he demurely answered that it's because most people complain about her, but then ask Shelter staff not to confront her for fear of retaliation just like I had asked Deanna in my note. I replied that I had asked Deanna to discard my former complaints in hopes that the situation with Lavermine would get better on its own, but that I had changed my mind and needed him to go speak to her. Now.

Cannot believe that when Mr. ShelterDirector reluctantly came upstairs, Lavermine swore that I made up the whole story because she has been sleeping all along. "I know you," he countered, point blank. "You do enjoy tormenting others." He then said that he was tired of hearing complaints about her, and was going to move her to bed 19 if she doesn't stop. The thought of moving to bed 19 seemed to have sent a chill down Lavermine's spine because her voice was a bit shaky when she replied that I should be moved to bed 19 since I am the one complaining. Do I need to say that Lavermine is sleeping like a baby as I write this while I am left wondering why Mr. ShelterDirector didn't even threaten to put her out?

About to leave St. Thomas More where I spent the past hour praying, meditating, cajoling, begging and bargaining with God to get me out of The Shelter. On a lighter note, a new convert I've never seen before came to me after Mass, placed both hands on my shoulder, and told me that God is sending me a blessing through her, did I want to receive it? I was so bothered by the incident that I don't recall a word she said. Something about asking Lord Jesus to bring me to him. I outwardly thanked her while I inwardly told Lord Jesus to inspire her to simply do a silent prayer for me the next time she worries about my unsaved soul. Looking back, maybe I had such a hard time receiving her "blessing" because I am so consumed with anger and rage. In a nutshell, electric chair and lethal injection are two of the things that come to mind whenever I think of possible punishments for Lavermine. Why do people who tried to take someone's life get locked up while spirit killers get to walk around free? The Sermon of the Mount, my most palatable biblical passage, just came to mind. Dear God, please help me keep in mind that even the Jesus of the Gospel didn't always turn the other cheek, and none of us knows for sure who the real Jesus was.

Bombshell du jour: JP and Angie have decided to move in together, and because I am such a failure of a mother, I have no authority to voice an opinion about him officially shacking up at such a young age.

Heartbreak du jour: JP and Angie have decided to move in together, and because I am such a failure of a mother, I have no authority to voice an opinion about him officially shacking up at such a young age.

Embarrassment du jour: JP and Angie have decided to move in together, and because I am such a failure of a mother, I have no authority to voice an opinion about him officially shacking up at such a young age.

The words "depressed" and "disappointed" don't even begin to encapsulate what I am feeling at the moment. Cried all day over the reality that I had allowed my God obsession to overshadow my better judgment. And the only way I was able to keep a cool façade at the madhouse was by faking a migraine and pretending to go to sleep right after dinner. Everyone I know thinks that I made a mistake when I left the bank to follow a call from God. Everyone. So why can't I agree with them when all the mounting evidence has proven them right? While I still have no regrets six years later, in spite of the fact that the bank was very good to me and I was very lucky to have worked primarily under Diane Sénécal and Tessie Marfori, two of the best admins ever, I do regret getting acquainted with you, God. Simply put, you're not my type. If I had to do it all over, I would rather die from food addiction than turn my will and my life over to a being with whom I cannot have a logical conversation, eyeball to eyeball.

4:55 a.m. – Lavermine "tormented" me directly or indirectly throughout the night. She was fussing at an epileptic woman named Valerie (real name) around midnight because Valerie was apparently going in and out of the big bathroom for no reason. She then suspected that a new Shelter guest was smoking in the dining room bathroom and made a commotion over that, too. She later exploded with rage at a woman from the back room because the woman was dragging her feet. (Lavermine can be heard from a mile away, dragging her feet.) And when I did finally fall asleep, I had one disturbing dream after another, including one in which I had just adopted a baby and found myself on the verge of eviction and was hoping against hope that God would spare us.

10:36 a.m. – At The Chain of Parks—as far away from the main library as I can get—and I just finished reading the testimony of Joseph Smith that was given to me by the two Mormon missionaries two weeks ago. I hate to be so upfront about this, but my morning would have been far less stressful if I had remained blissfully ignorant about Joseph Smith. To sum things up, the Mormon prophet has been visited by angels several times in his lifetime and even watched one ascend into heaven right before his eyes, was blessed with a live experience of Jesus and God in a vision, and let's not forget that John the Baptist himself came down from heaven to baptize Joseph Smith. Dear God, how can I be sure that my own spiritual experiences come from you when the first question that usually comes to mind when I read about other people's is: What have they (or their devotees) been smoking?

8:41 p.m. – Kaycee Boneheaded is in the front room again, whining about toilet paper. Toilet paper can be a rare commodity at The Shelter some evenings, that's for sure, but the woman has a job, a cell phone, a laptop, collects food stamps, shops at Old Navy on a regular basis, gets her nails done every two weeks and, by her own account, spends many of her days off from work relaxing in the best motel rooms that the city of Tallahassee has to offer, why can't she buy her own toilet paper? Her determination to be the best parasite that she can be while contending that she's a very independent woman who's just going through a hard time and does "not depend on The Shelter for nothing" doesn't cease to astound me.

Grateful for the beautiful homily from Father Shaw at the 8:30 Mass this morning (I finally know the names of the priests.) His message that we should accept all surprises God throws at us with grace even when they obliterate our plans, crush our hopes, shatter our fantasies, and turn our lives upside down touched me so deeply that I went to the altar after Mass and copied down his exact words, in spite of feeling guilty of sacrilege as I did so. Dear God, please help me learn to accept the surprises that you have in store for me, even when I can't stand them.

Grateful for a day free of fear and anxiety, though the fact that I spent hours this afternoon reading about Brother Lawrence and Jean-Pierre de Caussade, the two spiritual giants I was just introduced to, probably had a lot to do with it. Also grateful for a voice mail message Lulu left just to say that she was looking at the pictures we took when she came to New York to spend her birthday with me two years ago, and that she misses me more than I know.

Grateful for the wisdom to ignore her when Lavermine stepped out of the dining room bathroom around 5:30 this morning, recoiled in horror when she saw me standing in front of the lockers doing my stretches, then said, "Oh Lord, not her again!" The she-wolf is convinced that I exercise at The Shelter because I want to draw attention to myself when the reality is that I exercise because I would have been crippled with back pain by now if I didn't.

Grateful that I didn't take the bait when Doublefaced Lizzie, the new blonde in bed 2, said that Mr. ShelterDirector told her that I was a "safe" person to make friends with. If true, I hope she didn't believe him because I am not looking for Shelter friends. What did she want from me? The names of women she can "safely" talk to at The Shelter, and the ones she should avoid.

Grateful for the resolve to not get involved when two members of the Black Shameless Club came close to go into battle a few feet away from bed 6 because the more level-headed one at long last decided that she was "too grown to operate like a fucking fifth grader" and walked away. Still, my heart bleeds for my race.

A second day free of anxiety and fear until it dawned on me while showering that I've been at The Shelter three whole months. I was blinking away tears of rage minutes later when someone asked a drunk Lavermine if she had a good day and the answer was: "Girl, I had a great day. If it was any better, I would get scared for my own self." And what is she doing at this instant? Sitting at the dining table with Kaycee Boneheaded and joking about how she sold everything in her grandmother's house after her grandmother's death and kept all the money. "I sold her shit, I sold my shit, I sold everybody's shit and there was nothing they could do about it and I didn't feel no shame."

Does society do more harm than good by enabling bare-faced bloodsuckers like Lavermine? If welfare mothers were forced to go to work, why give free food, free clothing, free toiletries and free shelter for life to a homeless person while asking nothing in return?

Suspicion du jour: That Z'Laitah may be mentally ill. A case in point: Z'Laitah goes running daily, sometimes twice a day. Yet she now places a blanket on the floor near the emergency door every evening and does a multitude of sit-ups and push-ups while The Shameless make lewd remarks about her sounding like a mad woman having intercourse. She also got into arguments with Shelter staff over the mispronunciation of her name at least twice this week, spoke to a mesmerized Labrina about the capacity of some fax machines to alter the text one is trying to send out. And to cap it all off, she just told Ninabelle, "This is the last conversation we're going to have, ever. You have hurt me to the core." What did Ninabelle do to stir up such strong feelings? It's not even worth recording. I think it's time to do some research on mood disorders.

Vexation du jour: Listening to Gwen who is excessively proud of the fact that she is a "doctor's daughter," and whose only goal in life is to go back to a size two, tell a woman from West Africa who is spending a few nights in the madhouse that The Shelter must seem like a palace to her, compared to the living conditions in her homeland. The African woman timidly smiled in response, but I purposely broke into their conversation just to comment that I would rather live in a shack in the poorest country on the planet than at The Shelter because a certain level of dignity can be carved out from poverty, but not from homelessness. (Gwen, a plumpish natural blonde from Arizona, is the front room's latest guest. Kichelle went to live with a relative after she got approved for Social Security benefits.)

Wonderment du jour: Mr. ShelterDrillSergeant told Lavermine that he has "plans" for her. I wonder if it's plans to move her to bed 19. Her reaction? "The voodoo woman must have done something." (The new rumor making the rounds is that I stay up late at night to read *vodou* books.) She even said that she told her lawyer—one of her loaded friends—that I should be held responsible if anything bad happens to her. In a way, Lavermine is lucky to be on the breadline because somebody would have sued her for psychological abuse long ago if she had anything to lose.

Absurdity du jour: Many residents of The Shelter claim to be spokespersons for the Almighty, and as stated by the new Shelter mystic, all God's children looked alike at Creation, but after the "Disobedience," God split us apart in different part of the world, and cursed the people who disobeyed with paleness. And the reason why the pale people enjoy a higher living standard than the dark people is because their protector, Satan, gave them the earth as their heaven. Dear God, do you have any idea what it feels like to live among the stupendously stupid?

Highlight du jour: That I was able to use JP's phone to call Lulu, Mama, Joline and Lucy. Grateful that Lucy readily understood when I told her that I stopped looking for a job so that I can focus on the work that I think God wants me to do. Though upon reflection, she could have been professing empathy just because it was the Christian thing to do.

Gaffe du jour: Telling Sabine that I just started a part-time babysitting job when she asked if I was working because moments later Lavermine began to sing about people who are lying about having a job while they go sit on FAMU campus all day. She got the name of the campus wrong, but I am pretty sure that she was talking about me.

Silliness du jour: Introducing "my son" to a bus driver when JP and I boarded her bus because I am always walking up and down Tennessee Street since my bus pass expired and told myself that all the bus drivers now think of me as a vagrant. (I began to take the back streets thereafter.)

Amusement du jour: Seeing the look on Sabine's face while Lavermine excoriated her for sneaking in booze. Let's just say that Sabine, who languorously denied the charges, did not look as if she was praying for Lavermine.

Still feel guilty more than twelve hours later over what I did to Louvern this morning after I saw her standing at a bus stop in Frenchtown and literally ran the other way—and she saw me running. I keep asking myself whether I was wrong to assume that she was up to no good the moment I saw her, but what was Louvern, a white drug dealer, doing in a black neighborhood before 9 o'clock in the morning? Yes, it's possible that she too could have been on her way to Barnes & Noble and simply stopped in Frenchtown to buy a pack of cigarettes from Time Saver, but I've never been one to believe in other people's crap, let alone my own.

A day filled with surprises that not only upset my plans, but shocked the hell out of me:

Surprise No. 1 – That I woke up feeling perfectly fine on the eight anniversary of the day that changed the trajectory of my life forever. The day when you, God, introduced me to *Out of the Trenches*. Even more surprised that I am not feeling like a failure today. Strangely enough, I think that I am doing relatively well in your eyes, though that can only be confirmed by you.

Surprise No. 2 – My heart jumped in my chest and all the muscles in the back of my neck locked into place when someone placed a hand on my shoulder while I sat at a table at the main library late this morning. It was only JP, thank God, but my excitement about seeing him quickly faded away after I told him that I was going to stop by apartment 6 the next two days to help him with the move and he nicely hinted that he did not need my help.

Surprise No. 3 – I can't say that I was terribly surprised to find out that I didn't win the lottery when I stopped at Publix around 8:30 this morning, but I was a bundle of nerves when I bumped into Jacqueline Edwards. I managed to keep my sangfroid when she asked for the phone number of my new employer once again, but what an awkward encounter that was. (I told her that the people I work for don't know that I am homeless, and I don't want them to get a call about me from an organization that deals with the homeless.)

Surprise No. 4 – That Lavermine interrupted my conversation with Julie, an older woman who recently moved to The Shelter, to tell me that she knows that God is trying to get her attention, that I have no idea how bad she feels when she acts evil (Yes, she actually used the E-word), and that she knows that it's time to change because warning always come before the fall. Cannot believe that I've been so wrong about this woman. I will not go as far as saying that she has a conscience, but she does obviously have a teensy weensy bit of goodness in her that is struggling to come out and even prevail.

Surprise No. 5 – Shocked myself even more by giving a card to Lavermine. Didn't plan to do so, but felt sorry for her after she told Mr. ShelterDrillSergeant that "It's time. It's past time. I can't be a fool forever," and he cynically replied that he hopes that she was not trying to fool him. Forgot what I wrote in the card (something about the inability of most human beings to effectively change themselves until they turn to God for help), but Lavermine was so touched that she vowed to reread my card whenever she feels down (I told her to talk to God instead.) She also said that she doesn't deserve "something so nice" from me after all she has done, and out of the mouth of a woman who sounded very much like me but could not possibly be me came the following: "How can we expect Him to forgive us when we're not willing to forgive each other?" The only prayer I could say for Lavermine up to now was: God, please give her the gift of shame. But I have a new prayer tonight. God, please give her the gift of emotional healing for she does have potential. Potential that I could not see prior to today because I am not You.

3:18 p.m. – Sitting in front of computer No. 36 with the clock tickling, but had to take time to jot down the following. "I hear you, Ma'am, and I am sorry," was the answer the teenage boy on computer No. 37 just gave me after I told him, among other things, that people who behave like he does give the black race a bad name. JP once told me that all teenage boys are obsessed with sex, but curiosity about sex is not a good enough excuse for what he was doing while a woman old enough to be his mother sat right next to him. Come to think of it, why is it so easy to download pornographic materials in a so-called Christian country to start with? One more proof that too much freedom isn't necessarily a good thing for the soul of an individual, or a nation.

4:47 p.m. – At STM, waiting for the 5:15 Mass to begin, and brooding over today's disappointments. It still bothers me that JP kept silent when he asked how my job search was going and I answered that I am no longer looking for a job. His silence shook me up more than anything his roommate could have said out loud for it was a confirmation that he, too, had come to think of me as a "worthless freeloader." He also did not bother to thank me for the three hours I spent cleaning up the kitchen and living room, and even got huffy when I said that it didn't look like they'll be out of the apartment by August 1st since his roommate's bedroom still looks like a dumping-ground and no packing has been done. On another front, I am grateful that I was finally able to say a short prayer for the women at The Shelter when I got here. I guess last night's conversation with Lavermine was enough to persuade me that they are not the incorrigible *âmes perdues* that I categorized them to be. Besides, I've probably been too hard on them just because of my own unrealistic tendency to expect everyone to strive to be their best, no matter what their circumstances.

8:07 p.m. – Spent the past few minutes talking to Julie about her grandchildren whom she misses a lot because she was the one who raised them while her daughter went out partying for weeks at a time, she said. She also said that her lifelong dream was to work overseas as a missionary, but that she got married and raised children instead. I can't help thinking that Julie is a woman who had missed her calling in life, but I could be wrong. After all, I was more than sure that my calling was handed down to me on a silver platter the morning of July 27, 1998 when an inaudible voice, but a voice nonetheless, told me "You are going to write a novel!" while I showered in the gym of the World Bank's H building after a workout. Yet look where I am eight years later. Dear God, why didn't you just kill me?

Enragement du jour: Watching a white Shameless who just got out of jail playfully place a four-year-old black boy against a wall and read him his Miranda Rights while his mother, a black woman with a husband and a brother in prison, looked on with a smile.

Disgust du jour: Watching an ebullient Lavermine sell a pair of pants to Kaycee Boneheaded for $2. A pair of pants that Lavermine had just picked up from a donation bin. (Sabine later told me that she sometimes sees Lavermine taking orders from customers at the bus terminal.)

Irritation du jour: Breakfast at the Haven of Rest. (a) There were so many homeless men in line that I gave up counting after forty. (It took me a while to realize that a good number of people who stand in line with the homeless to get free food are not necessarily homeless or hungry.) (b) Ed, the guy who usually makes some of the best looking pancakes I've ever seen, didn't come in today and the pancakes were burned. (c) The people serving the food were so stingy that you would think they were being court-ordered to serve the homeless. (d) An older white man walked up to me after I joined the long line to get seconds (women eat first the first time around), and told me, "Thank you for coming. We're glad you're here." But I was feeling so much shame that what I heard was, "Thank you for coming. We're glad you're homeless because you're making us look good by feeding you." And when he added that I could get my nails done next Saturday because "a few ladies were coming to do nails," I gave him such a cold stare that he must have concluded that I was just a mean and unappreciative homeless woman. I later felt some compunctions when it occurred to me that the poor man was just being polite, but he did rub me the wrong way when he took it as fact that I would be glad to get my nails done when the reality is that I was silently wailing, as I watch myself lose my faith in God's mercy and power, to say nothing of God's love, when he approached me.

Astonishment du jour. Hearing that the young prostitute I once saw in the news found herself a steady boyfriend and is now pregnant with her second child. (I haven't seen Darla in weeks but rumor has it that she got tired of working the streets and moved in with her drug dealer.)

Flashback du jour: My 2000 trip to Haiti during which I gave money away as if it really grows on trees in America. Old motto: It's only money. New motto: Like it or not, money does matter. And I need to learn to give it its due respect, if I am ever going to learn to face life on life's terms.

Was so enthralled with the book I began to read last night, *The Practice of the Presence of God*, that I temporarily forgot my troubles. Sorry to say that my good spirit vanished shortly after I came back to the madhouse and an argument broke out between Z'Laitah and Kaycee Boneheaded after Z'Laitah, who's getting more paranoid with each passing day, accused Kaycee Boneheaded of stealing her socks from the laundry basket (their clothes were washed together.) And while Kaycee Boneheaded stoically stuck by her no-profanity rule, she essentially sat back and watched her entourage, fellow members of the Black Shameless Club, tear Z'Laitah to pieces. And in an effort to show her loyalty to Kaycee Boneheaded, Lavermine has been glued to her bed since the 8:15 smoke break, singing some of her most recent compositions, which include her jaw-dropping masterpiece: "Ugly ass, ugly ass, fuck that ugly bitch." Though she did find time in between songs to yell "I don't want to look at no damn hamburger, if you don't have a hot dog, stay away!" when she spotted Doublefaced Lizzie getting off her bunk in panties and bra. (Shelter guests are required to be fully clothed at all times, but Doublefaced Lizzie can't stop bragging about her recent weight loss and makes it a point to show off her new bod daily.) "We're all in the same boat," Lavermine is now singing. "If anybody was better than the other, they would not be here." This particular song is for all intents and purposes dedicated to both Z'Laitah and me since Z'Laitah also made it clear that she wasn't interested in joining the Black Shameless Club. I would love to tell the devil incarnate that she's gravely mistaken if she thinks that we're all in the same boat because she's on a boat of her own, The Perdition Boat, but she's been going out of her way to be civil to me, and it would be counterproductive to provoke her.

PS: Shelter dinner was fit for a king, and at my request Rashad agreed to serve his signature dessert—banana pudding—separately, rather than just add it to the side of the plate. I shamelessly ate my banana pudding and Sabine's, and my stomach is paying for it now.

Sitting on the usual bench in front of Westcott with my mind running a mile a minute:

- I was too afraid to check the lottery result yesterday because I didn't want to spoil my good mood, but it's official: I wasted one more dollar on another losing Florida Lotto ticket.

- I left JP a message last night asking if he's sure he didn't need my help, but he didn't return the call. I need to stop trying to mother adult children who no longer need mothering.

- I love books. I've always loved books. Throughout the years, books have surrogated as my parents, my friends, my teachers, and even my shrinks. And by extension, I love libraries. Yet I can't stand to be at the main library lately because I feel as if I am soiling it with my presence, just like the others.

- Lots of new students on campus, map in hands. And as you would expect, many of them are accompanied by their parents, an experience that my own children never had because of choices that I made. "Mass has ended, go in peace," were the priest's parting words this morning. How can I be in peace when I have so much turmoil inside me?

- Still sweating from the ten-minute walk between the main library and the Westcott Building. Even the sun in the middle of the desert didn't burn so intensely. But then again, maybe I just didn't feel it. After all, the wives of The Few and The Proud in 29 Palms, California, do not habitually hang out on the streets. (ExHusband spent a few years in the Marine Corps in what now feels like a whole different world.)

- I asked Mr. HornyBoy last night why the new teen at The Shelter was staying in the men's section and not in the family section with his mother. He said it's because the boy's mother is old-fashioned and didn't want the boy to get distracted by the two teenage girls. I find it hard to accept the reality of a fifteen-year-old boy sleeping among drunks, addicts, and criminals. A fifteen-year-old boy whose only mistake was to be born in the wrong family.

- Planned to walk to TCC this morning, but my left foot hurt so much that I took a seat in front of the College of Medicine in spite of myself and remained there until the sun chased me away. I risked going inside the building for the first time because I had to use the restroom, and am grateful that I was able to sneak in and out without seeing anyone. (Being as technology-challenged as I am, it didn't occur to me that just because I didn't see anyone did not mean that my visits went unnoticed.)

- Z'Laitah was arguing with The Shameless in the dining room again last night. Dear God, please grant her the gift of gentleness because her combative attitude is hurting her more than anyone ever could. And while you're at it, please also send some my way for while I am not a hostile person, I am more known for my straightforwardness than for my gentleness. (A year or two later, I became so hostile that I couldn't even look at Mr. ShelterDirector, much less say hello. And I openly let his subordinates know verbally and in writing that they couldn't talk to me "any kind of way" because I wasn't staying in their private house and The Shelter was not being financed by them.)

- Done reading *The Practice of the Presence of God*. I agree with Brother Lawrence that when suffering comes from God, only God can remedy it. Share his belief that people in pain should focus not so much on praying for deliverance, but on asking God for the courage to go on, trusting that relief will come on God's timetable. (That's not saying it's a belief I actually put into practice.) And I am completely blown away by his certainty that we can all learn to shoulder the insufferable, even be consoled by it, once we realize that our adversities may be the vehicle that God uses for our salvation. Yet because I am a woman, because I am a mother, because I am black, and because I am destitute, I can't help feeling that I have much more to bear than Brother Lawrence and people like him will ever have.

In the words of The Shameless, Lavermine is completely off the chain this evening, and I am beginning to feel as if I have entered into a tacit partnership with evil just to keep her off my back. She was fulminating against the whole shelter the moment she came in because she left her pajamas and makeup bag in the dining room bathroom this morning and they were not waiting for her on her bed as she had hoped. She berated a new Shelter guest moments later because the woman was sitting on the trunk that she keeps on the side of the bunk. She started an argument between Ninabelle and another girl when she nonchalantly, yet calculatingly, mentioned that the girl was gossiping about Ninabelle in the big bathroom, then came back to bed laughing about how babyish Ninabelle is. She ranted forever about "Shelter rule violation" when she saw Kaycee Sourpuss heading toward the back room with a cup of coffee. And when she couldn't think of anything else to do, she went back to huffing and puffing about whoever stole her pajamas and bag. "I hope those motherfuckers scorch their pussies and can never get hot again," she just screeched.

If I was given a choice to drop dead right now, or continue to share a bunk bed with this woman indefinitely, I would have chosen death without a blink.

Cannot believe that The Shameless are as addicted to more as anyone else. Eleven women dashed out of the dining room right before dinner when a Shelter staff brought in another bin of donated clothes. Z'Laitah got out of bed so quickly you would think her bunk was on fire. Lavermine nearly fought another woman over a pair of brown boots with four-inch heels—boots that she clearly can't wear, but can surely sell. Even Zhouli who has been zoned out all evening snapped back to reality once the prospect of getting more clothes and shoes flashed in front of her eyes. Doublefaced Lizzie was all smiles when she ended up with most of the clothes because they turned out to be too small for most of the women, too big for Z'Laitah and Zhouli, but perfect for her. I just don't understand these people. Young or old. Sane or insane.

Cannot believe that Deanna told Lavermine "I still love you," after she explained that she can no longer do after-hours laundry for Lavermine because whenever she does agree to wash two things, Lavermine brings a whole load. Does Deanna really love that ignoble woman or was she trying to pacify the beast? I just can't get over this one. But then again, I keep forgetting that Lavermine gets along well with almost all Shelter staff and even stays behind in the morning to help them clean up, though some say it's to maximize her chances to steal. And others swear that it's because she's having sex with them, which I doubt. The woman is evil, but she's not stupid.

Cannot believe that Gwen was smiling when she told me that it took her ten years to accept her fall from rich kid to homeless woman, but that she has finally resigned herself to her fate, and feels a sense of peace as a result. Gwen may have earned her homelessness through a series of bad choices like most of The Shameless, but I did not. Put another way, I am willing to endure, God, but I will never accept. (Other than the fact that she was born in a million-dollar home, Gwen doesn't say much about her past, but it once slipped out of her mouth that she hasn't seen her eighteen-year-old son in over five years because she had "messed up" and the boy was "in state custody.")

Cannot believe that both the Black Shameless Club and the White Shameless Club assembled in the dining room tonight to reminisce over their recent and not-so-recent sexual escapades. There were plenty of laughter, and some of them even tried to outshine each other with more outrageous stories. And, of course, not a word was said about all the heartbreaks, unwanted pregnancies, STDs, and stunted emotional growth that went along with all the fun. A tragic example of why the sexual revolution was the very worst thing that happened to women in the 20th century, whereas the average man has handsomely benefitted.

Cannot stop crying. Could not even hold back my tears while dinner was being served, and I know that Lavermine can't wait to throw it back to my face. On the one hand, I perfectly understand the dark-night-of-the-soul concept. Yet on the other hand, my heart is broken in a million pieces and my mere existence has become my greatest burden. On top of everything else, my daughter's birthday is coming up and it's hard to accept that I, whose only girlhood ambition was to be a good wife and a great mother, ended up giving birth to a rebellious and egomaniacal child who seriously believes that the fact that her second-grade teacher once used the word "sassy" to describe her is evidence that the common folks have felt enfeebled by her greatness since childhood, and that all I did as a mother was to encourage her to see the worst in her. An acquaintance once told me that she chose not to have children because she didn't want them to inherit her family's dysfunctions. I told myself, then, that she was being selfish, but now I wonder. I was so happy while I awaited the birth of my first child. I wanted a daughter. I expected a daughter. I named her even before the first sonogram. And I did everything in my power to be a good mother, my own mother being such a perfect model of what kind of mother not to be. What happened to all my good intentions and hard work? What the hell happened?

Disbelief du jour: JP was unable to meet with me this afternoon because he and his roommate were too busy cleaning up the apartment they were supposed to vacate days ago. Grateful I stifled the urge to say: I told you so.

Foolishness du jour: Scribbling a desperate cry for help right on the bunk while The Shameless gleefully watched a new music video on TV. Do I need to add that I am already fretting over how I am going to get rid of the marking—an all-too-clear telltale sign of my dismal state of mind—before Lavermine spots it?

Befuddlement du jour: Listening to Shelterqueen flaunt her Shelter clout all evening long. Mel knows her for years and she doesn't keep anything from him. Mel accepts her for who she is because he knows her heart. Mel knows that The Shelter is filled with nasty-ass bitches and whores and does not believe any of the lies that are being told about her. Mel, Mel, Mel, Mel, ad nauseum. Are they really that close or is she trying to shut me up?

Annoyance du jour: Being told by Doublefaced Lizzie that I was wasting my time going to church after she heard me talk to Lydia Pollyanna, a self-declared devout Catholic who showed up a few days ago, about Sunday Mass schedule. Yet minutes later, Doublefaced Lizzie was asking me for the phone number of Catholic Charities because she's hoping they can give her gas money to go visit some friends. (I think they laughed at her when she called.)

Mystery du jour: I told Deanna that I needed to speak to Mr. ShelterDirector, better known as Mel Eby, when I checked in at five. Why is it that Lavermine was made aware of my request even before I got to see Mr. ShelterDirector over four hours later? (Deanna said she wasn't the one who told Lavermine.) Even more puzzling, why is it that Mr. ShelterDirector himself seemed to be willing to discuss everything but Lavermine when we finally got to talk?

Lavermine is right. I can't touch her. The Shelter is hers. I lost again. And I am getting more and more curious.

6:33 a.m. – Already dressed and ready to go, but I can't leave yet since Mass isn't until 8 o'clock on Saturdays. Went to bed with Mr. ShelterDirector in mind. Woke up with Mr. ShelterDirector in mind. What on earth did . . . Lavermine and Sofunda, the new loony/crackhead/jailbird in bed 7, are at it again. "Go suck something sour and don't fuck with me about a fucking pen," an antagonistic Lavermine answered when Sofunda asked for a pen Lavermine had borrowed from her last night. "Go suck your own pussy," Sofunda growled. I think I am going to go for an early morning walk after all, before I end up biting much more than I am willing to chew at this time of day.

7:46 p.m. – Lavermine is back in bed, and the galling monologue has begun. She can stop worrying about her lost pajamas because Mel promised her a new pair. She thanks the Lord for being so good to her because he helped her find the right pair of earrings to match her outfit tomorrow. She is flat out scandalized by the conduct of some of the stupid-ass bitches and nasty-ass whores at The Shelter who refuse to leave her alone because they're blue in their hearts since they're not getting any hot dogs. "Sexual pills!" she concluded in a booming voice. "They need some sex-boosting pills." There is no denying it, the sleazebag is talking to me. After all, I was the one who was telling Julie a few minutes ago that I was enjoying celibacy more than I anticipated because I was quite disgruntled with all the pitfalls that go hand in hand with romantic love.

8:43 p.m. – Lavermine didn't shut up when she came back from smoke break, and I didn't mince my words when I told her that my days of hiding under a sheet just to avoid trouble at The Shelter were over. "You don't know who I am or who I know," I yelled as the other Shameless stared at me, dumbfounded, since they had clearly assumed that I, too, was afraid of the viper. "I can get you kicked out of The Shelter, in spite of all your connections." Upping the ante, I added that her soul was more rotten than the teeth in her mouth, that she's so noxious she doesn't even qualify for the Jesus salvation plan, and that I was going to make some phone calls tomorrow morning to find out why city officials were permitting a garbage can on legs to roam so freely on the streets of Florida's capital city. (Little did I know that two years later Lavermine would actually get, er, picked up by a super-smart garbage truck right off a Tallahassee street, a story that must sound familiar to readers of the *Democrat*. There, I said it.) Much to my surprise, a calm and collected Lavermine simply strolled over to the dining room, took a seat at the heinous table, then told the usual crowd of TV watchers that I must be losing it because she hasn't said a word to me all evening.

As expected, Lavermine is behaving like an angel tonight. Ignoring her for so long was a big mistake. Evil should be at least contained, if it can't be destroyed. I just don't understand why almost all Shelter staff give this woman the kid-gloves treatment when they don't hesitate to give a thirty-day ban to women who behave half as badly. I say all that to simply say that I am growing more irate at The Shelter for allowing Lavermine to do whatever she wants whenever she wants than at Lavermine for being who she is: an old bitter woman who insists on mentally torturing others in a desperate attempt to give some meaning to her inconsequential existence. Actually, those were some of the words that Mr. ShelterDirector himself used to describe Lavermine when I spoke to him the other night. He also corroborated what Louvern had told me when he revealed that Lavermine used to do "tricks" to support her habit. Yet why am I under the impression that he, too, expects me to learn to put up with The Shelter's favorite vermin since the only promise he could make was that he was going to start making Lavermine's life "increasingly difficult," and that sooner or later she will start asking herself why she's losing her privileges and change her ways.

I was already in a bad mood before I made it back to The Shelter, but being told by Lydia Pollyanna that the flavorless "Shelteroni," salty green beans, cheap slice of white bread and two chocolate chip cookies we had for dinner was a wonderful meal is threatening to send me over the edge. Also on my mind:

(1) Wish list – Kaycee Sourpuss's primary complaint this evening is that her new bunkmate has gotten everything she wanted from the wish list, even though she has only been at The Shelter a few days. Yet she, who has been there four years, is still waiting for the black backpack she asked for a month ago. Grateful that my name has never been on that list for The Shelter has nothing to give that I wish to have.

(2) Holy shamelessness – "In God's eyes there is no big sins and little sins. Just because you've never been locked up don't make you better. Your shit stinks as much as mine," a black Shameless who only comes in once a week to do laundry said a moment ago while a group of them gathered in the big bathroom, which is not all that big, to comment on something that took place during smoke break. "Ain't that the truth!" Bekkie-Sue enthusiastically threw in. "I know that's right!" an inebriated Labrina concurred.

(3) Layoffs and lawsuits – And guess who no longer has a job? Kaycee Boneheaded. It's almost funny in a way considering that she's always so quick to ask others to go get a job and stop depending on The Shelter for everything, even as she does just that all

along. She went on to say that she's not worried about money because she has "two cases open," and three other women confessed that they too had lawsuits pending. (The Shameless are always looking for ways to sue somebody, especially when they're not eligible for a check from Uncle Sam.)

(4) Mothers and madness – My mind is so filled with the fifteen-year-old boy whose mother, I suspect, is getting ready to leave The Shelter, in spite of not having anywhere to go, that I've successfully managed to ignore the main drama in the dining room until the star player, the mother of two who shamelessly spends her child support check on weed and motel rooms, indignantly exclaimed: "She said I would rather take care of a man than my children and that's a fucking lie. I can't believe she's doing this to me. She said she wanted them and I made a way for her to have them and four years later she's threatening to leave town and let them go to foster care. What kind of sister is she?" And of course no one dared to ask her: "What kind of mother are you?"

9:25 a.m. – Sitting on a bench across from TCC's Computer Technology Building with my heart pounding. Summer classes at FSU are already over, and a student just told me that summer classes at TCC are over as well. Where am I going to spend my days until the fall semester begin? I am not one of those people who have no qualms about imposing my homelessness on others at the main library all day. Even more worrisome, where will I go once the temperature start to drop and I can no longer spend my mornings outdoors? A life suffused with madness-inducing afflictions is definitely not what I had in mind when I decided to turn my will and my life over to God.

1:51 p.m. – JP just called to ask what I was doing. "Writing!" I said. (I was actually pacing the floor of the restroom on the first floor of the Computer Technology Building, waiting for 2 o'clock to roll by so I could head back downtown, toward the main library.) "I just want to know if you would like to go see a movie," he hastened to say with all the half-heartedness in the world. I cheekily replied that I was busy, and that he should have called yesterday to inquire about my schedule. I am way too fed up to play the all-is-well game just because he wants to take me to a fifty cents movie. Besides, I heard Andrelene say last night that she had a movie date, and whenever a woman at The Shelter say on a Monday that she plans to go to the movies the next day, it's not too big of a stretch to expect to see her and whoever she's sleeping with at Movie 8, locally known as the Dollar Theater, because it is half price on Tuesdays. I don't want to sound like a bitter and reproachful mother, but it's hard to accept that my own son can't bother to spend seven or eight dollars to take me to a real theater after all the money I spent entertaining him during his high-school years alone. (By the summer of 2010, the Dollar Theater had evolved into the $3.50 Theater, 50 Cents Tuesday was replaced by $2.50 Tuesday, and by then I only went to the movies on rare occasions.)

5:38 p.m. – Thundering heavily out. Grateful I got here before the rain. New Shelter rule: Only two bags per bed, beginning tomorrow. Don't care. I don't keep anything on the bed during the day. The small bookshelf next to Sabine's bunk has also been taken away, along with all her books, and she uncharacteristically went berserk, especially since the pile of romance novels on Lavermine's trunk remained untouched. I cannot stand The Shelter. Nothing is terribly wrong with the facility itself, but the people here make me sick, residents and staff. I either gave up everything for you, God, or lost everything as a result of putting you first, and I don't deserve to be punished for my loyalty.

Relief du jour: The fifteen-year-old boy and his mother did leave, but they came back because the boy, Mr. HornyBoy told me, didn't want to go back living in the woods.

Anxiety du jour: Running out of pen, and not enough money to go to Dollar Tree to buy a new pack. I have too much pride to be a thief, but I am not too proud to steal pen for I will literally die in this hellhole if I can't write.

Incredulity du jour: That an amiable Lavermine kindheartedly pointed out that my towel was about to fall off the bunk. The most unsettling thing about this woman is not knowing when she's going to strike. "If you can't beat them, you got to join them," I once heard her say. I hope she's clever enough to know that she can't beat me or join me.

Confirmation du jour: Louvern and Kaycee Sourpuss are right. White women at The Shelter do get treated unfairly by some Shelter staff. "Does this look like a hotel to you? If you want special privileges, you've got to get your own place," a Shelter staff who shall remain nameless told Gwen a minute ago. And what kind of special privileges did Gwen, who didn't come in last night, request? The privilege to disinfect the rollaway bed that was assigned to her because it was last occupied by a woman with lice.

Resentment du jour: "Even Jesus once asked why God had forsaken him," I icily replied when Lydia Pollyanna answered that the Bible says that we should not complain after I told her that I was beginning to feel more and more like Job. And she downright blanched when I added that I was so angry at God yesterday that I wished I could take him by the shoulders and shake him. Dear God, why is this woman taking my feelings about you so personally when I know without doubt that you do prefer my raw honesty to her disingenuous devoutness?

Disturbance du jour: Being told by a smiling Doublefaced Lizzie that she had a gift for me, which turned out to be a used dress that someone gave her. Okay, I don't really know where she got the dress from, but there she was forcing me to try it on as if her next breath depended on it. "If you have a decent home to give away I'll take it," I said to her in reply. She asked for my bra size in return because she also has some bras—used bras—she thinks that will fit me. Thank you, God, for using this woman to remind me that compulsive giving is even more cunning than compulsive eating because it's a weakness of character that is incredibly adept at masquerading itself as a virtue.

Grateful that I am still able to set high standards for myself, in spite of my surroundings. The longer I stay at The Shelter the more I realize that the lack of money could very well be the least of the problems facing America's poor.

Grateful that I can still get away with sitting in front of the College of Medicine while school is out since the med students seem to be on a different schedule than the rest of campus, meaning that people are still coming in and out of the building.

Grateful that the fighting spirit in me is back. "I already said I was going to be there," Mr. Jejune hollered when I went back downstairs after the 5 p.m. check-in to tell him that the showers were still locked. "I didn't know that, and you didn't have to yell," I shot back. Would not have spoken to him that way a week ago for fear of being "put out."

Grateful that I did not believe Lavermine when she announced that she plans to take her pills and go to sleep soon after dinner. She is in bed all right, but she's very much awake. "You know what I actually think?" she just asked herself with deadly seriousness. "I actually think that I am going to wear my sexy blue pants tomorrow."

Grateful I managed to rein in the impulse to scream "WHY ARE YOU PEOPLE SO DUMB?" while listening to one black woman from the back room tell another black woman that she always suspected that being black was a curse and her suspicion was confirmed when a nice white lady from her church told her to stop feeling bad about her blackness because the curse will be lifted when she gets to heaven since everyone in heaven is white.

Grateful that Deanna is wearing her God-given hair today. Her real hair does not look as glamorous as all the fake hairs she's been donning, but isn't it time for black women to learn to accept that our hairs, au naturel or processed, will never pass the world's beauty test and it's okay because it is the hair that you, God, chose to give us, and that you must surely have your reasons for depriving us from the long and soft hairs that you so freely gave to everyone else as their "glory." (Deanna, by the way, is so pretty that she would look just fine with no hair. And I earnestly believe that a woman's glory is her character, not her hair.)

Woke up crying after I told someone in a dream that I didn't think that *Out of the Trenches* will ever get published, and it looks like I am going to cry myself to sleep, again. It hurts like hell to admit it, but my mother is right. I would have been a Ph.D. candidate by now if I had left the bank to go back to school rather than to focus on finishing that stupid book. . . . A little boy in the family room is throwing another temper tantrum and I just heard the mother say that she loves him, but that she's going to send him to his dad if he doesn't shape up. Wish I knew before I became a mother that babies are not the blank slates that they appear to be at birth, that some children come into this world with more psychic baggage than others, and that, ideally, it would be up to the parents to teach such children how to cope with, and eventually rise above the difficulties ahead. Who knew that it takes much more than love to be a good mother? And who knew that life was so damn complicated?

Annoyance du jour: Listening to an elegantly dressed black lady who came to donate several large cans of sweet potatoes tell a male Shelter guest, who was in the driveway inquiring as to whether or not Mr. ShelterDirector had time to get his prescriptions filled, that there is no difference between the two of them because she could have easily been in his place. I wanted to ask if she, too, was a drunk, a drug addict, and a criminal. Or whether she would have a problem with it if her beautiful daughter, who had accompanied her, would start dating the blue-eyed *vaurien* in front of her since he was her "brother in Christ," but I silenced my thoughts.

Frustration du jour: Listening to Kaycee Boneheaded and Labrina practically complimenting Sabine for getting drunk. "You've got to love her," Kaycee Boneheaded cooed in between bouts of laughter. I don't want that kind of love; I don't practice that kind of love; I don't even understand that kind of love. Watching such an intelligent woman destroy her life with alcohol is more than I can bear sometimes, and the way I would express my love for Sabine is to force her to get sober by any means necessary.

Observation du jour: That a suddenly-friendly Z'Laitah seems to be hell-bent on becoming a member of the Black Shameless Club while remaining ill-disposed toward me. "Has anyone ever told you that you have beautiful eyes?" she asked out of the clear blue sky, prior to wishing Lavermine a good night. I purposely glanced at her with a frown on my face, as I pondered over her game plan.

Affirmation du jour: A part of me, in spite of the countless disappointments, will never accept that OOTT, a book for which I have sacrificed my livelihood, turned out to be such a monumental failure. Put differently, I still have a dream. The dream that you gave me, God. The dream to see *Out of the Trenches* on the best-seller list.

Exasperation du jour: "We're all just one ticket away from winning millions, why waste time complaining?" Lydia Pollyanna pompously stated after Kaycee Sourpuss declared that we've been eating so much rice they might as well ship us all to Vietnam. The woman doesn't even play the lottery.

Insanity du jour: Reminiscing over Deceitful CJ's breathtaking bedroom skills throughout the day. My head is getting sick again, God. Please fix it before it takes me back to where I no longer want to be.

7:03 a.m. – Can barely keep my eyes open. Was awaken shortly after midnight by Valerie who had another seizure, prompting Shelter staff to call for an ambulance, and, as usual, it took me forever to go back to sleep. Zhouli, in contrast, woke up looking like a rose and with a smile on her face, totally oblivious to the realities of homeless life. Losing one's mind does have its benefits, I am finding out. Lizzie Licehead, for instance, is, on the face of it, the most pleasant and coolheaded woman I know.

12:34 p.m. – Left Bethel before the 11 o'clock service was over and I am currently standing in line with the usual group of homeless men in the side yard of First Presbyterian, waiting to go in the basement of the church for lunch. I am not in the mood for more fried chicken or TV dinners, but I can't afford to skip a free meal since Shelter dinner is usually not eatable on Sundays. Do I need to add that their *sujet de conversation* solely consists of sports, booze, women, and jail? Pure hell on earth.

4:22 p.m. – About to leave the main library because I must check in early for laundry. Spent the past few hours doing the usual reading and note taking, and kept hoping that JP would show up since he knows exactly where to find me on Sunday afternoons, but he did not. While listening to Father Shaw this morning, it came to me that God may have stripped me of everything that matters in order to teach me to stop being so attached to certain people, places and things. Yet why am I still so hurt?

6:07 p.m. – The more Lydia Pollyanna talks about the wonderful time she had in the parish hall after the 10 o'clock Mass, the more I resent her for trying so hard to fit in at St. Thomas More when I try to be as invisible as I can be. I don't look back on my decision not to attend the farewell reception for Father Shaw, but am grateful for what I've learned about detachment just by watching him. Father Shaw seems to have enjoyed his stay at STM, yet he also seems excited about moving on. I wish I were so flexible.

8:10 p.m. – Well, well, well, it was a great dinner. Rashad not only cooked, he set up a table in front of the lockers and served the food buffet-style. In addition, I chose to eat dinner at the diabolical table in a preemptive act of humility since Mr. ShelterDrillSergeant has yet to give up on his campaign to pile up as many women as he can in the dining room. And thank goodness I waited until after dinner to take a shower because I honestly feel as if I have slept in the same bed as Estelle and Pamelia just for sitting so close to them.

8:52 p.m. – I just realized that the family of nine who has been staying in the family section the past week or so didn't check in tonight. Dear God, please grant that woman the wisdom to raise those children right so that her family doesn't become another statistic in a society that only expects the worst from single mothers, especially when they are poor and black. It would also be nice if you do give her the wisdom to get her tubes tied since she has made it frighteningly clear that she has no willingness to use birth control, nor the ability to keep her legs closed.

Grateful for the tinge of hope inside of me today. The hope that I did not delude myself as far as you are concerned, God, and that you did not abandon me, in spite of all the evidence to the contrary. But best of all, the hope that you will provide in a miraculous way at the end of the day.

Grateful to have received five pen from Sabine who was about to throw them away because she's "downsizing" in order to conform to the new rule (Sabine did get her books back.) I am even more grateful to have heard her say that she's ready to give sobriety another try. My heart goes out to her for I can only imagine how hard it is to get sober and stay sober in an environment where it is acceptable and even cute to be a drunk.

Grateful I was able to smile when a woman who is to all appearances a professor at the College of Medicine walked past me on her way to the building and commented that she was proud of me "for being so studious." In passing, the three murals next to the main entrance of the College of Medicine have been installed, and the workers did such a great job that it looks as if the murals have always been a part of the wall. Curious to know who the people are, two men and one woman, and what are their contributions to medicine. Also grateful for the hope that I, too, will have something meaningful to contribute to this world, someday.

Grateful for the confirmation that Z'Laitah is, in effect, mentally ill. She was beside herself last night because of a Shelter staff's "deliberate refusal" to properly pronounce her name. And tonight's song and dance is her premonition that someone has figured out the combination of her lock and has been stealing "quality clothes" from her locker with the help of Deanna. She didn't exactly accuse me of anything, but who else could she be referring to when she says that only a person sleeping next to her could have guessed her lock combination? It should be noted that while we are about the same height, I am at least fifteen pounds heavier than Z'Laitah, but she's evidently too whacko to take that into factor. It should also be noted that Z'Laitah, like most of The Shameless, came to The Shelter with barely nothing, yet she has so much stuff these days that she's storing clothes underneath her mattress and now needs a half-hour to get dressed in the morning, just like Lavermine.

Relief du jour: That Israel and Hezbollah finally agreed to a cease-fire agreement (with both sides claiming victory). About a thousand people have been killed since the latest round of fighting began on July 12. God have mercy on us all for we are not well. (Call me what you like, but I at times wonder if the Jewish people would not have been better off had they chosen to build a Jewish state outside of the Middle East. A piece of land is just not worth all that trouble.)

Bemusement du jour: A male Shelter guest, who once asked me why I leave so early in the morning and where do I go, stopped on Park Avenue this afternoon to offer me a ride on my way back to The Shelter from Borders. I didn't take the ride, but I was thunderstruck at the sight of him driving a nice looking Jeep with his air condition on. Who the hell are these homeless people with cell phones, laptops, cars and money for motel rooms?

Enchantment du jour: Reading Paulo Coelho's *The Alchemist*. I don't believe that the universe converges to make our dreams come true, or that a bed of roses is waiting for us at the end of each setback. But I enjoyed the story immensely, and only wish that I had read it six years ago when I was getting ready to leave the bank because by now I've already learned most of its lessons the hard way.

Flashback du jour: JP's ex-roommate telling him on the day of his high school graduation: "You don't want to face it, but she [me] doesn't care about your future." Meanwhile it looks like she and JP are finally on the same page since he stopped calling me altogether.

Wish du jour: That someone had warned me years ago that the same people who are pointing the finger at you today for being distrustful will be laughing at you tomorrow for being too naïve—once you listen to them and let your guards down.

Perplexity du jour: I saw the fifteen-year-old boy in the driveway at check-in time, and didn't notice a bookbag or any sign that he started school on Monday like the other children at The Shelter. Is he even in school?

"I thank the Lord for blessing me with a good day," a black Shameless waiting to see the nurse said moments ago while flashing me a smile, which I did not return. "People around here are so miserable," she smugly added, as she looked away. "But the Lord blessed me with a joyful heart. Can't anybody do it like King Jesus." I am so sick of listening to these women talk about Jesus I don't know what to do. If King Jesus is so good to you, why is he taking so long to let you know that you should not be selling your food stamps to go get drunk, I want to ask. But, of course, I said nothing. After all, many of The Shameless already think that I envy them because they're so full of joy when what they call joyfulness, I call obliviousness. (They also think that I give blowjobs in cemeteries for cash. Hello, Mama Bear the nasty drunk. I still want to see that picture you have of me.)

"I am not judging you, honey, I understand. Only the Lord has the right to judge," Gwen had similarly said to Pamelia earlier after Pamelia told her, with no apparent shame, how she once went to jail for stealing a diamond ring—from someone who was trying to help her get permanent housing—and sold it to her "dope man" for $200. The Shameless seem to think that they'll get brownie points from God for their reluctance to judge right from wrong when the main reason they don't judge each other is because of their common lack of moral consciousness. Too exhausted to go on. I've been up since before 3 a.m., again. God, please help me get some sleep tonight for I won't be able to function in the morning if you don't.

Don't feel like writing, but the following needs to be recorded before a new wave of drama completely eclipses them from my memory bank:

- Full house at The Shelter once again since many of The Shameless are back, including Mi-Kum and Lissa who had quietly disappeared a few weeks ago. And while Lissa has been keeping a low profile so far, Mi-Kum is already bleating about people who are always staring at her because she's Asian, and I am one breath away from telling her that the reason people stare is not because she's Asian, but because she looks like a clown.

- I watched Kaycee Sourpuss hurl racial epithets at Estelle for no reason then told Shelter staff that Estelle verbally attacked her because she's white. I watched Sofunda turn the TV back on, yet swore five minutes later that she didn't touch it and all her buddies kept quiet. (Shelter staff sometimes turn the TV off when the hurlyburly in the dining room spins out of control.) I watched one of the black Shameless call a white woman a cracker and when the woman went to complain, the Black Shameless Club testified that the white woman made up the story just to get them in trouble.

- Z'Laitah finally found a listening ear to vent out her litany of troubles: my cousin Didi. It so happens that they both have experience with government agencies conspiring to screw up their lives. Wish I could have heard all the juicy details, but they were not speaking loud enough. By the way, I spent an hour at the main library yesterday morning reading about bipolar disorder and paranoid schizophrenia online after I woke up in the middle of the night and found Z'Laitah sitting up in bed in what appeared to be a catatonic state. And the mild discomfort I felt about sleeping so close to her grew by leaps and bounds after I went to Barnes & Noble and found myself skimming through Ronald K. Siegel's *Whispers: The Voices of Paranoia.*

- "Skip just asked me about a few things and I had to tell him the honest truth," Shelterqueen trumpeted a short time ago when she came back from downstairs. Why did she make the comment? Because she "caught" me talking to Mr. HornyBoy, again. I was tempted to reply that it's rather dumb of Mr. ShelterDrillSergeant to rely on a crackhead for information about what goes on in the women's section when a Shelter staff should have been placed on the floor at all times to begin with, but I didn't want to give them a reason to put me out. (At least five Shelter staff are on duty every evening, in addition to Mr. ShelterDirector who allegedly has not taken a night off in all his years at The Shelter, but they primarily stay downstairs even though the male guests, although greater in number, do not cause as many problems as the female guests, at least from what I've heard from Shelter staff. I could be wrong, but I sometimes think that Mr. ShelterDirector allows such decadence to flourish in the women's section just so The Shameless can feel at home and keep coming back.)

Grateful for my inclination to question everything that I've been told—once a source of pride but now a burden—rather than embrace every set of beliefs that has been passed down to me. Did King Solomon become one flesh with each and every one of his seven-hundred wives was the thought that came to me this morning while the priest spoke of the sacredness of marriage. (I do, however, believe in the social, sexual, psychological and financial benefits of marriage—if one is in a good marriage.)

Grateful for the courage to almost always be consistent in my behavior wherever I am. A born-again Shameless who recently showed up with a smile on her face and the Gospel on her lips is in the dining room right now, browbeating another woman. Yet she managed to pass herself off as the most Jesuslike when "The Church Lady" was here not long ago. The Church Lady a k a Wendy Campbell comes to The Shelter once a month to serve Subway sandwiches, but does a Bible study before and during the meal, which annoyed me greatly, at first, until I've learned through talking to her that her heart is in the right place.

Grateful that I am not a white woman living in America. To come to the point, I found myself going to the website of isitreallydepression.com after coming across their very tantalizing three-page ad in the *Democrat*'s weekend magazine, featuring a frazzled white woman staring in a mirror, as if questioning her sanity. I don't care what the experts have to say about people who believe in conspiracy theories, and care even less about the lack of empirical evidence to support my hypothesis, but there is clearly a consensus in this country among pharmaceutical companies, in tandem with many mental health providers and far too many pill-pushing primary care physicians, to use depression—AND THE FEAR OF DEPRESSION—as a weapon to keep women genuflecting at the altar of emotional insecurities, forever and ever. Amen. (And I have a sneaking suspicion that Peter Breggin, a Harvard-trained psychiatrist and a fierce critic of psychiatric drugs, would probably agree with me on this one.)

5:42 a.m. – Dreamt that Lulu called to say that Mama was back in the hospital, but there was nothing I could do because I had no means to get to my mother. (This dream actually came to pass the following year.) Do I need to add that the dream unleashed fears that have been dormant for years, as well as an extra dose of shame? I am afraid that my mother is going to die alone, and am terrified at the thought that her last memory of me will be that of a failure. I am also apprehensive over the safety of my old journals and pictures, though I am first and foremost concerned over the fate of the one hard copy of *Out of the Trenches* that is also in storage in her apartment because I would not be able to rewrite the novel from scratch for all the money in the world. (I used to carry the novel with me on a diskette at all times, but the diskette went bad while I lived in New York. And, yes, I nearly lost my mind the day I found out.)

8:05 p.m. – "Goddamn fake ass phony motherfucker, find somebody else to mess with and leave me the fuck alone," is the song Lavermine is singing at this moment in time. Who is she talking to? Her new target: Doublefaced Lizzie. Listening to her voice alone is enough to make me want to puke, yet I am going to have to go sit in the dining room with her and Ninabelle and Kaycee Boneheaded and God knows who else in just about an hour if I want to watch Lifetime's *The Fantasia Barrino Story: Life is not a fairytale*.

11:31 p.m. – I was so intrigued by the unflattering movie review in yesterday's *USA Today* that I felt compelled to see Fantasia's movie just to form my own opinion, and I have one question: How dare Robert Bianco disparage an entire family's triumph over tons of obstacles for not being entertaining enough? I loved the movie, though I do regret initiating a conversation about Robert Bianco with Lavermine and Kaycee Boneheaded afterward. Hope they don't think that we're friends now for I would rather be their enemy than their friend. I was so fired up that I threatened to email Robert Bianco to give him my opinion on his baseless criticism of Fantasia's coping strategies and acting skills. In the meantime, I trust that you, God, will give that young woman the tools that she will need to navigate though her newfound fame for celebrityhood is oftentimes nothing more and nothing less than a well-disguised malediction.

Spent the last hour talking to Julie, and she is in so much pain that I should pat myself in the back for taking the time to listen since I am usually so stingy with time. Julie, by the way, is one of the few women at The Shelter who actually cares about the status of her relationship with her children. In fact, those women speak so rarely of their children that I keep forgetting that most of them are mothers, including Ninabelle. Needless to say that Julie's dilemma brought my own strained relationship with my children back to the forefront of my mind. And what is Z'Laitah doing as I write this? Painting her toenails, as if she didn't have a care in the world. Bertha once told me that since her family doesn't celebrate Christmas she and her mother went to a homeless shelter one Christmas morning to bring gifts to the women and stayed around to help them put their makeup on. "What was the point of bringing them makeup?" I remember asking, as I struggled to conceal my growing irritation. And as Bertha expounded on how feeling beautiful contributed to the women having a better Christmas, I told myself that she was embellishing the story just to magnify her perceived impact on the women's lives because physical appearance couldn't possibly be on the list of priority of any woman living in a homeless shelter. I was wrong. And speaking of artificial beauty, I hardly heard a word from the sermon at Bethel this morning because I was too busy inspecting hairdos.

Dear God, what do you think those black Christian women would do if the sky opens up and Jesus himself drops down and implores them to stop wearing fake hairs out of respect for you and the hairs that you saw fit to give them? (To be clear, I would have been less distressed by the fake-hair pandemic if black people owned the factories that manufacture those hairs, but we don't. Now that I think about it, we don't own the factories that manufacture the guns we use to kill each other either. And we certainly don't reap the financial benefits of the illegal drug trade since in this area, too, we are predominantly consumers, not producers.)

"All right, ladies, come in, there are enough empty chairs for everyone!" Mr. ShelterDrillSergeant just said to the group of women who usually stand in the front room to eat dinner, as he motioned for them to go inside the dining room. Sabine and Lydia Pollyanna were the first ones to comply, and Kaycee Sourpuss the last. I chose to climb back into bed. My nerves simply can't take these women up close tonight, and I am not about to make myself feel worse over a plate of crappy food. Bertha, by the way, remained on my mind all day.

Did she finish graduate school and land a job with an NGO in Ethiopia, as she envisioned?

Did she get married and have a baby? She wanted babies so much. Did she not get married and adopt?

"So Much Trouble in the World," one of my favorite Bob Marley songs just popped into mind. Knowing what I know about this depressing world, I sometimes wonder if the people who are not depressed are the ones who are mentally ill. Taking this standpoint one step further, I daresay that if you're a woman over the age of thirty and you're not slightly depressed, you are, in all probability, very much out of touch with the reality of what it's like to be a woman in a not-female-friendly world. (Read *The Road of Lost Innocence* or *Half the Sky* if you don't believe me. Or just pay attention to how girls talk to their mothers on TV shows.)

Paranoia du jour: That my email to the editor of *USA Today* in response to Robert Bianco's unfair movie review is going to be published, and all the folks I owe money to will rush to Tallahassee to track me down. Am I turning into Z'Laitah?

Shamelessness du jour: Sneaking into the diner across from the College of Medicine, along with the proud parents of a group of students attending "Orientation 2006," for a free lunch. Even snatched a few pastries to eat for breakfast the next two days.

Sadness du jour: Reading a few chapters of *Luther: The Life and Longing of Luther Vandross*. Luther Vandross, it seems to me, literally killed himself with his obsession with food and fame. God have mercy on his mother, a woman who gave birth to four children and buried all four in one lifetime. (Luther's mother has since passed away.)

Mortification du jour: Seeing the beautiful raven-haired girl who used to be at The Shelter nearly every evening a few months ago on FSU campus, and she did not only remember me, she asked if I was a student. I told her that I was waiting for my son to get out of class, but I was too embarrassed—for both of us—to ask why she had to work at The Shelter as a CS worker.

Proposition du jour: Peggy, a regular at the 7 a.m. Mass, wants to know if I am interested in attending RCIA classes (the formation process that non-Catholics must go through if they're interested in joining the church.) Dear God, why am I being told by my intuition that religion is merely a brilliant tool to keep the masses appeased and malleable and has very little to do with you, if nothing at all?

Discombobulation du jour: Being told by two bellicose women, seemingly older college students, that I am infringing on their freedom of speech, that I should go back to my country, but that in the intervening time I could go rot in hell for all they care. Who knew that it was even possible to get into arguments in the QUIET STUDY AREA of a library? One more reminder that higher education doesn't always lead to better behaviors.

Flashback du jour: Being told by ExHusband that he does not like to mix apples and oranges when I had asked why he didn't introduce my children to his second wife before they got married. (FourteenYearOldWifey is ExHusband's third wife and my children didn't meet her until her son, my children's half-brother, was four years old. And they have yet to meet their two half-sisters as of this writing.) Dear God, please help me overcome all the valid and invalid feelings of anger, resentments, humiliations and pettiness that have infiltrated my life for too long.

Hunch du jour: That depression can also be a learned behavior (or a self-fulfilling prophecy in the case of a society that is always on the lookout for mental illnesses), and that some women have fallen deeply in love with their mentally-ill label. "I must call my lawyer and plead with him to find me a place because I have a mental illness and these women will get me hospitalized if I stay here," an older woman who just arrived at The Shelter alarmingly said to another older woman who has been staying at The Shelter for years while she waits for retirement. And what's her mental illness? Clinical depression that was set in motion when her husband of thirty-two years left her fifteen months ago. I was tempted to tell her that her depression is a perfectly normal reaction to a very painful situation, and that she'll be a much stronger woman fifteen months from now if she just accepts the depression as part of a down payment for a different but, perhaps, better life, rather than fight it, or, worse, fear it, but I didn't waste my breath since she seems to revel in her pity-me-I-am-depressed identity.

Cannot believe that I've deluded myself for so long about the lottery that I actually saw it as an omen when I took a shortcut to Borders this morning and found myself in front of the headquarters of Florida Lottery.

Cannot believe that I caught a cold again, in spite of all the precautions I've been taking to avoid another one. The plan was to take a shower and go to sleep once I got here, but, of course, that was an exercise in wishful thinking.

Cannot believe that JP doesn't even pretend to want to see me anymore, and I can't even blame him for his need to avoid me since I pretty much created it. If this isn't more painful than a physical death, I don't know what is.

Too sick to do any recording except to say that today marks four months at The Shelter and that it feels more like forty years. And what did I dream about? Of being chased by men in dark suits and dark hats. And the fastest I ran, the more they multiplied. Men from the I.R.S.

Barely 8 a.m. and I am already on the bench in front of the College of Medicine with too much on my mind:

(1) Bullying at The Shelter – My nerves are so frayed that I already know that I will not be able to take Lavermine's verbal abuse tonight, even if it's not directed at me. Plus, I still have a headache and running nose. Dear God, do you have any idea what it feels like to be sick and have nowhere to lie down?

(2) Triviality at The Shelter – Doublefaced Lizzie does not make her bed in the morning, wears donation clothes right off the bin, and the inside of her car that is parked in the parking lot next to The Shelter's driveway looks like a junkyard, yet the woman feels so sorry for me not having enough clothes that she's always talking about it.

(3) Starvation at The Shelter – Okay, I am not exactly starving, but I am hungry. And, no, it's not the food monster trying to get out of its cage. I am really hungry. And what was served for dinner last night? Pasta salad with more onion than pasta, potato chips, a hamburger and a cookie. I gave the hamburger to Sabine, trashed the cookie and potato chips and gobbled down the cold nasty pasta because I had no other choice.

(4) Insomnia at The Shelter – Pamelia was caught smoking in the back bathroom shortly before midnight and was consequently kicked out by Mr. Aloof, a Shelter staff The Shameless think is awfully nice because they're too stupid to realize that he just doesn't give a damn. Took me forever to fall asleep only to be awakened around 4:15 by Shelterqueen yelling at those "nasty motherfuckers" for making too much noise in the big bathroom . . . lots of pretty girls on campus . . . "Where are you ladies going so well dressed?" I nosily asked the last two who just walked by. "We're rushing for sorority," one answered. I don't quite know what a sorority is since I didn't make it to a community college until I was in my late 20s, but I do know that it's one more thing that my daughter didn't get to experience because of me.

(5) Ghetto mentality at The Shelter – I didn't realize that Andrelene and Estelle were watching a news documentary on the AIDS epidemic in black America until I went to use the dining room bathroom around 10:30 last night. From what I understand, most of the people who died of AIDS in the eighties were white gay men. Today, most of the people dying of AIDS are black heterosexuals. In other words, white gay men changed their sex habits in order to save their lives, but black people didn't. "The government isn't doing enough," was the conclusion Andrelene came

up with at the end of the program. My riposte came tumbling out: "Is the government forcing black people to have unprotected sex?" She conceded that they were not, but adamantly argued that they could have done more to prevent HIV spreading. I just stood there looking at her—and at Estelle who was nodding in agreement—doing all over again what we, black folks, managed to become experts at: shifting the blame for our failings to anyone but us. And I couldn't help thinking that the biggest hurdle facing black people in the 21st century is even more devastating than slavery because it's something that only we can change: our mindset.

Grateful for the dawning realization that I, too, am being a coward whenever I sit back and let Shelterqueen do whatever she wants in a homeless shelter that advertises itself as a safe haven for the needy on its website.

Grateful for the bravery to ask Mr. ShelterDirector to step away from the bunk and go talk elsewhere when I woke up around 1:20 this morning and found him standing next to bed 6, chatting with Shelterqueen about Pamelia who was begging him to let her back in.

Grateful for the backbone to ask Mr. Grouch why is it that The Shelter doesn't enforce it own rules after I watched Doublefaced Lizzie complain to him, and all he said to Lavermine was "You need to leave that white woman alone," and walked away while Lavermine chuckled.

Grateful for the chutzpah to later tell Mr. ShelterDirector that I gave money to the United Way for years and hope that my money wasn't used to support people like Lavermine because it would have set my teeth on edge. (I read online that over fifty percent of The Shelter's budget comes from the United Way.) But more than anything else, I am grateful for the gutsiness to tell him that the fact that

Lavermine is able to get away with so much makes me seriously question the leadership of The Shelter.

My most satisfying day at The Shelter. Lavermine, former queen of The Shelter, has been moved to bed 19.

Hallelujah! Hallelujah! Halleeeeeeelujah!

4:06 a.m. – Awake since 2:34 because it was when Shelter madness started. And when I was about to doze off an hour later, Doublefaced Lizzie knocked on the bunk to ask if I could loan her a dollar to buy two cigarettes because she wants to go to the next smoke break but just remembered that she gave her last cigarette away. (Only a nicotine-addicted weirdo would start smoke break at 4 a.m. in a homeless shelter.) Furthermore, Z'Laitah must have read my mind when I decided that I might as well go wash up and get dressed because she leapt out of bed the moment I was getting ready to go down, and I am still waiting for her to exit the bathroom. And who spent the night in bed 5? Labrina, the prostitute granny. And she can't wait for the weekend because she plans to rent herself a motel room and "get shitfaced with a couple bottles of Jack Daniel's."

4:43 p.m. – Sitting on the usual bench in front of the College of Medicine after a very interesting day spent attending classes on TCC campus. Did I register for classes? No. But the way I see it, no one will know whether I am a legit student or not the first few weeks of class—I hope. Accidentally found myself in a math class at some point, and listening to the professor talk about algebraic equations brought back to mind the grim reality that my brain doesn't work in some areas and that I should stick with what comes to me naturally: reading, writing, and judging. Speaking of which, I forgot to record that I got chided the other day by Mr. Irresistible, Sabine's nickname for a new Shelter staff since many of The Shameless have a crush on him, though I strongly believe that Mr. BabyDaddyWithTheWanderingEye would be a more fitting sobriquet. At any rate, Mr. Irresistible said that I was being rude and judgmental—my middle names at The Shelter—after he asked the women in the front room to be quiet while The Shameless in the dining room said a prayer before dinner, and I replied that I didn't want to hear no phony prayers.

7:07 p.m. – "You reap what you sow!" an overwrought Kaycee Boneheaded just told Sabine with all the self-righteousness that she could muster. "My sister could tell you that. The bank just took her house from her and her husband and now she's homeless." I think she's trying to insinuate that something bad is going to happen to Mr. ShelterDrillSergeant for giving her the third degree earlier. What did she do? According to Shelter staff, she used her cell phone to call Hooligan Linda, a two-legged mad dog who once called Z'Laitah a "psychosomatic psycho bitch," and who nowadays lives in Frenchtown, and asked Hooligan Linda to go buy her a bottle of soda and to throw it over the fence during smoke break. But a livid Kaycee Boneheaded said that she was framed, that the soda wasn't hers, and that she will ultimately have the last word in Jesus's name just like she did with her sister and everyone else who has ever done her wrong. Kaycee Boneheaded has been living at The Shelter since she completed her 11/29 two years ago. Does she not realize that she, The Saved One, went homeless long before her sister? (Translation: 11/29 is another way of saying eleven months and twenty-nine days in jail.)

Misdeed du jour: Crashing into a "Theories of Personality" class on the ground floor of the new psychology building this afternoon after I sort of felt obligated to go inside to take a look. It was a delight to hear the very knowledgeable Dr. Boroto talk about the affairs of the mind, yet I couldn't help feeling a bit restless as I listened to more of mankind's theories on mankind's behaviors after having spent the past few years learning about the true nature of mankind from the greatest Professor of all time.

Nervousness du jour: Lydia Pollyanna went to church with me this morning and had such a good time that she plans to go to Daily Mass from now on. I quietly sat in my usual seat, a back pew near the parking lot entrance, while she headed for a pew right in front of the altar where she nodded and smiled during the entire service and I already know that she, too, is going to have an issue with me once she realizes that I don't take communion. And of course she had to go say hello to the priest after Mass.

Hilarity du jour: (a) Listening to Estelle tell the story of a young woman who pensively muttered "Shit!" when she was told that Lavermine was moving to the back room, and hasn't been seen at The Shelter since. (b) Being told by Sabine, who is back from "the hospital," that she's very proud of me for getting Lavermine out of the room because she tried to get rid of her several times with no success. (c) A very contrite Baby Bush going on TV to say that he took full responsibility for the failure of FEMA in New Orleans a year ago. Uh-huh.

Confirmation du jour: One vermin is gone and others are being born. Kaycee Boneheaded must have told at least three people how elated Lavermine is to be in the back room because she very much wanted a change. (I know for a fact that Lavermine hates the back room.) Kaycee Boneheaded also said that people who were in need of "peace and tranquility" should not be looking for it in a homeless shelter, but need to go rent their own house. And a very talkative Z'Laitah made so many comments about judgmental people that I had to create an opportunity to let them all know that I've never been skittish about judging the misconduct of others, and wasn't about to start now out of fear. For good measure, I added that I was actually looking forward to the day when God will judge me by the same measure that I judged others, and that for the time being anyone at The Shelter was welcome to judge me when it's my turn doing wrong. (Lavermine started to mock me for eating too much and too fast from then on, even though she's the one who is shaped like a cross between a hog and an overstuffed turkey.)

I was too tired and hungry to walk to TCC and ended up spending the entire day on FSU campus attending classes in real estate, history and psychology. Decided to go to the main library around 4 p.m., and was more than a bit puzzled when I came face to face with my son who was so thrilled to see me that he had tears in his eyes. He said he hasn't been able to call me because he lost his charger and he didn't have money to buy a new one since he was saving for rent, but that he has been coming to the library more often in hopes to run into me. He laughed when I answered that I had resigned myself to the fact that he, too, had turned his back on me, and reassured me that he was going to love me forever. Yet in spite of his poignant display of affection, I couldn't help thinking that if he was really worried, he would have used Angie's phone to call his ex-roommate whose phone number he knows by heart and ask her for my number, or simply call The Shelter to see if I was still alive. But I told him no such thing, not wanting to spoil the moment. And I am very grateful for the forty dollars he gave when we said goodbye an hour later, which means that I can now go buy the usual necessities.

PS: Julie was already gone when I got here, and I am happy for her because she was as miserable as I am in this hellhole. She left a note on bed 6 saying that she'll be staying with friends while she waits for a transitional home to become available.

PPS: The fifteen-year-old boy doesn't go to school because he's being homeschooled by his mother. I still can't stand the thought of this boy living among those dangerous looking men, but I am afraid to contact social services lest he'll be worse off if they take him away. (He went to live with a local family that took a liking to him a year later.)

Cannot believe I am living in an environment where drinking water is a transgression (I was caught "drinking" on Shelter premises and Mr. Irresistible was very disappointed in me for having a water bottle), but harassing and bullying aren't frowned upon. Or drinking yourself to death. Sabine got drunk again after spending a few days in rehab and she was their biggest source of amusement. "Sabine don't drink," Mr. Jejune derisively spat out right before dinner. "She swallow that stuff." They all laughed, black, white, and yellow. Dear God, how much longer will I have to wait for you to deliver me from this living hell? How much longer will my children have to remain the unwitting casualties of my relationship with you? How much longer will I have to be ashamed of the person I have become in your name?

Cannot believe that a group of women who claim to have such great faith in God can be so easily satisfied with mediocrity. Bekkie-Sue is in the dining room talking about how proud she is of her baby brother who had never been in trouble with the law (as if going to jail was something that was expected of him at birth), never had a D on his report card (a perfect C student. Wow!), and who plans to move to Atlanta to become a rapper after he graduates from high school. (Double wow!) And what does twenty-eight-year-old Bekkie-Sue hope to be when she grows up? A cashier in a hip department store, just like her big sister, so that she can get discounts on all the new clothes. I think it's time for the gazillion of preachers in poor black neighborhoods to start asking members of their congregations to pray the good Lord for a different kind of blessings, namely for aspiration and brainpower.

Cannot believe that "hope" has become my least favorite word in the English language after every modicum of hope I've ever had was crushed over and over day after day, week after week, month after month, year after year. Cannot believe that it has been almost a year since I walked away from my post-eviction career as a domestic worker in New York City and the quality of my life has deteriorated even further. Cannot believe that my expectations of God are still so terrifyingly high that they cause me more pain these days than homelessness and hopelessness combined. And I definitely cannot believe that Lydia Pollyanna told me in all seriousness that we are not homeless because homeless people live on the streets, but we don't. Evermore sanguine, she added that God just performed a miracle for Julie; therefore, hers and mine could not be too far away. And I didn't have the guts to tell her that I had no interest in chickenshit miracles.

Mass just ended, but I didn't hear a word Father Cayer, the new priest, said because my mind is so filled with The Shameless that I might as well still be at The Shelter.

(1) Sunrise gathering of the Black Shameless Club – Ninabelle slept in bed 5 last night, tossed and turned all night, and because she's so heavy the whole bunk rocked with each toss, as if I needed one more reason to stay awake. And true to form, she was already running her mouth below me long before 6 o'clock, and I even had to tell some of her buddies that it was much too early to start congregating around the bunk. She also went to sleep farting and woke up farting.

(2) Burning hot shamelessness – *"Hot Lavermine No. 19—Nothing But Love,"* Shelterqueen wrote on her

locker as I got ready to leave. She even referred to herself as "hot" while talking to a fellow Shameless about her very active sex life. (Her man finds her so hot he wants a piece of her at least three times a week.) The woman is in the winter of her life on all fronts, and she's still clinging to her out-of-commission sexual attractiveness? I now understand why Kaycee Sourpuss shrills "Sicko! Psycho!" whenever she sees Lavermine lately.

(3) STM's homeless invasion – Lydia Pollyanna already found herself a wonderful friend at St. Thomas More and her wonderful friend took her out for breakfast after Mass this morning, which means that I can hopefully enjoy a solid hour of solitude before the groundkeeper shows up. Lydia Pollyanna has been spending the whole morning in church all week, forcing me to head out right after Mass since I truly believe that there is not enough room at St. Thomas More for two homeless women. Moreover, she casually mentioned on our way here that it saddens her that some people don't take communion because they don't feel worthy of Christ when all they need to do to clear up their conscience is to go to confession and be granted absolution. And I unashamedly replied that I personally did not take communion not because of a dirty conscience, but because I was more interested in the spirit of Jesus than in his body and blood.

(4) The ugly side of niceness – Doublefaced Lizzie has been avoiding me since Lavermine got moved to the back room, yet there she was knocking on bed 6 again right after midnight to tell me that she was on the verge of an anxiety attack. I got out of bed and spent the next twenty minutes in the dining room trying to calm her down while she swallowed down two more pills and spoke of her contentious

relationship with her parents and adult children. She said her family still resent her for behaving "like a girl in a woman's body," in spite of doing what they wanted her to do by becoming sober. She also admitted that she couldn't stand it at The Shelter because the women use her and steal from her. "I am fucking tired of being victimized wherever I go just because I am nice," she sanctimoniously stated in closing. One of these days I am going to have to tell her—as nicely as I can—that being nice is not all that it's cracked up to be, especially when one is being nice in order to avoid looking at oneself, or in a near-obsessive effort to obtain attention and praise.

6:50 p.m. – Z'Laitah is in the middle of a very intense conversation with Monica, a newcomer who already got into trouble this morning because she had the TV on CNN and Lavermine who hasn't been able to watch her favorite morning show since Monica "appeared with her CNN obsession" let her have it. From what I gathered, Monica, who is passing through Tallahassee on her way to South Florida, had asked Z'Laitah about something last night and Z'Laitah bitingly replied that she didn't feel like talking, and Z'Laitah is now apologizing for her rudeness. Oh, my God, Z'Laitah just found out that Monica, a cute and perky blonde of Swedish descent who speaks with no detectable foreign accent, is originally from Columbia and they're now speaking in Spanish (Z'Laitah's ex-husband is from Spain.) Do I need to add that Monica, who is also fluent in French, suddenly looks as if she had hit the jackpot now that she found an *amiga* who speaks her mother tongue and that the meanie in me can't wait to see how long it's going to take Z'Laitah to turn the tables on her?

10:44 p.m. – "I am here in the basement, cleaning out!" Doublefaced Lizzie just cried out in her sleep, her Paxilinduced sleep. I don't find it hard to believe that Double-faced Lizzie even people-pleases in her sleep, but I simply could not believe my ears when I heard her take credit for being the one who got Lavermine out of the room when the reality is that she was so jumpy in the days after the move that she barely spoke to me for fear that Lavermine exacts vengeance on her, too. It's true that Doublefaced Lizzie was, as far as I know, the last person who formally complained to Mr. ShelterDirector about Lavermine. But it was I who unapologetically interrupted their conversation to report how Lavermine was so out of control that the first thing I heard when I woke up that morning was Lavermine telling Valerie (quiet, fragile-looking, sickish Valerie): "I HOPE YOU HAVE A SEIZURE AND DIE!" In fact, Double-faced Lizzie instantly came to the defense of Mr. ShelterDirector by insisting that it was not fair to hold him responsible for Lavermine's behavior when I later dropped the line about questioning the leadership of The Shelter. I find Doublefaced Lizzie's propensity to lie to herself astonishing. Maybe she's just one of those "unfortunates" they talk about on page fifty-eight of the Big Book. People who have lied to themselves for so long that they no longer know the difference between fact and fiction.

Stupefaction du jour: Betty-Lou, the young and polite black woman with the gorgeous smile who came in about a week ago is three months pregnant with her third child (she's as thin as a rail.) I was even more stunned when she told me that her parents, the legal guardians of her two children, are begging her to come back home but she actually likes it at The Shelter because some of her best friends are here. (Many Shelter guests first met each other in jail, but a few of them actually went to the same high school.)

Insult du jour: "A tune-up from within rather than a paint job is what we need to pray for" was the message from St. Thomas More this morning, at least it was the message I heard. And I sat there once again thinking that I did just that and look what happened to me. Bethel later followed suit with "Prayer can do what money, friends, education can't do . . . crisis don't last forever . . . nothing is too hard for God." Nothing except making me win a meager Florida Lotto jackpot, I guess. (The Powerball did not come to Florida until January 2009. The Mega Millions followed in May 2013.)

Regalement du jour – Hot Lavermine was in front of her locker (she can't stay away from the front room) when Andrelene who just came back from one of her monthly "Shelter breaks" asked how she liked her new bed. Lavermine boasted that the back room was a lot quieter and that she sleeps much better. For some unknown reason, Andrelene then asked if Lavermine was the one who asked to be moved, or did she get moved. The devil in Lavermine immediately came out, and next thing I know she was accusing a bamboozled Andrelene of trying to intimidate her by "instigating shit that were over and done with."

Awkwardness du jour: Speaking to "Pastor Beth," the good-looking wife of Glenn Burns, Director of the Haven of Rest Rescue Mission, about the prospect of moving in a subsidized trailer when my expectations of you, God, is so much bigger than anything those people can offer me. How did I end up in Beth Burns's office? Julie now does volunteer work at the Haven of Rest and is getting ready to move in their new Christian home for women, and would love me to come along. Felt completely trapped during the entire conversation, especially after Beth Burns mentioned that she was in the process of looking for sponsors to pay the first month of rent for women who didn't yet have an income. I would not want to share a mobile home with my best friend in the world if I still had one, let alone with anyone I met at The Shelter. Besides, I have a great aversion to the word "sponsor," which is why I never wanted one in OA, to the great disgust of OA old timers.

Sitting in front of the Dollar Theater while I wait for *The Devil Wears Prada* to begin at 1:15. Mentally and physically exhausted. Shelter drama lasted all night. No details necessary except to say that these women are determined to teach me what smarter folks have discovered long ago: some people are just not worth the trouble of trying to help them out. Another mistaken belief that had to be uprooted so that reality could prevail. And to make a bad day even worse, I found myself staring at the lottery billboard as I walked out of Barnes & Noble half hour ago and the jackpot is back at three million. I must have been a horrible person in one of my past lives for nothing I've ever done in my present life deserves such indescribable suffering.

"If you can't enjoy your days, what's the point of having them?" a more-jovial-than-usual Kaycee Boneheaded just said to Lavermine who is again standing at her locker, looking for something sexy to wear tomorrow. (I am 100 percent sure by now that Lavermine concocted the story of the superlatively amorous boyfriend just to aggrandize her Shelter sphere and, of course, to make the other women squirm with envy.) Kaycee Boneheaded, however, is clearly making the most of her early retirement and had a great day "chilling with friends," and plans to do the same, tomorrow while she waits for her unemployment checks to kick in. "Go it with your bad self, girl!" Lavermine wittily egged on. "You're a hot mess." Conversely, anguish bordering on agony plagued me every minute of the day, even as I listened to Dr. Esposito's peppy discussion of Renaissance and Baroque art (I just can't see how looking at Bernini's St. Teresa in Ecstasy or Tintoretto and Da Vinci's very different portraying of the Last Supper can enhance my life in any way.) I got even more depressed after I sneaked into a room at the TCC student union, along with a group of students from a speech class, to listen to a best-selling author who is trying to break into the motivational speaking circuit. And according to Don Yaeger, taking a look at who you associate with can give you a good idea of who you are, and if you have a yen for success, you need to hang around successful people. Not exactly a newsflash, yet his words gave me goose bumps because they brought The Shameless back to mind when the main reason I like to be on TCC campus is because it's far enough from The Shelter that I can temporarily forget about those people when I am there. And why did I not meet with JP today as planned? Because he called to reschedule under the pretext that he missed the bus. It never once crossed my mind that this boy would be treating me like an old shoe one day, something he's still fond of, but no longer has any need for.

Spent my morning in church and at Borders and I am currently sitting at my favorite spot at the main library where I spent the past few hours catching up with articles of the past two days, and the following are worth recording:

- The I.R.S. is sending collection agencies after people who own back taxes. How long will it take them to find me and demand that I cough up money that I don't have?

- Immigration, which has been the No. 1 national preoccupation of late is being taken off the political agenda. I guarantee that it will be back in the headlines as soon as there is a need to distract the American people once more.

- Katie Couric made her debut as the first sole female anchor of CBS Evening News. Barbara Walters must be proud. And the viewers who still have issues with a woman sitting in the anchor chair must be wishing that they could turn back time.

- A "permanent" artificial heart that must be replaced within five years was just approved by the FDA with a $250,000 asking price. Hard to believe the lengths some people are willing to go in an attempt to delay the unavoidable. For my part, I would rather die a sudden and unexpected death at fifty—if I have no dependents under the age of twenty-one—than to be "alive" at eighty, but hooked up to a machine just to help the health care industry fulfill its demented wish to extend life at any cost.

- Rosie O'Donnell reportedly told a cameraman on *The View* to not worry about her causing trouble because she has been taking her medication. The mental health experts must be grinning from ear to ear now that they got women to brainwash women about popping pills, and to joke on TV about their real or imaginary mental illnesses. And speaking of mental illnesses, why do they group everyone with a mental health challenge (and many without any) under the term "the mentally ill" while they don't use the words "the physically ill" to describe people, say, with erectile dysfunction or prostate cancer?

Already 6:43. Must now brace myself for the trip back to The Shelter. Must also brace myself for a possible showdown with Z'Laitah who has slowly fallen into the habit of breaking into my conversations just to refute my point of views, and I've ignored her long enough.

Grateful for the privilege to spend the day in the company of my kind of people, educators and students, in spite of the additional level of stress that comes along.

Grateful for my five-minute conversation with Lulu this morning in which she confirmed what my mother told me the last time we spoke: that my Patoutou is turning out into a smart, beautiful and even-tempered little girl.

Grateful that teaching the new generation about diversity is paying off, at least on FSU campus. Was worried that FSU students were going to stare me away from their classrooms, but they don't even give me a second look.

Grateful I didn't flinch when Mr. ShelterDrillSergeant say last night that he would be assigning seats in the dining room beginning today. The control freak, who only works part-time at The Shelter, but whose omnipotence seems to be omnipresent, didn't even come to work.

Grateful that Z'Laitah did jump in my conversation tonight while I spoke to Lydia Pollyanna about Charlie Crist, her favorite politician on God's green earth, which gave me the perfect opportunity to say: "Z'Laitah, I would really appreciate it if you would learn to ignore me as much as I ignore you." I think she was too embarrassed to think of a reply, but I know that she won't remain tongue-tied for long.

Grateful that I still trust you, God, in spite of being scared shitless that you will not come through for me, and that I will end up living at The Shelter forever just like Lavermine. Even more grateful for the confidence to say to Doublefaced Lizzie that "I don't do the system because I am waiting on something better" when she, too, told me that I need to go apply for food stamps. (Having a food stamp card is akin to having a free ATM card in the world of The Shameless, perhaps because selling food stamps is such a surefire way to earn cash for cigarettes, marijuana, beers, crack, phone cards and motel rooms.)

8:17 a.m. – Cool out this morning, which prompted me to take refuge at the Robert Manning Strozier Library, Florida

State University's main library, for the first time in my Shelter life. Lydia Pollyanna was right: anyone can go inside Strozier. Interesting how I hardly felt any scruples sneaking into their classrooms, yet I wrongly assumed that one needed a student ID to use their library. Do I need to add that I am getting even more antsy about winter clothes and winter holidays?

12:02 p.m. – Getting ready to go meet JP at the main library, and he better there because I am tired of him taking my time for granted. Spent the past hour reviewing the notes I took yesterday about the Catholic roots of the Anglican Church, the formation of the puritans, the fact that John Calvin and Martin . . . Speaking of Martin Luther, I perfectly understood why he came to the conclusion that salvation can only be achieved through divine mercy while eating my third piece of cake on my way to church this morning. A continuous fall from grace is a hard thing on the ego.

3:49 p.m. – At the main library while I wait to go have a meal at the Haven of Rest at 5 o'clock because Julie said I could and I don't exactly want to deal with Mr. ShelterDrillSergeant in the event that he does show up. JP left with the 3:40 bus since he had to be at work at 4. I don't really know what to say about the time we spent together except that he showed up an hour late, and I felt dejected and trivialized all over again. I also wish that I had kept my mouth shut when he mentioned that he didn't think that his ex-roommate approves of him playing house with Angie, and I forthrightly replied that perhaps ExRoommate has a good reason to be oppositional for a change.

7:47 p.m. – Many of the Shameless didn't check in tonight, but the atmosphere in the front room is still insupportable because Zhouli has been quarreling with her unseeable tormentors all evening. She's also skinnier than ever, and looks ten years older. I told Marguerite a few days ago that Zhouli needed psychiatric care, and she said that she was going to talk to Mr. ShelterDirector to see what kind of help The Shelter has available to people with such serious mental illness, but she hasn't said a word to me on the matter since and I don't want to look as if I am pumping her for info. In addition, Mr. ShelterDrillSergeant did come to work, and he did assign seats to all the women standing in the front room. I did not bother to get out of bed and ate crackers and peanut butter to supplement the small meal I had at the Haven of Rest. Of course, the free meal wasn't free. More later . . . Kaycee Boneheaded and Sofunda just started a screaming contest, which I can't afford to miss.

8:24 p.m. – Well, Kaycee Boneheaded got exactly what she wanted: Mr. ShelterDrillSergeant just kicked Sofunda out. What did Sofunda do? All I know is that the two of them were arguing in the dining room when Kaycee Boneheaded swore that Sofunda pushed her, sent one of her acolytes to go get Mr. Jejune, and to her dismay Mr. Jejune simply asked Sofunda to apologize. A riled Kaycee Boneheaded then asked to see Mr. ShelterDirector and basically told him that she would be willing to forget the whole thing if he would just give her a voucher to go spend the night at the Holiday Inn. Mr. ShelterDirector sarcastically replied that he too would like to go relax at the Holiday Inn for free, and Kaycee Boneheaded began with her list of threats, which included going to the emergency room, filing a police report, calling the state attorney office, and suing a short white woman whom she believes privately owns The Shelter. (Sofunda, for the record, is roughly half the size of three-hundred-and-sixty-five-pound Kaycee Boneheaded.) And going back to my experience at the Haven of Rest, one of the men who lives at the mission flopped himself across from me the moment I took a seat, and proceeded to hound me all over again about going out with him, even after I told him that I was the most boring woman at The Shelter and that a good looking man like him could easily find a more exciting woman to spend his time with. (He said we could get bored together.) Dear God, do you have any idea how frustrating it is to be a woman in a world that pursues us and demeans us all at once?

Disappointment du jour: Being told by Mama that JP hasn't called her since Mother's Day and she hasn't heard from my daughter in a month. My mother has been good to my children, and she deserves so much better.

Astonishment du jour: Being told by a peevish Deanna that the reason Mr. ShelterDrillSergeant thinks he can control everybody is not because he's the manager of The Shelter, but because he's the Shelter staff with the longest seniority. Who knew?

Gratitude du jour: For a peaceful morning on a bench next to the FSU's Alumni Center, my new hiding place that is conveniently located on West Tennessee Street on the right side of St. Thomas More. (And that was where FSUPD eventually caught up with me on a Sunday morning in the spring of 2007. Hello, Officer Brimm.)

Annoyance du jour: Watching the eyes of Doublefaced Lizzie filled up with tears as she expressed her deep gratitude for being at The Shelter where she can have a roof over her head and food in her belly. May God forgive me if I am wrong, but I am not grateful for free food and free shelter, and I am not going to pretend that I am just to be nice. Only lazy and crazy people enjoy receiving handouts and I am neither. In fact, the more handouts I receive the less dignity I feel.

Reality check du jour: The food monster is out of its cage again. Ate a bagel and a banana for breakfast, yet I was starving by noon, and ended up spending $3.20 at the Wendy's (now closed) a block away from The Shelter to buy fries, nuggets, and a frosty from their 99 cents menu. I was asked if I wanted a chocolate or a vanilla frosty; I didn't even know they now had vanilla frosty. (Grateful that I found out weeks later that I could buy a decent serving of rice and beans for $1.50 at G & G, the Jamaican restaurant next to The Shelter, and special thanks to Juliet Brown for treating me, my three "Tallahassee wannabe grandchildren," and their mother with compassion and friendliness, always.)

Irritation du jour: Watching Lavermine behave in The Shelter's kitchen as if she owns it when no other guest has the right to even linger in the kitchen. Mr. ShelterDrillSergeant actually scolded me once just for coming too close to a box of plantains. (I was so happy to see something that used to be a staple in my diet before the eviction that I impulsively reached inside the box to touch a plantain.) Yet there was Lavermine standing in front of the refrigerator at 6:19 this morning, looking for ketchup to put on the hamburger she was fixing herself. One of these days, I am going to have to ask Mr. ShelterDirector—in writing—why is it that Shelter rules apply to everyone at The Shelter but Lavermine.

At the little park right behind the main library again, and making every effort to put out of my mind the three creatures who are either sleeping or passed out in the gazebo forty feet behind me. Grateful it finally stopped raining. It was pouring when I left Bethel around 12:30 and rained on and off all afternoon. Also grateful for the courage to tell Julie when I saw her this morning that while I am very happy that she had found herself a home, I am choosing to stay put at The Shelter because I think that's where God wants me to be for now. A stream of nauseousness swept through me when she mentioned that Pamelia will be one of the three women with whom she'll be sharing the two-bedroom trailer, but I made no comments, not wanting to be caught passing judgments on my way to church. Especially after Monica asked me last night why I was sitting up in bed with a sheet over my head and I told her that it's because I didn't want to see The Shameless, and she snootily replied that she stopped judging people years ago because it goes against the big plan that the universe has for all of us. (And, I am sure, against the big picture she has in her head vis-à-vis the spiritualist she thinks she is.)

PS: It still bothers me that I felt pressured to thank a lady at the First Presbyterian Church at lunch time for giving me two sandwich bags filled with toiletries because she acted as if she was doing me a big favor by giving me an extra one. I've never given to others what I didn't want for myself, and it hurts like hell to say thank you when I don't mean it. Cannot stand it, God. Cannot stand it at all. I don't have the mental constitution of a pauper, and you know it.

PPS: Sabine didn't come in last night and Lydia Blackvan, a tall Canadian redhead from the back room who is collecting two checks from God knows where, drives a nice car, yet claims she doesn't have enough money to rent her own apartment, said that she saw a smashed Sabine dodging traffic on East Tennessee Street yesterday morning. Dear God, please do for Sabine what she cannot do for herself because she's going to drink herself to death if you don't.

9:32 a.m. – Just arrived at Tallahassee Mall and I am sitting on a bench near the customer service desk, waiting for Barnes & Noble to open at ten, and hoping that security won't notice me since the only other people here so far are the mall walkers. Other than that, it has been a good morning free of fear and anxiety, and Father Cayer even rekindled my hope in a better future when he said in his homily that the best healers are healers who have been wounded themselves. He also asked everyone to say a prayer for the families of those who died in 9/11, but I am also asking you, God, to bequeath mercy on the survivors because the ones who die in a natural or manmade disaster are sometimes better off than the ones who survived.

6:17 p.m. – Lydia Pollyanna just told me that Pastor Beth came to The Shelter this morning to pick up the deaf woman who has been in bed 5 the past few nights and thank God because the poor woman was too old to be at The Shelter. I heard Marvy, Monica's new Shelter best friend since Z'Laitah stopped talking to her two days ago, say that the deaf lady was a battered woman who came to The Shelter to hide from her husband, but I was afraid to confirm it with Lydia Pollyanna since gossiping is not one of her vices. But I did ask her why she calls Beth Burns "Pastor Beth," and she cheerfully answered that it's because Beth Burns is so wonderful at counseling people that she might as well be a pastor.

6:48 p.m. – The laundry basket came up during the 6:30 smoke break, and I just found a pair of Z'Laitah's "quality panties" in my clothes while putting them away (she has twenty-one pairs of quality panties.) I threw them on her bed while she had her back to me, but I still feel thoroughly repulsed considering that I used to do the laundry of my own children separately when I was using my own washing machine in my own home. And guess who will be sleeping in bed 7 and 5 tonight? Crackhead JiBonnie and pregnant mother of six Chelsea (real name), respectively. "The 'hood is moving to the suburb and hell is going to freeze over!" they giddily agreed on as they changed the sheets, a hint that they, too, are aware that I don't allow certain behaviors to go on in the front room.

9:08 p.m. – Chelsea is on the phone with her baby's father, who stays at the Haven of Rest, for the third time since the 8:15 smoke break because she's bored out of her mind while she waits for the 9:30 smoke break. (Most pregnant women at The Shelter smoke, and that, too, is normal in the eyes of The Shameless.) At the same time, a cantankerous JiBonnie just came back from the back room and is threatening to beat up "all the bitches in here getting checks." I never had to deal with a vociferous crackhead before, and don't even know where to begin. How did I, a person who has always been so conscious of how she invests her time and her mind, end up in the company of such wasted human beings? Human beings who, one can assume, make God ashamed to be their Creator.

A good day spent on TCC and FSU campuses, learning and relearning about things such as the Pequot war of 1637 during which the colonists exterminated an entire tribe in order to take over their land, the King Phillip's War, which ended with King Phillip, the first Native American king who dared to challenge the colonists, being decapitated and his wife and children being sold to slavery. Dr. Esposito spoke about Louis XIV's major achievements, which left me indifferent, but I was glad to learn that he had moved the seat of French government to Versailles partly because he hated the stench of Paris since sewage used to be dumped in La Seine back then. And my God, what a big relief it was to confirm that I don't need a TCC ID to enter the TCC library. And because he's one of those professors who insists on making eye contact with every student and I have trouble meeting his gaze, I was a bit nervous about crashing into Dr. Boroto's class again, but I am grateful that I was there to hear him talk about the three basic assumptions of human nature. And most important, to be reminded that "great successes and miserable defeats" are both parts of the learning process . . . Mr. Jejune is here to turn off the lights and Z'Laitah just apologized for the way she lunged toward the tray he was carrying at dinner time just so he would not serve me before her. But, of course, she didn't mention me in her mea culpa.

Just arrived at Strozier and must take time to record the following before I even glance at today's paper.

    (1) Laverminesque cheekiness – Lavermine has been trying to ingratiate herself with me again by broadcasting to be a changed woman, but she must have sensed that she can no longer rely on ruse to win me over because she's back harassing me. "Washing your clothes again? Mel is going to know about that," she groaned after she caught me drying another dress on the bunk late last night when I was relatively sure that the sickopsycho had gone to sleep for good. The woman is taking clothes and shoes from the donation bin to sell inside and outside The Shelter and she's not worried about being caught, but she wants me to worry about washing clothes by hand? Could kick myself for not thinking of a retort fast enough, and now she probably thinks that she got something to hold over my head.

    (2) Preposterous fidelity – As told by Dr. Boroto, Fred Adler believed that our goals are always based on fiction, but that we do show courage and common sense if we know when to hold on to a fantasy and when to fold it. Why am I thinking about Fictional Finalism at 8 o'clock in the morning? Because I dreamed that I was still living at 2900 Upshur Street months after the eviction, but that my heart practically stopped every time I heard a car door slam and I was constantly checking the front porch, the sidewalks, the streets, and the driveway (just like I had done in real life during the nail-biting months between foreclosure and eviction while I feverishly prayed for a miracle.) And I woke up wondering if my stubborn determination to pursue God no matter what is not in and of itself a sign of mental illness.

    (3) Historical revisionism – Let's just say that I would not be surprised if my great-grandchildren learn in

history class that new evidence shows that the Native Americans were the ones who invited the English over after all, and because they proved to be such gracious guests, lands were offered to them. And who killed the Native Americans? The evil black slaves, of course. And how did the evil black slaves end up in America? Anticipating that the New World would be in need of manpower for agricultural purposes, the king of Africa himself had contacted Jamestown and offered to sell his people to the new settlers. I guess what I am trying to say is that the more history classes I attend, the more amazed I am at the ability of white America to maintain the nice image it has of itself even when doing nasty. (We're going to bomb Iraq, but don't worry, we do plan to stick around long enough to help them rebuild. And to shove our political system down their throats, whether their people are ready for democracy or not.)

(4) Unconscientious babymamahood – The mother of four, who was joking about being as high as a kite at check-in time, spent a long time in the stairwell after the 10:45 smoke break, chatting with Labrina. And after listening to her recount the sanitized version of the events that rendered her homeless again, I found myself thinking about the undeniable correlation between grinding poverty and family planning, or lack thereof. I bet most of The Shameless would have agreed to be sterilized if the government was willing to pay them $5000 to stop having babies that they cannot provide for in any area that I can think of. And why am I placing the blame for irresponsible baby making solely on women? Because we are the ones who do get pregnant, and we should be the ones to keep all the disastrous consequences of sex in mind before we

place ourselves in situations that can lead to irreparable blunders in the name of love or pleasure.

Cannot believe that the quiet and angelic-looking black lady with the beautiful voice who is assigned to bed 5 tonight is crazy, too. It all started with her singing in the shower about being a living miracle thanks to the love of Jesus, then preaching to everyone who would listen about all the tricks Satan uses to lead us astray. And it culminated with her standing in the doorway of the big bathroom and brandishing her Bible as she castigated the people in the dining room for watching the devil's television. As if I needed one more proof that God is an all-time favorite subject among prophets and saints, as well as simpletons and loonies.

Cannot believe that JP didn't show up for our 2 p.m. appointment, and didn't even call to reschedule. I recently came across an essay in which a woman told the story of the hell she put her mother-in-law through just to prove that she was the No. 1 woman in her husband's life. I wonder if Angie is capable of that kind of manipulation, though in all honesty I don't really care what she's capable of. I gave birth to JP, not Angie. I raised JP, not Angie. I have loved JP for the past twenty-one years, not Angie. So JP is the one I am casting all the blame on, and no one else.

Cannot believe that Dr. Phil's wife has a half-page ad in today *USA Today,* promoting her new book on how to live a passionate and purposeful life. It goes without saying that there was a tiny picture of Dr. Phil in the ad, asking readers to tune in to his talk show for more info. I cannot stand it when people who have nothing valuable to say write books just because they know they can sell books. And why would Robin McGraw even think of using the word "purpose" in the subtitle of her book after Rick Warren unequivocally milked that word for all it's worth?

Cannot believe that Sabine is drunk again after she told me that she has finally reached her nadir, and was going to stop drinking again for at least a year. (She said she was sober for several years until stress about her financial situation propelled her back to the bottle.) I swear I am beginning to wonder just how hard she's trying.

Cannot believe that even Patoutou who has always been very eager to speak to me was too busy to come to the phone today—too busy watching *Dora*. And I absolutely refuse to believe, nor accept, that the God I gave up my livelihood for is nowhere to be found when I need him the most. My life has become my worst nightmare.

Challenge du jour: Trying to get acquainted with the real Monica after she took me for hostage since there was no one else to talk to because Marvy was drunk to the point of being incoherent and Z'Laitah is still giving her the cold shoulder. Monica, who is very proud of her ability to pack up and go at any moment, actually started her bicycle trip from Minnesota nine weeks ago with $18 in cash and less than $200 on a credit card. She also confirmed something I've suspected all along: she has no idea where she's heading, and is simply looking for a place where she can feel completely free just like she felt when she lived in France in the '70s. She also considers herself to be "*une intellectuelle*" as well as an expert on a variety of religious beliefs, and even has a guru in Nepal whose work she would like to share with me in the future. Monica is not a *sans-abri*, either. She actually owns a three-bedroom, two-bathroom condo that is being rented out by two of her nieces while she's on her exhilarating quest for freedom. Monica doesn't seem insane but what do I know? Meanwhile, I can't wait to be enlightened by her guru.

Satisfaction du jour: Reading that Whitney Houston finally filed for a legal separation from that train wreck of hers. Her mental, physical and spiritual recovery can now begin, I hope. I also hope that the "thin ban" that has been placed on anorexic-looking models by the organizers of the Madrid Fashion Week will start an international trend. It's hard to believe how far some women are still willing to go for money and fame. Or to simply gain validation from a mercurial world that will never remain satisfied with them for long, even if they somehow or other manage to morph themselves into becoming who it wants them to be.

Exasperation du jour: Listening to Lydia Pollyanna gloat over Charlie Crist's decision to select a running mate whom she thinks is Catholic because he was recently awarded the 2006 Defensor Vitae Award from the Florida Catholic Conference. She was swollen with so much pride that you would think that the presumed lieutenant governor was a friend of hers, and that he promised to hire her as his personal assistant if Charlie Crist get elected, but what followed was a long monologue about the pro-life movement. Dear God, how can I, in good conscience, invest my time and energy in the unborn when the physical, mental, and intellectual development of millions of strikingly visible children is being impaired as we speak through chronic malnutrition alone? To put it bluntly, I would have been much more disposed to listen to what the pro-life folks have to say if most of them had made a meaningful contribution to the world by adopting one child—and treat that child like they would treat their own biological child—rather than merely talk crap about the evils of abortion.

Gwen is back after more than a week of "vacation." For someone who claims to be saving money for an apartment she and her "husband" sure spend a lot of money on motel rooms, but that's not the point. The point is that she's been driving me nuts all evening talking about her long hair, which is indeed blond and long, but rather dull and unremarkable. (Monica's blond hair is long and thick and nice-looking, but she apparently is not defined by her hair since she hardly talks about it.) She also can't stop talking about her weight. Gwen may have lost five or six pounds since she showed up at The Shelter two months ago, but wants everyone to believe that she's on her way back to a size two because she has lost fifteen pounds in the past thirty days alone. In addition, I felt quite lucky last night at the chance to watch the John Stossel Special on *20/20* about race, sex and stereotypes, but in retrospect I wish that I, too, had stayed in bed. Was I startled by any of the findings? No. They were simply some ugly truths about the real nature of mankind that some people would rather deny, but that I had already figured out on my own through cheer observation. What I do find intolerable, however, is the reality that I am sharing a roof with a group of people who are, for the most part, the perfect embodiment of the stereotypes that the world has created of them.

12:08 p.m. – Already in line at the First Presbyterian Church because the Bethelites at the 11 a.m. service were so boisterous in their praise of the Lord that, as my headache intensified, I found myself wondering if Jesus would have had to wear earplugs if he were in their midst in the flesh. I just have a hard time understanding how anyone can get so passionate about stories that they haven't witnessed, much less experienced. And what was the topic at STM earlier? We must remain fascinated by Jesus because while he doesn't offer us a life free of pain, he does offer us a successful life. Needless to say that I clenched my teeth throughout the homily. (No offense, Jesus. It's not you. It's them.) Yet I found myself smiling a few minutes later at the sight of five women on the altar, helping Monsignor Tugwell, the rector, prepare for Holy Communion. A reminder that while the Catholic Church enjoys preaching about the importance of humility, the Church itself has no intention to be humble. If they can change their rules to include altar girls and if female Eucharistic Ministers can now serve the body and blood of Christ right alongside the male priests, why can't they change their rules to ordain women when women do the bulk of the work that enables the Church to keep proclaiming that it provides more assistance than any other institution on earth to the sick, the poor, and the illiterate. Most significantly, does it ever occur to the Vatican that the Church would not have been embroiled in the most appalling religious sex scandal of the new millennium if more women were in charge?

7:54 p.m. – "Thank you, Sir!" was how a very meek Z'Laitah thanked the white man who handed her a box of chicken at the First Presbyterian Church at lunch time. Yet what did she do when she was being served dinner by a black woman twenty minutes ago? She essentially repeated the same behavior she acted out with Mr. Jejune, except that her aggressiveness had nothing to do with me this time. (She hates Deanna so much that she didn't want Deanna to touch her plate.) Deanna asked her to place the plate back on the tray, and Z'Laitah rambled on about the inefficiency of Shelter staff until a hot and bothered Labrina asked her "to shut the fuck up and show some respect."

11:57 p.m. – I made the mistake to assume that today's shenanigans were over when the TV went off at 11:28 and was about to doze off when Blabbermouth Mary, a new guest who already made it clear that she doesn't have all her marbles, ran past me hollering that she had to get out of The Shelter because "that woman back there who runs The Shelter and has been here a hundred years" was going to kill her. Two members of the White Shameless Club are currently in the big bathroom, consoling Blabbermouth Mary, while Lavermine went downstairs to tell her side of the story. What really happened? I put my earplugs back on just so I would not hear the specifics.

Shelter quotes of the day:

"My mother always said that I would not amount to anything, and she turned out to be right." I was about to tell that young woman that it wasn't too late to prove her mother wrong but it occurred to me that the statement was made to educe pity, not as an expression of grief.

"You niggers ain't shit!" Lissa allegedly told JiBonnie during smoke break, and JiBonnie is boiling mad and she's going to knock Lissa's old motherfucking ass out. Did I mention that the black Shameless use the verb "knock out" so often that you would think they're being trained to fight Mike Tyson?

"You know what he sang to me today?" a white Shameless who just got off crack after seventeen years (but is still drinking) told another in reference to the Hispanic mendicant she met in The Shelter's backyard a month ago. "He sang 'You Are the Sunshine of My Life,' and I cried. He's so good to me, and he's so good for me."

"I think the motherfucker wants to turn me into a white woman, but that ain't going to happen. I was born a strong black woman and I am going to die a strong black woman. Those niggers are always looking for somebody to control." Dear God, please do my race a favor and let all belligerent black women know that yelling and cussing and bulldozing is only a sign of strength in the decaying subculture that they have created for themselves and nowhere else.

"There is only one way to react to any situation and it's love," Monica pointedly opined while she tried to make a better person out of me, again. Yet she showed no love and plenty of judgment an hour later when she was forced to shower in the filthy big bathroom because Lissa purportedly locked the door of the dining room bathroom again, out of spite. And it didn't occur to her that she could have grabbed broom and mop and clean the big bathroom herself if cleanliness was such a major issue for her.

"Don't you fucking tell me how to raise my child. It's my child!" a mother from the family section barked after one of The Shameless told her that she should not spank her children so often. I wish someone would tell these women that there is much more to motherhood than getting pregnant and giving birth. (Many Shelter mothers, black or white, do not tell their children "go sit down," for instance, because it is acceptable in this hellhole to tell your child "go sit your ass down," or "I don't want to hold your big ass," or "shut your ass up."

"Well, I told you. People who are prejudiced die with cancer. If your sister is not prejudiced and she has cancer, then you must look at your parents, or your grandparents, or some other family members down the line. The Bible does not lie. Just be glad that she finally accepted Jesus and got baptized in holy water because she would have burned in hell if she didn't." Religion is not only the opium of the poor, the notion that God loves us so much that he sent his only begotten son to die for our sins (and give us everlasting life to boot) is, inarguably, the mother of all fairytales.

"At least if I am pregnant now I know who the father is. The last time I thought I was pregnant I was so high and shit that I had no idea who could have knocked me up and my mother nearly went bonkers." I just don't understand the soil on which this kind of shamelessness is rooted. Oddest of all is the fact that The Shameless erupted in laughter when the comment was made by the latest arrival, a scarily thin white woman with spiked jet-black hair and the tattoo of an orange butterfly on the back of her neck, and worse was to follow in the form of more sexually-loaded remarks. It's enough to make you wonder if these women do not have a genetic inability to develop and retain a moral compass.

"You're being a real shithead tonight," was the comment a suddenly brave Doublefaced Lizzie made around 8 p.m. while Mr. Jejune walked through the room griping about something that I don't recall. "What did you say?" he turned around and asked. "You heard me. I said that you're being a real shithead tonight," Doublefaced Lizzie flippantly replied, as if she was desperately looking for a reason to be kicked out. His answer came at once: "Pack your bags." Nearly two hours later, I still can't believe that a master bullshitter like Doublefaced Lizzie decided to tell the truth when she should have lied. And in typical white Shameless fashion, she donned a frozen smile as she said her goodbyes, and told everyone that she'll be just fine, sleeping in her car.

"If God eludes someone, who moved? He told us in the Bible that he will never leave us nor forsake us," Lydia Pollyanna gaily answered when I told her in a moment of weakness that I feel as if I am wasting my time pursuing an incomprehensible God. What angers me the most is that I had to underscore the inner conflicts of St. Augustine before she even tried to identify with my pain. And of course she tried to shush me when I later asked if she had read the front page story of today's paper. Looking at her, you would think that I was the one who had advised Pope Benedict to go quote some medieval text that associates Muslims with violence. And as you would expect, she nearly blew a gasket when I added that it wasn't fair of the pope to single out Muslims because the hands of both Christianity and Islam were tainted with blood, not to mention all the ghastly blood baths in the Old Testament.

Grateful for a lovely hour in JP's company (he finally remembered that he had a mother and called to ask if I wanted us to meet for lunch.) Also grateful that he's showing plenty of "critical thinking skills," in spite of being financially unable to sign up for even one class this semester. (I heard a TCC professor say that critical thinking skills should be a goal for all students.)

Grateful for the realization that I am being educated beyond my level of interest on the two topics that I've never been inclined to learn about in the past: religion and money. I even read the Bible from cover to cover while I lived in apartment 6. Also grateful for the realization that my financial crisis is perhaps the greatest thing that has ever happened to me because it brought me closer to you, God, than I ever thought possible.

Grateful I kept humming—my latest tool in my constant struggle to keep my sanity in the heart of Bedlam—and pretended that I didn't hear her when Z'Laitah warned, "Do it again and somebody will be on the floor," after a T-shirt disappeared from her bed. I am trying very hard not to let this woman scare me, but unlike Lavermine whose harassment is mostly limited to verbal abuse (she has been accused of spitting at two different women since I got here, but Shelter staff said they couldn't pursue the matter because no witnesses would come forward), Z'Laitah seems willing and able to knock somebody out at any time.

Grateful for the decision to spend the day reading Martin Luther's bio, rather than go sneak into classes at TCC and FSU. What a relief it was to find out that he too went through bouts of confusion during which he didn't quite know which path to take, and that he also felt useless when all he was able to do for an extended period of time was reading, thinking and writing. Yet while I do have great admiration for the courage of the young Luther to question the then-practices of religious leaders and demand changes, part of me can't help feeling that the main reason the old Luther seemingly ruined his health in his efforts to demonize his roots is because he didn't have what it takes to walk in the footsteps of the saints. (Presuming that the saints really earned their saintliness fair and square.)

Just arrived at St. Thomas More and I am seething with rage, to say the least. (a) A "foreign reject" is what I was called by Lavermine after she began a loud conversation in the big bathroom with Estelle after 11:30 last night, and I asked them to lower their voices. I let the comment slide in view of the late hour, but got worked up all over again when I saw her eating a big plate of last night's leftover dinner in The Shelter's kitchen a few minutes ago on my way out. (b) The people at STM now know that I am homeless thanks to Lydia Pollyanna who was invited to some evening function at the church and instead of saying that she couldn't make it and leave it at that, she felt the need to divulge that she lives at The Shelter and couldn't stay out past seven (she didn't know that she could ask for permission.) I always part ways with her at the door when we enter the church, but people driving up the hill on Virginia Street see us walk together every weekday morning, and I have no doubt that the big smile Peggy gave me when our eyes met earlier was a pity smile. (c) Forgot what else I am pissed off about, but it doesn't matter since Mass is about to begin.

7:45 p.m. – Back in bed 6 with the rawest of nerves. The dining room was so packed that sixteen women stood in the front room to eat (the room is roughly twenty feet by twenty.) Felt so discomposed I went to eat in the stairwell. And guess who are once again the best of friends? Z'Laitah and Monica. They've been speaking in Spanish all evening, though Z'Laitah did briefly switch to English when it was time to share that she finally figured out how they have been able to steal clothes from her locker: The Shelter must have a master key. Meanwhile, a drunk Sabine is in the midst of a very lively conversation with an equally drunk Labrina about what they would do with the money if they had the guts to go rob a bank, and listening to them alone is enough to make me want to pull my hair out. Newsflash: Monica just told Z'Laitah that she must go see the nurse before it's too late because she can't sleep without her pills. Now, that's a surprise. Can't love put her to sleep?

8:23 p.m. – "It's a discovery. What do you mean what I think?" Lydia Pollyanna just said to me when I asked what she thought of the "Dikika Child," the oldest fossilized remains of a child that was found in Ethiopia not long ago. "Do you have any opinion on the discovery?" I pressed on. She said she didn't. She, however, had plenty to say an hour ago when I mentioned that I had gone to the Haven of Rest to inquire about winter clothes, and was told to go speak to the "information specialist on duty," who turned out to be a clean and sober Pamelia. To put it simply, Lydia Pollyanna was too envious of Pamelia's new title to care about the unearthing of "Lucy's baby." A reminder that underneath her perpetual blitheness, Lydia Pollyanna is a cold fish who doesn't give much thought about anything that doesn't have a direct impact on her.

9:06 p.m. – I just read an article about the suicide epidemic that has been affecting farmers in India in recent years as it became more difficult to earn a living through agriculture. Those downtrodden men most likely killed themselves because of their inability to provide for their families while shameless people in Tallahassee are being fed, clothed and sheltered for free just because they happen to be born (or live) in the US of A. Life can be such a bitter pill to swallow. One more thing, there was a box of used underwear among the piles and piles of junk that Information Specialist Pamelia showed me when I had followed her into the basement of The Haven of Rest's main building this afternoon, and a frisson of horror coursed through me when she benevolently asked if I needed any undies. Dear God, in case you think you're being funny, I can guarantee you that you're not.

Daresay du jour: I finished reading *The Happiest People on Earth*, a book that was recently donated to The Shelter, and suffice to say that Demos Shakarian's happiness didn't rub off on me one bit. We already have more than enough trouble communicating with each other even when we speak the same language, why would God add to the confusion by sending us a spirit who speaks in an idiom unknown to mankind? More to the point, aside from all the fun that it provides to people who are predisposed to use Jesus as an excuse to keep indulging their senses, how did the tongue-speaking movement benefit the world at large, or even the quality of life of its speakers and interpreters? Dear God, I hope you don't take this the wrong way, but certain good-for-nothing blessings, I just don't want.

Wonderment du jour: The black Shameless at the dining room table doubled over with laughter when the following was said by one of their members: "I don't give a hoot if I fuck twenty motherfuckers a day, that's nobody's business. I have a hyper pussy and I am going to take care of it if I need to." Yet why did the same group of black Shameless acted as if their dignity has been attacked when somebody farted a few minutes later? In blunter terms, why is it that black women at The Shelter—I am reasonably sure that black people outside of The Shelter do not behave this way—think nothing of it when another black person is behaving like a piece of shit, yet make such a big deal out of it when somebody, God forbid, fart?

Disappointment du jour: My fantasy to see Z'Laitah's mug shot didn't come to pass simply because there is no such thing as a free background check online as far as I could tell, but it's good to know how easy it is to dig up dirt on others for as little as $9.99. Felt quite a bit of relief when I found out that Chrisnel Muller and all it variations (Chrisnel M. Muller, Chris Muller, J. Chrisnel Muller) virtually died with the eviction, meaning that there is no current information about me on the Web. Does this mean that I will stop dreaming about the I.R.S.?

Acknowledgment du jour: That I, too, am a bundle of contradictions. I hate religion, yet I not only find solace in church, I would love to have a priest at my bedside (with Charles Aznavour's *"La mamma"* playing in the background) at check-out time. I believe in God, but have the cynical disposition of an atheist. I have great compassion for most people, yet nothing but disdain for some. (Learning to replace disdain with empathy as I revised the first proof of this book in October 2015.)

Amusement du jour: I usually act as if I don't know The Shameless when I see them outside of The Shelter, but found myself speaking to Monica when I ran into her at the main library this afternoon, and in next to no time she was reading my horoscope and printing out my birth chart with a promise to help me interpret it at a later time. Come to find out, Monica is also an expert in astrology and was flabbergasted when I didn't know what a birth chart was.

Supplication du jour: Saw one of the male Shelter guests who usually hangs out at the main library all day on the second floor of the FSU library this morning. Worse, I also saw the white Shameless from Jacksonville, who is in town visiting her married boyfriend, smoking a cigarette in front of the building on my way out around 2 o'clock. Dear God, please don't let those people take over Strozier the same way they took over the main library.

Incredulity du jour: "Don't I deserve to spend some time in your company?" was the question a male Shelter guest who must be new in town, since the rest of them pretty much leave me alone by now, asked on my way out of The Shelter this morning. The man is homeless and jobless and has no shame about it, and now he deserves to get laid? Some people ask way too much out of life.

An emotionally and spiritually fulfilling day spent on FSU campus in the company of Joseph Campbell until I went back to the madhouse and found Estelle in bed 1. According to Deanna, Estelle just got back from another hospital stay (I didn't even know that she was gone), and Mr. ShelterDirector transferred her to the front room because he feels that she needed a quieter atmosphere to recuperate. The problem is that Estelle already turned the front room into the back room. Labrina and Chelsea were sitting on her bed when I arrived, and Ninabelle just pulled herself a chair from the dining room and joined the fray. Can I break up the party? Yes. Shelter rules are on my side: Only one person per bed and no chairs in the sleeping area. But I don't have the nerve to risk upsetting a woman who just got out of the hospital, even if she's faking the severity of her illness just to get a check as it is rumored. Though to her credit, Estelle did stop going on smoke breaks, and I even heard her tell her drug dealer to go to hell when he came to The Shelter a few weeks ago and tried to cajole her into buying more crack while we waited in the driveway to check in . . . Estelle just said that she misses her family and will be going back to Michigan at the end of the month. I just hope that I don't lose my mind before then because her laughter alone is loud enough to wake the dead.

PS: Today's accomplishment: a thorough cleaning and spraying of the bunk since no one was assigned to bed 5 tonight. I think the roach problem is solved for now.

Grateful that I am finally learning to measure people's characters by their actions rather than their words. It is a known fact that Kaycee Boneheaded is very fond of

Sabine. Well, Sabine was so drunk she couldn't stand up for dinner, sat in bed to eat, made a big mess all over the floor, and went right back to sleep. Kaycee Boneheaded did come over to kiss Sabine, and to emphasize that Sabine can have a good night sleep secure in the knowledge that she has someone who cares about her deeply at The Shelter. But JiBonnie, who turned out to be a fairly good-natured person when she's not high, was the one who cleaned the floor.

Grateful for the presence of mind to walk away from a table at the First Presbyterian Church when a brimming-with-confidence April, whom I haven't seen at The Shelter in a while because she supposedly got sick of living in sin, gave her life to Christ, and left Tallahassee to start over in a new city, far away from old temptations, began to speak about the phenomenal ass-kicking she recently gave to another woman who was flirting with her old man. Monsignor Kerr was the celebrant at the 8:30 Mass this morning. His message: We must love and respect one another, in spite of our differences. I bet even Monsignor Kerr would have been flooded with disgust if he was forced to be in April's company outside of the confessional booth.

Grateful for the assurance that I will survive this month even if my money miracle doesn't come through—a major improvement from September 2003 when I planned to commit suicide by October 1st if I was still homeless. Also grateful for a quiet afternoon on my new bench next to the Alumni Center, reading more of Joseph Campbell. And while I don't necessarily agree with all he said, I am thankful for all the work he has done and the legacy he left behind because learning about the myths of other cultures give me a greater understanding of the ones around me. Likewise grateful for his perspective on the need of a boy to distance himself from his mother in order to become a man. Is that what JP is doing?

Grateful I didn't feel guilty this morning after I mordantly replied "Why don't you go eat at The Shelter for free?" when a woman I often see around The Shelter, but never inside, came to St. Thomas More to beg for money because she hasn't eaten in two days. I just found out that she was telling the truth about not being able to eat at The Shelter because she was indefinitely banned for a drinking-related mischief, but that she does receive food stamps as well as a disability check, and currently stays with relatives. (Many people who left The Shelter years ago still go there to eat lunch and dinner because The Shelter's credo is to feed anyone who shows up for a plate whether they are homeless or not. Many former residents also continue to use The Shelter's mailing address long after they move out and regularly stop by to pick up their mail.)

1:01 a.m. – Wide awake and hurting. Spent the past two hours musing on salvation vs. nirvana, social duties vs. social temptations, Buddha vs. Jesus, two men who lived five hundred years apart, so they say, yet conveyed many of the same messages. I also spent a long time reflecting on whether or not I would be happy if I were able to create a psychological paradise for myself right here on earth where I would liberated from all desires and fears. I think I am overdosing on Joseph Campbell, and need to take a break. Yet, what did just come to mind? The long conversation I had with Monica before lights out about "the great shift" that is due to occur in the world's consciousness in 2012. It's going to be another sleepless night.

3:29 p.m. – Sitting in front of the College of Medicine with my head spinning. Betty-Lou was actually walking away from the building as I approached the bench. What was she doing on campus? She and her husband (she pointed to an outcast sitting at a picnic table in front of the Education Building across the street), bought some food at a nearby restaurant, and decided to come to eat it on campus. She then needed to use the restroom, felt too self-conscious to go inside the Education Building since a group of maintenance workers were standing in front, so her husband suggested that she goes to the College of Medicine, but the side door was locked when she tried to open it. I felt a slight pang of guilt, but I wasn't about to tell her that the front door on the other side of the building is wide open, and I still have trouble breathing long after they headed back to West Tennessee Street. (A security desk clerk has since been planted in the lobby of the College of Medicine, and I have reason to believe that it's because of yours truly.)

5:00 p.m. – Getting ready to walk to the main library, but I must take a moment to record the encounter I just had with a young woman who walked up to me in the past few minutes and asked if I ever gave any thought to what would happen to me when I die. To my big surprise, we ended up having a very nice conversation, once I was sure that she wasn't another loony walking through campus on her way to The Shelter, just one of those atypical FSU students who feel duty-bound to spread the Gospel wherever they go. Of course, I told her that I was a student. I also threw at her one of the questions I was mulling over in the middle of the night: "If God only has one son, what are we to Him?" It didn't take her long to reply that we are all born sinners, but that we do become children of God once we accept Jesus Christ as our Lord and Savior. She, however, didn't have a clichéd answer when I came back with, "Then, why are we so desperate to take away women's rights to abort if the fetus is not even a child of God?" (This is not to say that I am pro-abortion. I am not. All I am saying is that *Roe v. Wade* is a necessary evil in a hell of a world.)

Cannot believe that an exuberant Lydia Pollyanna, who now has her very own information specialist badge and was recently seen on TV at a church event, was so stunned when I mentioned that I have visited the Canterbury Cathedral as well as Notre Dame de Paris that you would think I had told her that I was born with two heads. Who do those women think I am? Parenthetically, Lydia Pollyanna is not the average woman at The Shelter. She doesn't have any visible substance abuse or behavioral problems, and she's not mentally impaired. In fact, she said she went back to school after her last child left home, and only came to Tallahassee after graduation because it has always been her dream to work with elected officials.

Cannot believe that Gwen, who spent a long time standing in front of the wall mirror next to the entrance of the big bathroom, casually commented that the reason why black women usually look younger than their age is because their skins are so dark their winkles can't be seen. I told her that many white women look younger than their age, including herself, but she did leave me speechless when she then asked if I knew what black people were calling themselves these days because between negro, colored, black, and African-American, she could not keep up. I've heard about people like Gwen before, but I've never had any direct contact with them until my life went south, so to speak. Grateful this is her last week at The Shelter; she won't be missed. (Gwen didn't come back to The Shelter, but the last time I saw her she was in deep conversation with a young man whose main occupation is to walk around the city all day in bright-colored suits. Maybe she was asking him why he feels the need to dress in all his finery every morning when he doesn't have a job to go to as far as anyone knows.)

Cannot believe that Z'Laitah intentionally removed my flip-flops from where I had left them at the foot of the bunk, gave them to Labrina in an apparent attempt to foment more friction between Labrina and me, then swore that she had found them near a trash can in The Shelter's driveway, and didn't know that they belonged to me. If Z'Laitah had indeed found a pair of expensive flip-flops (I actually "borrowed" them from ExRoommate when I found myself needing "shower shoes"), she would have kept them for herself because that's just who she is. I think I need to let her know that her moodiness and physical threats don't ruffle me anymore than Lavermine's character assassination. (Lavermine recently told me that I think I am somebody, but people are talking about me "like a dog" after I told her that she can't be standing in front of her locker at 5:20 a.m. wondering out loud what color of wig she should wear.)

Highlight du jour: Seeing a nearly unrecognizable Sonya-Bette at the main library. She hasn't been at The Shelter in months, and I heard that her drinking had gotten so bad that she was sleeping in cemeteries and parks, but that was then. She told me that she finally got sick and tired of living like an animal, went back to AA with a new determination to make the program work for her, and got herself a job. She added that she hates The Shelter so much that she would rather sleep on a friend's couch than come back here. She went on to say that helping the homeless get back on their feet does not seem to be the objective of Mr. ShelterDirector because "all he cares about is body count." (In the interest of honesty, I must add that Mr. ShelterDirector has always been very nice to me—at times, too nice—and that SonyaBette is one of the few Shelter guests I know who ever spoke poorly of him since he more or less enjoys godlike status at The Shelter.)

Humiliation du jour: Being denied entry at The Shelter because I came in late, they said, when I was standing in The Shelter's driveway at exactly 7 p.m. I eventually went in, but Mr. Redneck, the one and only Caucasian staff at The Shelter who's fond of saying that all Shelter guests are "cut from the same cloth," called me a liar who's trying to blame him for my lateness when I told him that he can't fault me if my registration card shows that I do come in after seven sometimes because it's just the time they let me in. Must email Mr. ShelterDirector tomorrow because I am not about to let this man get away with insulting me just because he thinks he knows who I am in view of my skin color.

Stupidity du jour: Wasting nearly an hour of my time talking to Monica about relationships and astrology. I am grateful for the chance to underline that there is a whole spectrum of emotions between love and hate when she contended, again, that people either react to a situation with love or with hatred. But I should have cut the conversation short after she asserted that people need to learn to solve their problems through astrology because it is a more reliable field than psychology.

Irritation du jour: A jubilant Monsignor Tugwell began his homily by joking that at the exception of the three nuns present, he's relatively sure that everyone else has dreamed about winning the lottery, and ended it by urging us to set our sights on heavenly treasures. Yet according to the church bulletin, doesn't Monsignor Tugwell need thousands and thousands of earthly treasures in the collection basket every week in order to keep the church running?

Shelter drama du jour: Face-off between Kaycee Sourpuss and Lavermine. "I don't care what you do," a gushing-with-pride Lavermine came back with when Kaycee Sourpuss said that she was going to call TPD to file a police report after Lavermine vowed to beat her up outside. "I love doing things I don't get no business doing." Let's hope that she will remember those words when it's time to pay for her Shelter sins.

Heartbreak du jour: Seeing the picture of a one-year-old African baby with a bullet wound in her lower back. Dear God, where were you when that bullet was heading toward that child who is much too young to learn whatever lessons she could have learned from the incident? And where is your love and mercy for the millions of people who are living in hell right here on earth?

So sick with another cold that I chose to put out of my mind the article I read this morning about how an increasing number of women are taking and putting their children on ADHD drugs, and hobbled to the nurse's office and got myself some cold medicine. The two pills feel as foreign inside me as I feel inside The Shelter, but my nose stopped running and the headache has subsided. Too depressed to go on. On second thoughts, I am sleepy, not depressed.

Exhausted *à en mourir* and still too sick to write, but feel compelled to record the following:

(1) Madness-free madhouse – A quiet evening so far. From what I heard, a group of Shameless were waiting in the driveway for Mr. ShelterDirector to come in with the mail, and subsequently left for motel rooms.

(2) FSU homeless invasion – Saw the brown-haired young woman with indigo blue highlights who spent a few nights in bed 5 before she got moved to the back room take a nap on a couch on the second floor of Strozier this morning. It is not my imagination. I am seeing more of them on FSU campus.

(3) Winter shopping – My irrational fear of freezing to death in Tallahassee got so strong that it led me to the Salvation Army office, located a few blocks from the back entrance of The Shelter, then all the way to their thrift store on the other side of town to use the voucher that was given to me. I still need a jacket and a decent pair of shoes. (Thinking that North

Florida was as warm as South Florida, I donated my winter clothes to a thrift store in New York the day before I left for Tallahassee.)

(4) Phony bravado – Z'Laitah is eerily quiet since the flip-flops occurrence, and my mind is whirling with all kind of thoughts about how she's going to crack up one of these days and who's going to be her first victim—especially after I heard Lavermine say that she stopped "messing" with Z'Laitah because Z'Laitah looks like someone who is about to "go off her rocker." Dear God, please remind me that you did not keep me alive all this time just to have me killed in a homeless shelter by a mentally ill woman with violent tendencies.

(5) Serendipitous decampment – I was so hungry after all the walking I did this morning that I went to the Haven of Rest at 5 o'clock to get something to eat. The food was awful, but my conversation with Betty-Lou more than made up for it. In brief, she just spent a few nights in jail, was so unruly when she got there that they put her on "lock down," and is mad as hell because TPD was downright profiling her. She's also mad at Ninabelle because she went to jail a year ago for carrying Ninabelle's crack and Ninabelle is not showing any appreciation. I was beyond shocked, but a surge of relief washed over me when I asked how her pregnancy was going, and she said that she had miscarried. Smart baby.

1:46 p.m. – Sitting at my favorite spot at the main library, waiting for JP. Was trying to avoid Monica when I came in, but she did see me. Sabine tactfully remarked last night that "Monica *est très bavarde*," but Monica is more than *bavarde*, Monica has a serious case of verbal diarrhea. In a few words, she had a map on the screen and wanted to show me some of the roads she had traveled on her bicycle trip, and I was about to nod off when her hour on the computer thankfully came to an end. Lydia Pollyanna is also here and for once she's not feeling wonderful. She apologized for not waking up on time for Mass this morning, and said that she's exhausted because they have been working her too hard at the Haven of Rest, adding that she may have to take a break from volunteer work because it's limiting the time she could be spending looking for a real job. I think I like her better when she's being real.

3:21 p.m. – Angie just called. I could have picked up to say that I am sitting on a bench outside the library while JP is at a computer downloading songs, but I am choosing to treat her like she treats me.

3:24 p.m. – Angie's 3rd call.

3:33 p.m. – 4th call.

3:34 p.m. – 5th call.

3:59 p.m. – Calls No. 6 to 11 came in while I spoke to Lulu. The girl has the boy to herself seven days a week, yet she always finds a reason to call him whenever he decides to spend a few hours with his mother. If she's so territorial at her age, what will she be like in ten years? She even broke my own pathetic record. I once called . . . oh, my God, Bobbie is turning fifteen next week. Love her as much today as I did then, and hope that she's a content and well-adjusted teen. She was such a delightful baby. In any case, I once called Bobbie's father ten times in one hour. Did not like the guy, had no respect for him, but boy did I "love" him. And of course I had all these plans about how I was going to make a responsible man out of him. Plan No. 1 was to teach him how to be a good father by inculcating him with a desire to start paying child support. If God can fix my head as far as the bondage of romantic love is concerned, I guess I should trust that he will ultimately fix my money problem. In the interim, how am I going to deal with the Angie conundrum? Did I mention that JP now carries a wallet? I once bought the boy a wallet and he never used it. She bought him a wallet, and he's suddenly a wallet carrier. Mystifying. (He did stop carrying *her* wallet, too, once he got comfortable in the relationship.)

Mr. Redneck just came up with the laundry basket and didn't behave like a jackass for once. Mr. ShelterDirector must have had a talk with him after he got my email. Much more to record, but I can't concentrate. Estelle is laughing again. Let me rephrase that: Estelle is cackling again. And who is she cackling with? Kaycee Boneheaded and Labrina. The man who promised to buy Estelle a bus ticket did pay the bill on one of her cell phones (she has three), but changed his mind about giving her the money to go back home and she's going to have to wait for her check to come in, which could take as long as thirty more days. Monsignor Tugwell spoke this morning about some of the things the pope is doing in the hope to bury the hatchet with Islam, which includes inviting twenty-one representatives of the Muslim faith to his summer house for a parley, and I had to wonder why I have no home when the pope has a summer house in addition to his papal apartments if we're both living out the calling of a just and loving God. I got even more disturbed when Sabine later told me that the papal summer residence is not just a house, but an upscale palace, which she once visited. Not sure where I am going with this, but I don't really care.

"Oh, God is good, God is good, and God is good!" Estelle just cried out with evangelical fervor. "All the time!" a suddenly pious Labrina trilled. "That's what I'm talking about!" Kaycee Boneheaded wholeheartedly chipped in. I had no idea that people living dirty lives like to talk about God so much. Deceitful CJ déjà vu all over again, I guess.

Grateful I didn't have any problem zipping up the two skirts and the two pair of pants I got from the Salvation Army when I tried them on this evening (had to get them washed first.) The thing is that I didn't realize that one of the skirts was a size eight and the other a size twelve since I didn't bother to check the sizes when I bought them, yet they both fit. A subtle but telling reminder that the fashion industry, too, is playing game with women's heads in the name of greed, and women are taking the bait in droves in the name of vanity.

Grateful Monica and Z'Laitah decided to converse in English this evening, maybe because Kaycee Boneheaded has thunderously expressed her displeasure with people speaking anything but English at The Shelter. Anyway, it sounds as if both Z'Laitah and Monica have found love right in The Shelter's backyard, and they're now hoping to have a good influence on their men since Monica's boyfriend is addicted to crack and Z'Laitah's practically lives at the liquor store. Also learned a whole lot about their past relationships, though a crucial difference between the two is that Monica whined about how much she has loved, in spite of getting hurt repeatedly, while Z'Laitah only spoke about how popular she used to be and how much she has been loved.

Grateful that taking advantage of the system has never been an inclination of mine. Sparky, a male Shelter guest with whom I exchanged a few words yesterday after I heard him say that he was studying for a test, came to talk to me on TCC campus this morning and couldn't stop bragging about how his tuition gets "wiped away" with a simple letter from The Shelter, and all the financial aid goes straight to his pocket. Did a bit of research afterward, and found out that the benefits of being homeless in Tallahassee also include free medical clinics and legal services, which means that I could perhaps use my homeless status to settle with the I.R.S. and the credit card companies and

Sallie Mae. Let's not forget Verizon and Pepco and Washington Gas and the water company, which name I can't recall, but do recall owning them money. But, Dear God, why should I take the loser route when I am an obedient child of the biggest Provider in the world? . . . Harold Kushner just came back to mind. What if he's right about God not being who I think God is? Did I mention that I have trouble praying lately? What if the only thing prayers avail to is false hope? Feeling not so grateful all of a sudden.

Disturbance du jour: (a) More school shootings. This time in an Amish community in Pennsylvania. More dead girls. A good thing I fell asleep before the 11 o'clock news last night because I couldn't bring myself to read about it in the paper. (b) Listening to Estelle joke about robbing a bank at the age of fifteen. And when Sabine asked how much time she got, she glanced at me who must have been gawking at her with my mouth wide open, laughed some more, then told Sabine that she would rather keep the particulars to herself. I can't believe I actually know these women, much less live with them.

Enigma du jour: I finally took a good look at the mural next to The Shelter's kitchen entrance, depicting a towering black woman looking up to a white angel, with a large number of black men, black women, and black children at her feet (and a handful of white people). "This place is designed to keep you depressed and oppressed" a Trinidadian woman who spent a few nights at The Shelter several weeks ago once said. I didn't think anything of it, then, since The Shameless are not exactly known for their depression or their oppression, but I now wonder if she was onto something. (The Shelter has since been adorned with a new mural that features a new towering black woman who represents "whatever you want it to represent," I was told by one of the designers. But no white angel.)

Disappointment du jour: Wasting 50 cents of Lulu's money (I received another letter from her along with $25 over the weekend) to go see *Little Man*. Hard to believe that the Wayans brothers cannot put their heads together to come up with a comedy that will heighten people's perception of their race, rather than reinforce existing stereotypes. (I don't find anything funny about a gun-toting grandmother either, and firmly believe that Madea ought to redeem herself by dying a slow and painful death from an accidental gunshot wound since she loves to fire her gun so much. I also hope that Mr. Perry realizes sooner or later that eliciting cheap laughs from the unenlightened should not be the primary goal of black filmmakers, and that less is sometimes more when it comes to quality movie making.)

Gratitude du jour: An older white woman who left The Shelter months ago to go live with her daughter is currently crying in the big bathroom because her daughter tried to beat her up this morning, in addition to calling her a "sorry-ass, blackhearted bitch." Grateful I spent the first nineteen years of my life in a country where you are expected to show a certain level of respect to your mother even if she didn't earn it. Who knew that the babies we women carry in our bellies, feed from our breasts, love with all our hearts, could grow up to be strangers that we don't even like? Yet we can't even talk about the albatross around our necks because the verbal and physical abuse of parents by their own children isn't a topic that anyone cares to discuss. In fact, doen't the entertainment industry loves to pit daughters against mothers on small and big screens when they know perfectly well that they're just fanning the flames of female agression?

Well, well, well, I learned more about Z'Laitah tonight than I ever thought possible. As a matter of fact, she talked for so long that Talking Machine Monica who had actually climbed into bed 8 shortly after dinner for a more intimate tête-à-tête was the one who ended the conversation long before lights out. In a word, Z'Laitah is exactly who I thought her to be. She even blames her children for choosing to live with their dad after she lost her home. And as you would expect, all her former employers were bigots who undermined her by sabotaging her career at every turn (some went as far as implying that she was mentally ill.) Even her alma mater contributed to her downfall by falsifying her transcript after a racist but very influential professor at the school found out that she had married a white man. Did I mention that Z'Laitah doesn't date black men? She simply never met a black man who was her intellectual equal, though one of her brothers theorized that she never showed interest in black men because she didn't want "chocolate babies."

5:24 a.m. – Standing in The Shelter's backyard in my nightgown (a t-shirt of JP) with a sheet wrapped around me. Oh my goodness, there is really a fire on the second floor of The Shelter where the business office is located. I don't see any flames, but smoke is coming out of the back windows. Dear God, do I need to remind you that my only valuables at The Shelter, my notebooks, are still in the locker inside the building?

5:57 a.m. – The drama is pretty much over, but one of the firemen is walking around, offering fifty dollars to anyone kind enough to return his missing cell phone. No takers. An indignant Lavermine, however, just went up to the fireman, and apologized for the miscreant who had the sheer effrontery to steal from someone so noble, which makes me wonder if she knows a thing or two about the whereabouts of the cell phone.

3:40 p.m. – On a bench in front of Westcott once again, and a girl just called me to say that she found JP's phone in a movie theater last night. Since Angie recently changed her phone number and I forgot to ask JP for the new one, I did the next best thing and left a voice mail message for ExRoommate, asking her to go to JP's and let him know where he can pick up his phone. Dear God, please remind me that I have done all that I can do and let it go.

7:09 p.m. – Mr. ShelterDirector was standing next to bed 6 when I got out of the shower five minutes ago. I don't know why he decided to grace The Shameless with his presence since he doesn't usually come upstairs when the insanity is at its peak, but I did hear him tell a woman who was asking him for a favor that he's tired of people who pretend they want to change just to get more stuff from the numerous religious organizations around the city.

8:38 p.m. – "Did the last one say that you were taking medicine?" a befuddled Deanna just asked after Z'Laitah told her to make sure that her new registration card states "No medicine." Z'Laitah made it compellingly clear that she simply doesn't want any misinformation in her file. I don't know why it took so long, but it just occurred to me that Z'Laitah may have come straight from a psych ward—as it is often the case—the day she turned up at The Shelter.

The lights just went out, moments after I finished reading a recent magazine interview with Martha Stewart in which she is reported to have said that it's hard for her to accept that Americans enjoy building people up just for the fun of tearing them down. Grateful that I have reached a point in my life where other people no longer have the power to make me or break me. Yet the fact remains that I woke up feeling very disappointed this morning because I didn't have the pat on the back I was hoping for in my dreams, spent the whole day waiting for some major revelation to seep through the thick wall of gloom that engulfed me, and here I am going to bed in complete agony because the day ended as uneventfully as it began. Dear God, do you have any idea what it feels like to be living among the lowest of the low after you unmistakably woke me up in the middle of the night five years ago to speak to me? And who's sleeping in bed 5 tonight? Andrelene's sister who already came across as the very opposite of Andrelene. Will this nightmare ever end?

Cannot believe that the first words that came out of Estelle's mouth when Mr. HornyBoy handed her the envelope that contained the check she has been waiting for so impatiently were: "Thank you Jesus. Now I can go shopping." Fortunately, she's also using some of the money to buy a bus ticket and give herself a going away party. I guess I should be thankful that you, God, are taking the time to educate me prior to set me free from the burden of poverty for I won't be using my deliverance money to go shopping or to throw parties. (Or to carry out the fantasies of others, especially the ones who had nothing to do with me when I was dying the daily deaths of homelessness.)

Cannot believe that Sabine, who is well known for her ability to overlook Shelter madness even when she's sober, finally took a stand after the 9:30 smoke break when Ninabelle went back to sit on Estelle's bed to continue where they have left off, and Mr. Aloof chose to side with Ninabelle. I was so upset that I didn't even take time to think of the consequences when I shouted, "It's almost 10 o'clock and the madness in this room got to stop." Gaining steam, I added that most women at The Shelter have no self-respect and only listen when they're being yelled at. Ninabelle quietly left for the back room while I was still talking, but I won't be caught off guard if they gang up on me tomorrow.

Cannot believe that Kaycee Sourpuss is still fuming because she didn't get a backpack when she attended the Seventh Annual Homeless Day celebration at HOPE even though she did get a haircut, a flu shot, a blanket, more clothes and free food. And speaking of self-entitled shamelessness, Kaycee Boneheaded finally bought a roll of toilet paper, but is debating whether she should use it because she does not want "to give anything to The Shelter for free." She's also bearing a grudge against Mr. ShelterDirector because her boyfriend's birthday is in a few days, and Mr. ShelterDirector refused to give them permission to spend the night out. So being the "grown woman" that she is, she's going to stay out anyway and lose her reserved bed.

Cannot believe that a fire at The Shelter did not pique the curiosity of any reporter at the *Tallahassee Democrat*. Funnily enough, it was just a week ago that Gerald Ensley, one of their columnists, wrote that too many bygone writers didn't apparently view themselves as historians, because they didn't apply what is known in journalistic jargon as the five W's (Who, What, When, Where and Why) in their writings. Yet when Lydia Pollyanna showed me the brief article in yesterday's *Democrat* about the fire at The Shelter, it said nothing about WHO started the fire. I bet they would have bombarded me with superfluous information right on the front page if "someone" has started a fire by emptying an ashtray in a trash can in a smoke free building on FAMU campus. (Isn't that right, Miss Cantley?)

The drama has been nonstop since I got here and here are a few of the highlights:

- Estelle's cell phones have been ringing incessantly, at times simultaneously, because she's trying to get in touch with all her friends in Tallahassee to say goodbye, and to inform her friends out of state of her impending arrival. The party is scheduled for tomorrow evening, and thank God I've already been granted permission to come in late.

- Both Marvy and Sabine are drunk. But while Sabine is sleeping it off, Marvy spent the evening sitting on the floor by the emergency door, next to Sabine's bed, complaining about how inconsiderate Mr. ShelterDrillSergeant is, and how she plans to go to "the authorities" to report him. (Reporting Shelter staff for real and imagined grievances is an ongoing menace from members of the White Shameless Club.)

- My cousin Didi does not drink or do drugs, but she's foaming at the mouth over the unfair treatment she's been getting from the U.S. government these past five years, in spite of being a very productive business woman who earns a minimum of $2000 a day, and she's thinking about taking her case to the Supreme Court. (I don't quite understand the nature of her business, but it has something to do with parapsychological research.)

- Z'Laitah spent the longest time in JiBonnie's arms, in tears. "They don't care about me. I worked so hard to give them a good upbringing, but they treat me like dirt under their feet." To be brief, she called her youngest child during smoke break since she's not on speaking terms with her oldest two, and the conversation didn't go too well. It's kind of sad that such an intelligent woman doesn't have the humility to accept that she has a mental illness, and either beg God to fix her head or seek psychiatric help.

- Lavermine has been causing a lot of problems for a lot people in the back room and Daneecia, a fairly complaisant young woman who also works at a fast food restaurant and claims to be saving money to open her own business, went up in arms. Daneecia was so incensed that she threatened to unleash her inner thug, who has been on hiatus since she found Jesus, if Lavermine even peeks at her. Lavermine heeded the warning and retreated to her bed by several accounts, but Daneecia is still expressing her outrage in the dining room an hour later with quite a bit of help from Lavermine's other victims.

- "Touch it again and get your ass kicked!" Andrelene's sister shriekingly said after Monica used some of her bottle of soap, thinking that it belonged to The Shelter. Monica apologized, but Andrelene's sister kept up with the verbal assault. Monica summoned a Shelter staff, but Andrelene's sister denied any bullying and no one dared to contradict her. The madness went on until I got tired of listening to Monica apologize and vehemently told her to stop acting like she had done something wrong because the soap should not have been left in the shower to start with. The good news is that Andrelene's sister who's quite proud of the fact that she's not homeless, just "in between apartments," will be gone next week. The bad news is that I was forced to reevaluate my opinion of Andrelene because she did confound me when she just sat there and silently watched her sister lambaste Monica for no reason. Added evidence that niceness doesn't always equate goodness.

The party was still on when I arrived at 9 p.m. Estelle had her music blasting and was happily chatting with Monica about the latest fashion. Kaycee Boneheaded was sitting on Sabine's bed, laughing her raucous laugh. A drugged-out-of-her-mind JiBonnie was talking to Ninabelle about why she masturbates even more often than BigBodyPartVilda, and completed her tirade by squealing, "I need some D.I.C.K. and I need it bad!" I even saw a giggling Marvy take a sip from a bottle, and I am moderately sure that she wasn't drinking apple juice. Disconcerted and furious, I went to take a shower and thank goodness the lights were off and a fatigued Estelle was telling them that she needed to get her beauty sleep when I got out of the bathroom. A story I watched on *20/20* years ago about street children living in sewers in Romania just came to mind. It infuriates me that poor children with no one to care for them are living below the streets in some parts of the world when shameless people in America have it so good.

PS: Lydia Pollyanna left me a note saying she won't be walking to church with me anymore because it's too long of a walk. Lucky me. She was getting on my last nerves.

PPS: Monica just asked if I was interested in going to work with her tomorrow because they need some extra hands. I told her I'll let her know in the morning.

Gratitude du jour: For the courage to continue to do what I believe you want me to do, God, rather than go pick mushrooms with Monica for fifty dollars.

Challenge du jour: Not give in to despair after finding out that two winning tickets were sold for the $14 million jackpot on Saturday. I didn't play, but I was hoping the jackpot would roll over.

Awkwardness du jour: Sparky came to sit at the nearest table while I was at the TCC library this morning. I acted as if I didn't see him, of course. Hope he doesn't think we're friends just because I spoke to him twice.

Amazement du jour: That Monica is already "engaged," though she's not interested in a legal marriage, but a spiritual one. Who knew that a fifty-one-year-old blonde from Minnesota could have so much in common with Brandy?

Observation du jour: That Deanna's unbounded patience with The Shameless is running thin lately. Even heard her say that she works hard to be as helpful as she can be, but "these ungrateful women are always bitching." It's so easy to fall in love when you don't really know who you're falling in love with.

Satisfaction du jour: Reading that the Amish have asked the media to leave them alone, and that they won't be giving any more updates on the surviving girls. The more I learn about those people, the more I admire them. Why should their pain be used to regale the public's taste for the ghoulish? May God continue to bless them with dignity and wisdom, and may he give some to The Shameless.

Insult du jour: Reading that the Runaway Bride received a $500,000 advance from a New York publisher a year ago to write a book about her ludicrous adventure, which has no value whatsoever other than cheap entertainment, when I couldn't get an agent for *Out of the Trenches*, a story that had the potential to be an inspiration to women worldwide. Dear God, have you taken leave of your sense of justice?

Discomfort du jour: Sitting in Dr. Esposito's class and wondering how long it's going to take her to expose me. She spoke of the Romantic Era, in which I had no interest. She also commented on a certain television reporter whom she feels is successful simply because he was "groomed for success," adding that a rich boy in Armani suit can't possibly relate to the suffering of the masses. She may be right, but the bottom line is that it's time for me to "drop" her class if I don't want to create more trouble for myself.

Respite du jour: That the Black Shameless Club did not convene in the front room now that Estelle is gone. I was reminded by a history professor the other day that slaves didn't have the right to congregate, which may explain why the black Shameless like to hang around each other so much. Still, it's a pity that they only come together to indulge their appetite for the boorish, not to commiserate over their mutual failure as children of God, or think of ways to build up their character and redeem themselves in the eyes of their Creator and their fellow citizens.

8:12 a.m. – In front of a computer on the first floor of Strozier, gnashing my teeth. "Excuse me, where the two of you being pernicious a moment ago when you compared being here to being in jail?" Z'Laitah unexpectedly asked Lydia Pollyanna and me last night. And perhaps because we both stared at her in silence, she cockily rephrased herself. "The two of you were not being serious when you said that The Shelter was like a detention center or a mental hospital, right?" Lydia Pollyanna gingerly replied that we were joking while I mumbled that we were not. What's killing me now is that I didn't know the meaning of the word "pernicious" until I looked it up a minute ago. Had I known, I would have come back with something along the lines of, "Crazy bitch, please stop barging into my conversations and mind your own business for the last time." Okay, I would not have said the first two words, but only because the B-word is one of those words that I do occasionally use while journaling, but prefer not to utter out loud.

9:05 p.m. – They actually turned the lights off on time and I couldn't be more grateful because Monica practically spent the last hour pounding on my ears since Z'Laitah was already sleeping when I came in, and Marvy was too drunk to hold a conversation. She had plenty to say, *comme d'habitude*, but let's keep the focus on the most exciting parts. Monica has been married six times, though two of her marriages were spiritual ones (her mother was legally married seven times.) And when I asked how things were going with her fiancé, she said she didn't see him the past two days because he was banned from The Shelter for reasons unknown to her, but that he had sent her a message to meet him at the main library tomorrow after work. And totally oblivious of her role as the latest victim of Shelter love, she added that her fiancé is such a nice guy that while he did stop smoking crack out of love for her, he still buys crack for his friends, and she's trying to make him stop. He's also illiterate, but his lack of education is part of his charm because "his mind hasn't been polluted and his spirit is pure, which means that he's teachable." I wish a new Dr. Spock would write a book encouraging parents to start teaching their daughters to learn to master their emotions at an early age—the same way they teach their sons—because it's a veritable tragedy to watch full-grown women behave like teenage girls in the name of love.

Going to bed with Father Cayer and Dr. Boroto in mind. Father Cayer who just got back from his two-week trip to China (I missed him more than I thought I would) urged us this morning to not only seek God out, but to go as far as telling him explicitly what we need him to do for us. So, there it is: Dear God, please find a way to get *Out of the Trenches* on the best-seller list, and/or make me win a big jackpot. And let's just say that I could have kissed Dr. Boroto when he said in class this afternoon that one can't change a situation by adapting to it because adaptation only maintains the status quo. And I nearly broke into applause when he added that "People don't take a stand on a behavior unless it's self-actualized, and if you're making a difference in the world, you're not going to get agreement from the world." God, I think I finally know why you wanted me to cross paths with this man, and I thank you. I also think that the time has come to stop giving FSUPD a legitimate reason to have a word with me.

On my mind at the moment:

(1) Psychological decimation – I received a picture of Patoutou in the mail today, took one look at her, and burst out laughing. Of course, I had to show the picture to some of the women, and they all agreed that she looks like a girl who is on her way somewhere. In short, the girl exudes self-confidence. Yet I find myself worrying about the woman she will

grow up to be in a world that is so proficient in undermining the self-esteem of women of all ages, but of young women most of all.

(2) Self-destructive comradeship – JiBonnie is leaving for rehab this weekend. She said a local church gave her a temporary place to stay with the promise of a job and transitional housing as long as she stays clean. She also spoke of losing her family (and of nearly losing her life) as a result of being on crack. Yet while JiBonnie does show a sincere desire for a better life, I don't think she'll be able to stay away from drugs for long because she doesn't have the willingness to change her playground and her playmates, like they say in the program.

(3) Star-studded adoption – In her efforts to constantly reinvent herself, Madonna is adopting a black child from Malawi. She finally faced the fact that she's too old to get naked and nasty in another coffee-table book or to be kissing girls on national TV, I suppose. I will not be surprised if she files for divorce before the end of the year because she seems to be a woman dangerously bored with her life. I bet Malawian officials would not have approved the adoption if Madonna was an African entertainer with middle-class income.

(4) Ear-splitting adoration – Kaycee Boneheaded, Labrina, and a new black Shameless who just got of jail for stabbing her uncle while they were both drunk are having another Bible study in the dining room, and I am about to jump out of my skin. These women's proclivity to worship the Lord as loudly as they can as if he was giving out extra credits for theatrical display of faith doesn't sit well with me at all. It is often said that Christianity brings the best out of people, but Christianity did not bring the best out of The Shameless. Christianity simply gave them

> a shield that can be used to minimize their ignorance, whitewash their sins and justify their failures.

> (5) Astrological dumbness – Monica spent a great deal of the evening pontificating about people who need to let go of preconceived ideas about God so that they can achieve spiritual success because God needs us as much as we need him, about Mars being a powerful sign that causes a lot of instability when it is the ruling planet of the house, and of all the good things that normally come to pass whenever Venus and Mercury are sharing the third house. I hardly understood anything she said, as usual, and could not be more floored when she momentarily stopped her conversation with Z'Laitah to tell me that she was writing a metaphysical book and would like Z'Laitah and me to review the first draft since we're the brainiest women at The Shelter. She has evidently overestimated my level of intelligence.

So flustered by all the madness around me that I taped the following note on bed 6 after dinner, facing the dining room.

Grateful that I am only homeless.
Not homeless and vicious.
And definitely not homeless and shameless.

You would think that it would give them something to think about, but it didn't. It doesn't help that I am constipated again from a diet of pasta and pastries. (It's not like I am going out of my way to eat sugar and flour—and that's the OA guilt speaking—it's just that sugar and flour and green beans are what is mostly served at The Shelter.) It also doesn't help that I spent the entire day reading about issues that are not conducive to my peace of mind. (The two-page ad for Cymbalta in the current issue of *Psychology Today*, accentuating the predicament of a young mother whose depression hurts so much she couldn't play with her children rattled my nerves so much that it brought forth another headache.) Today also marks my one-year anniversary in Florida, and while I am thankful for all the spiritual, emotionally and intellectual growth, and for the fact that I don't have to worry about rent and food while I wait for God to release me from the shackles of homelessness, I would rather die at this very moment than stay at The Shelter one more week. Worst of all, my biggest Shelter fear just came to pass: Kaycee Boneheaded did indeed choose to lose her reserved bed, spent the past two nights on a rollaway, has been assigned to bed 1 tonight, already turned the front room into the back room, and is also giving me the evil eye because she knows that I am not going to let her impose her shamelessness on me.

7:53 a.m. – Still in bed 6, but breathing a sigh of relief after Monica scared the pants off me a few minutes ago when she interrupted my journaling to congratulate me on wearing the correct color combination: jean skirt and a red sweater. Didn't fully understand her reasoning (something about the power of some colors to reconcile and rectify), but did quickly understand that I had to hide under my yellow and green floral sheet again and change because I am not about to start meshing with those women in any way, shape, form, or color. (The sheet actually belongs to The Shelter but I've been hiding under it for so long that I now claim it as mine, and even wash it with my own clothes when I do laundry. And speaking of sheets, I was literally wearing Shelter sheets a year later when it dawned on me that I would feel less humiliated if I start making my own clothes, rather than wear other people's throwaways. Besides, sewing considerably calmed my nerves down in the evenings while I wait for lights out.)

9:26 a.m. – Mass ended at 9:23 and Lydia Pollyanna just left with her wonderful friend Louise. Chose not to make a big deal out of it, but I still resent her for the way she brushed me off yesterday. To put it briefly, I didn't expect to see her sitting on one of the benches on my way out of church an hour after the end of Mass, and went to ask if she wasn't cold since she wasn't properly dressed. She abruptly cut me off in mid-sentence with "I've got to go. I'll talk to you later," and it didn't occur to me that Louise had pulled up in the parking lot until I saw her get in Louise's car. She later showed me her newest blessings from the Lord, a pair of prescription eyeglasses and a new haircut, which were paid for by Louise. Those women are all the same deep down: nasty and beggarly. And what did Saint Monica of The Shelter say when she saw me wearing a gray sweater? She accused me of "defiling something divine with profane thoughts."

9:37 a.m. – Monsignor Kerr is on his way out, and I wish I had the guts to go ask him why he doesn't persuade the bishop to sell off the church, the parish hall, the rectory and all the other surrounding assets so that he and his fellow priests can move to The Shelter where they can be of help to the poor around the clock. (Daily Mass can always be said at The Chain of Parks.) While he's at it, he should also petition Rome to sell Vatican City and give the money to the poor. After all, Jesus was homeless, churchless, and Vaticanless. Heck, Jesus wasn't even a Christian. I guess I didn't realize until now how much Monsignor Kerr soured my mood when he said in his homily that "we must have an appreciation for the poor." There is nothing poor about the quality of life of the leaders of the Catholic Church, and I am sick and tired of listening to them glorify poverty. (R.B. Holmes and his wife drive expensive cars and wear exquisite clothes, but they don't go around praising poverty.)

12:29 p.m. – In line at the First Presbyterian Church and my God, they're all here. Andrelene and her honey (the lazy jailbird she plans to marry once he gets a job), Ninabelle and her "husband" (last I heard she was through with him because he made a pass at one of the CS workers), Labrina, her new boyfriend, and her grandson (thank God I didn't raise my children with a beggar mentality.) Even Kaycee Sourpuss is all smiles as she chatters away with a group of white vagabonds (I don't recall seeing her smile before.) Z'Laitah, looking stunning in a red dress and red stilettos, is also here, but she is, sadly, very much alone because her "male friend" hasn't been seen in days. (He went on another drinking binge, according to The Shameless.) And guess who just arrived? Monica and her fiancé. Never laid eyes on him before, but I at once understood why Mr. ShelterDirector and Mr. Jejune ridiculed her mercilessly, she said, the first time they saw them together. If she were my daughter, I would give her a scolding.

Wish du jour: That I could go hike at Rock Creek Park like I used to do once or twice a week when I lived in the D.C. area. Or even better: at Bear Mountain in upstate New York. Tallahassee's moss-draped trees have lost many of their leaves, but I have yet to see any fall foliage. (On September 8, 2010, I was in The Shelter's driveway, waiting for the 6:30 check-in, and psyching myself up for a possible confrontation with LavermineTheThird, a pugnacious whale who kept badgering me since I gave her a note saying that I didn't want to hear her loud mouth after lights out, when my phone beeped. It was a text message from JP, and here's what it said: "*I just wanted to tell you that I miss our hikes. I'm glad you took us, despite our complaints.*" Since I still don't know how to operate the text message feature in the phone that he got me a year ago, I called him up and said: "You made my day!")

Confirmation du jour: My feelings about Lydia Pollyanna were right on the money. "Whatever!" she dismissively said to a woman who was complaining about something at dinner time. "You need to be more aware of your environment," the woman snapped. "I am very aware of the wonderful food I am eating," Lydia Pollyanna snapped back. And what's the real reason she no longer walks the four blocks to church? One of her wonderful friends gave her a 31-day bus pass. She also got quite testy when she remarked that one should do good deeds and simply wait for their rewards from the Lord and I came back with, "Would you still do good if there was no reward?"

Disbelief du jour: A quiet Bekkie-Sue sitting in a corner of the dining room, reading a book. And because she doesn't look or sound like the reading type, I had to create an excuse to go near her just to take a look at the book title. And what was she reading? Zane. Dear God, please have mercy on this young woman for being too dumb to realize that she needs to start praying for the capability to stay on a job for more than sixty days, rather than waste the few brain cells that she has left on erotic fiction. And please have mercy on Zane for using the writing skills that you gave her to further exacerbate the plight of her race.

Surprise du jour: Being told by Julie that many of the women I haven't seen at The Shelter lately now spend their days doing volunteer work at the Haven of Rest, including new information specialist Chelsea who is looking so poised that I almost felt a moral imperative to tell her to keep up the good work. She replied that her life has gotten better because she made the decision to renew her relationship with Jesus, stopped doing some of the things she used to do, and got her own place while she's waiting for the birth of her baby. (Her other children live with her mother, from what I heard.)

Realization du jour: That Zhouli is all but skin and bones. I spoke to Marguerite again, to Deanna, and even to Mr.

ShelterDrillSergeant. The consensus is that The Shelter can't force a guest to seek treatment (the poor woman is too sick to seek her own treatment.) Besides, it's hard to find help for Zhouli because she's an illegal immigrant.

Disgust du jour: Being told by Deanna that Kaycee Boneheaded wants to sue The Shelter for the damage that was done to her clothes during the fire. The woman is even more dangerous than I thought, which may help explain why she feels the need to camouflage her perjuring nature with more and more Bible studies.

Tonight's biblebabbling is taking place in the front room thanks to Ninabelle who had a long conversation with her grandmama this morning, which led to an overpowering desire to make things right with the Lord through studying "His eternal Word." And who did she turn to for help on the road to salvation? Shelter Bible Scholar Kaycee Boneheaded. True to their self-serving beliefs, they just spent the last hour reassuring themselves that God loves them just the way they are because he's a loving God who doesn't discriminate against anyone. (Dear God, why do I have this feeling that you do not love us as much as we think you do?) And plenty is currently being said about the Book of Hallucination, or is it the Book of Revelation?

Cannot believe that JiBonnie created such a scene because two pregnant women wanted to sit down on the floor in the front room to eat dinner since the dining room was full and no one at the devilish table was willing to give up her seat for a pregnant woman. And why was JiBonnie hurling obscenities at two pregnant women? Because she's still in a state over being turned down by the church-sponsored rehabilitation program at the last minute for reasons that she would not disclose. She was also high.

Yet to hear her say it, she "just wanted to start some shit to keep the bitches on their toes."

Cannot believe that I haven't heard from JP this whole month. I called him again this afternoon, and the phone went straight to voice mail. I bet he didn't even pick up his phone from the girl who called me. He did speak to his grandmother, though, but only because my mother had called ExRoommate a week ago while the two of them happened to be together. Wish someone had told me before I became a mother that motherhood continues to hurt long after childbirth. Wish someone had also told me that the day will come when I will have to learn to live without the people I think I cannot live without.

Cannot believe that less than twenty women attended the lecture on "Sex, Lies and Media Ownership" at the Student Services Building this evening even though it was advertized in the campus newspaper as part as the Love Your Body Week celebration. (I asked for permission to leave The Shelter right after dinner.) I find it strange that FSU Women's Center chose a man to deliver the lecture. A man who called himself a woman advocate with two degrees in women's studies, but a man whose topmost goal seemed to be the personal satisfaction he gets from hanging around a certain kind of pretty girls.

Cannot believe that Sparky came to sit on the chair right across from mine when he saw me on the second floor of the TCC library this morning. I didn't pay attention to him until we first spoke at the First Presbyterian Church, yet he knows quite a bit about me, including the facts that I am "always writing" and frequently go to Barnes & Noble. He also had plenty to say about "the losers at The Shelter who are drinking and drugging their lives away," but does he really expect me to believe that he walked away from a good-paying job and became homeless just so he can go to school for free? Homelessness by choice. I just can't wrap my mind around this one. (I later met a seemingly sane woman who claimed that she became homeless for the sole purpose of getting back at her family for being too stuck-up. And I will literally choke if I don't mention the "true prophetess" from Philly, a hyperreligious with a serious delusion of grandeur, who is so loved by God that demons are in the air trying to prevent prayers that have already been answered from getting to her, and who once told a psychiatrist that the devil, *who was sitting in a corner of the room during a therapy session*, was laughing at him because he thought she was crazy. Said prophetess also has a Ph.D. yet doesn't know what a dissertation is. She was also born with movie-star looks, but her beauty was cursed at birth by the same jealous aunt who stole the millions her godmother left her.)

Feel so dead inside I have no business being alive, but I need to write just to keep breathing.

- Mr. HornyBoy got himself fired for good. He once told me that he got kicked out of culinary school because of sexual misconduct, but that the girl was lying. I guess he'll keep getting fired until he learns to gain mastery over his sex drive.

- Dr. Boroto is also on my mind. "We don't mind being foolish," he had said in class a few weeks ago. "We just don't want an audience." Dear God, I know I don't need to tell you that I am my worst audience, and that I am feeling like the biggest fool on earth.

- The Shelter is so crowded that several women are sleeping on the floor, in between bunks, and in the hallway leading to the back room. I just don't have the stomach for that kind of existence. The only good news: Kaycee Boneheaded is back on a rollaway in the dining room, and Monica switched from the back room to bed 1.

- Deanna told me that she won't be working at The Shelter much longer because her mother wants her to go back to school next semester. I wish she had said that she was the one who wanted to go back to school, but I don't really care why she goes as long as she goes. I do love that girl, even though she cusses like a sailor nowadays when she doesn't think that I am listening.

- Darla and Nicolitta are back. I haven't seen them at The Shelter or anywhere else in months, and they're both as shameless as ever. They have also "hooked up." Nicolitta was at the dining room table joking about her latest LCJ vacation when I got here, but the tide has turned and she's in the big bathroom at the moment, yelling at Darla. It turns out that Darla used to go with Ninabelle, too. And Nicolitta suspects that they still have feelings for each other, in spite of them denying it.

- Father Cayer is on my mind as well. Let's just say that I am still troubled by what he said in a homily days ago. Something about people should not be expecting "spectacular signs" from God because the Word of God through Jesus Christ is enough. Wish I had gone to him after Mass just to remind him that the reason why Jesus is so revered 2000 years later is not because of his words, but because of all the "spectacular" deeds that have been attributed to him. (Deeds that none of his followers have been able to replicate so far, in spite of the Gospel's assurance that they could, as long as they believe.)

- Lydia Blackvan, who had stopped saying hello to me a while back after she heard me say that not all homeless people were created equal, surprisingly asked me if I knew anything about Machiavelli and King Lear because they were both mentioned in the novel she's reading. I told her the little bit I could remember from my days of studying Machiavelli, but admitted that I didn't know a thing about King Lear. I of course didn't tell her that because I wanted to become a sophisticated reader, I tried to get reacquainted with Hamlet several months ago, and had to make peace with the fact that I've never been the Shakespeare type. Dear God, please remind me that you will guide me to whatever it is you need me to know in order for me to be of greater service to you, not to conform to the world's idea of what sophisticated reading entails.

- It's official. Strozier has been invaded by the homeless. Saw one of the white pregnant women there this afternoon, strolling hand in hand with her durag-wearing, gangster-looking white husband. Moments later, I saw the other one with her equally creepy Asian boyfriend, sitting side by side in front of a computer. Mi-Kum was also there, as well as Z'Laitah and the red stilettos. (I think the shoes didn't have the success she anticipated them to garner on Sunday, so she gave them another try with dark blue pants, cream-colored blouse and red blazer, and I swear she looks more well-groomed than the average library staff.) I also saw the new religious freak who claims that hearing voices is a gift from God. And let's not forget the throng of male Shelter guests who walked past me during the two hours I spent at a table on the first floor. (In actuality, I saw four of them, but it was four too many.)

7:30 a.m. – The fifteen-minute communion service was done by Peggy's husband, but I hardly heard a word he said because I am still reeling from the maddening effects of 5 a.m. Shelter drama. (Lavermine cussed a woman out for taking too long in the back bathroom and got cussed in return by many of The Shameless for waking up everybody.) Lydia Pollyanna didn't come to church this morning, and hasn't been here since the priests went on retreat at the beginning of the week. But I bet she'll be here bright and early tomorrow morning because the priests should be back by then, and she needs them to think highly of her.

10:34 a.m. – In my purple chairs on the third floor of Strozier, the only place in this library where I am not continuously assaulted by the sight of THEM since there are no computers on this floor. (That, too, changed during the extensive first floor renovation in 2009.) In any event, I just read today's paper and wish I could go home and cry. Anna Nicole Smith finally buried her son. Cannot imagine what this woman is going through since I've never lost a living child. Dear God, please help her clean up her life for the sake of her new baby. And please let her know that only you can be her rock. (We all know how that story ended.)

6:12 p.m. – JP's bus left long ago, but I am still on a bench at the terminal. It was such a nice surprise to find him waiting at my favorite spot when I arrived at the main library around 4:30. He did not pick up his phone as I feared, nor did he call the phone company to report the lost of the phone. But I was so excited to see him that I didn't give him a lecture. I did not ask why it took him so long to contact me, either. Who would have thought that I would someday be complaining about this boy that I've birthed and raised the same way I've complained all my life about the handful of men that I have loved—or thought I loved.

8:06 p.m. – Finally getting settled in bed 6 because I was too busy arguing with Z'Laitah to take a shower before dinner. "You need to get on your knees and pray God to fix your head," I told her when she hinted, again, that I was stealing her clothes. In reply, she said that I was jealous of her good taste because it was clear that I had none, and even tantalized me with the labels of some of her quality clothes. She also said that I was the one who was mentally ill and concluded with, "Chrisnel, thank you for demonstrating so beautifully the defense mechanisms of denial and projection." I was so shocked my mind went blank.

9:55 p.m. – Mr. ShelterDrillSergeant just turned the lights back on to announce that they're going to start doing "random bag checks" because an empty can of sardines was seen in one of the garbage cans and he's not going to tolerate it. The Shelter houses forty to fifty women on any given night and most of these women are either alcoholics, drug addicts, prostitutes, outlaws, or insane. Yet they are allowed to run wild between 5 p.m. and 8:30 a.m. (now 8:15) with no direct supervision, and they're worried about clandestine sardines eating? Being under the control of self-applauding clowns is a bit of a hell, all right.

A very tense day followed by a very tense evening. Checked in the hellhole early because Mr. ShelterDrillSergeant also said that the staff will be checking beds today as part of the new two-sheets-one-blanket-per-bed rule and unbeknownst to them, I have at least a dozen sheets and two blankets on and underneath the mattress. Bed 6 was not stripped, but my nerves are still raw from worrying. Furthermore, Lavermine is pestering me again, and I am still mad at myself for not thinking of a comeback quick enough when she stood at her locker singing, "Oh baby, your psychological studies aren't taking you nowhere." What is she referring to? My earlier conversation with the nurse about the American Psychiatric Association exploring the possibility of classifying compulsive shopping as a mental disorder. (Have they ever thought of turning men's preoccupation with sex, sports, and power into mental disorders?) Anyhow, I was telling Marguerite that the danger with creating imaginary mental disorders is that once classified the experts will have no problems finding new victims through the power of suggestion alone when I noticed that Lavermine was staring at me with a smirk on her face. Next time I see her, I just may start chanting, "Oh Shelter devil, don't you think it's time to stop drinking, drugging, and conniving after half a century of shameless living."

PS: Too tired to elaborate on long post-dinner conversation with Monica, but the main point is that she finally realized that "le *mec est un gosse*" with no willingness to grow up. And she's utterly heartbroken, especially since he took her to his church last Sunday and the pastor spoke of the importance of marriage, and she took it as a sign that God was blessing their union. To cap it all off, Z'Laitah not only stopped talking to her without warning, Z'Laitah officially told her that their friendship was over.

PPS: "You don't have a life, just die!" Lavermine howled a moment ago as she stormed out of the dining room after another fiery argument with Daneecia. Daneecia is right behind her, and the pandemonium has been spilled into the front room. I feel as if I've been ambushed, and can already sense the emergence of another stress headache. Never in my life have I been around a group of people who are so tenaciously *sans gêne, sans souci, sans remord, sans le moindre scrupule.*

Ridiculousness du jour: Being given a list of "empowering activities" by Monica, which includes gazing into the eyes of my loved ones while saying things like, "May infinite love flow into me, into you and into all," and telling myself that all will be well once I get in touch with the goddess within. I will not waste another minute on this except to say that there is no doubt in my mind that JP would have me Baker-Acted if I would try to practice any of the exercises with him.

Event du jour: A double celebration at Bethel. The church has been in existence for one hundred and thirty six years, and R.B. Holmes has been its pastor for the last twenty. "You will not grow as long as you keep walking in darkness," the guest speaker, Pastor France A. Davis of Calvary Missionary Baptist Church in Salt Lake City, said at one point during his rousing sermon. I find it bothersome how even black people associate darkness with evil when it's highly possible that the ultimate Master of the universe can only be found where he is least expected.

Gratitude du jour: To be in my forties. Because I now know without doubt that there are more important things in life than HAVING A MAN, something I wish my mother had taught me long before my first heartbreak. "I may be fat, but I have a man. And I have had him for the past six years, thank you very much. You're skinny, and you still can't get a man," one of the black Shameless cried out after she was told that she was a bit too voluptuous for the pink mini skirt she was wearing. Hard to believe that having a man is such a colossal stroke of luck even when the man in question is in and out of jail and cannot get a job to save his life. (And when the woman in question was fooling around with another Shameless just a few weeks ago.)

Confirmation du jour: That Sparky is, in fact, the white male equivalent of Kaycee Boneheaded, a bizarre amalgam of shamelessness and pridefulness. He actually told me this afternoon that the government should take money from the rich to give to the poor because it would only be fair. What have those people done for society in order to feel so entitled? And why am I spending so much time talking to Sparky? Because he shows up everywhere I go. He also complimented me on my pretty skin today. My pretty light skin, to be exact. Since my skin is darker under the Florida sun than it has ever been, the only thing I can think of is that he was trying to make me feel good about myself because he's under the assumption that my mind, too, has been contaminated with the most universal cultural illness of all time: the disdain for black skin.

7:25 a.m. – Mass just ended, and the sight of Lydia Pollyanna on her knees in front of the altar is making me see red, but my early morning conversation with Monica is what I need to ruminate on right now. First, Monica was so inconsolable over Mr. ShelterDrillSergeant not letting an intoxicated Marvy in last night that she barely slept, despite being told by at least two other women who know Marvy much better than she does that Marvy will be just fine. Come to think of it, Marvy doesn't even stay at The Shelter all that much, which confirms that The Shelter is not her only pied-à-terre in Tallahassee. Second, Monica's love life is still in shambles and she's so hurt that she couldn't even talk about it except to say that LeMec is smoking crack again and she had to let him go. (LeMec, I later found out, has six children, and the youngest was conceived with a CS worker he met at The Shelter.) Third, the situation with Z'Laitah is beginning to wear her out because all she has ever done was to love Z'Laitah unconditionally, and try as she might, she cannot figure out why Z'Laitah is so mad at her. I wonder how many additional doses of Shelter reality it will take for Monica to finally accept those people for who they are. By the same token, I also wonder how many additional doses of reality it will take for me to accept that my beliefs about God are out of alignment with the sobering facts that life has presented to me so far. I've never felt so demoralized, so bewildered, or so bitter.

5:32 p.m. – Back at Strozier, but sitting at a table on the second floor because a real student took over my purple chairs when I left to go to the Haven of Rest. The food was actually worth eating (thanks, Bobby), and I was even enjoying the meal until a guy who once offered to take me to the movies accused me of being "a hardhearted and selfish woman" when I told him that it would be easier for me to give him my money, if I had any, than my time. Incidentally, while I seem to be the only Shelter resident in this section of Strozier at the present time, a group of boys about the age of ten are here, and they're embarrassing the hell out of me. In the event that these children's mothers (I dare not say fathers) are too busy toiling in fast food restaurants or cleaning Tallahassee's apartment buildings, hotel rooms and construction sites, where are their grandmothers, their aunts, their cousins, their older siblings? (Probably at The Shelter where they can enjoy their twisted version of *la belle vie* without any responsibility of any kind. I actually heard many of The Shameless say that they do not want to live with their children because they don't want to sit home all day rocking grandbabies.) Meanwhile, two of the boys are running back and forth to the water fountain. Dear God, please keep the anger out of my voice when I go tell them to go back to their computers, or to go play outside. Do I need to add that the dozen or so white FSU students scattered in the east side of the building (front section) are keeping mum because they are, almost certainly, too afraid of being painted as racists?

Cannot believe that my name and the word "gracious" were actually used in the same sentence today as in, "That was very gracious of you, Chrisnel, to simply hand them the napkins instead of telling them to pick up the food that fell off their plates." And that was a compliment paid to me by Sharon, a new blonde who seems so eager to be liked that she already comes across as a blend between Doublefaced Lizzie and Lydia Pollyanna.

Cannot believe that I can buy a cheese burger for 69 cents, a double cheeseburger for 99 cents, and a triple cheese burger for $1.49 at the McDonald's on West Pensacola Street this week. Never heard of triple cheese burgers until I saw the ad in the window of the restaurant on my way to TCC this morning, and once again I found myself wondering why is it so easy—and so cheap—to buy junk food in a country with an expanding waistline and, paradoxically, a puzzling obsession with thinness?

Cannot believe that Monica is so excited because Marvy wants to take her along to San Francisco next month. The fact that Marvy should not be inviting a total stranger to her mother's home when her "upper-class mom" is trying to save her from her demons doesn't seem to be an issue for Monica. All that matters is that Marvy is offering her the opportunity to go on an "awesome adventure," and it would be stupid to say no. Monica also made it a point to congratulate Z'Laitah on the "labor of love" Z'Laitah was performing this evening. What was Z'Laitah doing? French braiding her hair. Z'Laitah ignored her in reply.

Cannot believe that Lydia Pollyanna who had a wonderful day, and is feeling even more wonderful tonight, spent almost an hour standing by bed 6 before and after dinner to talk to me about the Moore case. More precisely, about the report Attorney General Charlie Crist recently released on his murder re-investigation of Harry and Harriette Moore, two civil rights workers whose house was bombed by the KKK on December 25, 1951—a chilling reminder that terrorism was present on American soil long before 9/11. She also showed me a letter Charlie Crist wrote to her, though she didn't let me read its content. (Maybe he was threatening to take her to court if she doesn't stop writing to him.) She did, however, let me read the two letters she had received from the pope and George W., thanking her for her well wishes. And speaking of the Bushes, she also shook hands with Jeb Bush once, and it was such a—you guessed it—wonderful experience that she'll never forget it. Did she, too, just escape from a loony bin?

Grateful that I didn't feel too mortified when I stopped at HOPE on my way back downtown from TCC and was told that Kelly Kearns no longer works with people from The

Shelter, but that I could come back tomorrow afternoon between two and five to see Jeff Franck who had taken her place. What did I want from Kelly? A voucher for a pair of shoes. Humiliating beyond words to be wearing used shoes when I don't even like to walk in other people's footsteps.

Grateful for the courage to be somewhat honest when Sabine asked if I was still babysitting and I told her that I had let go of the job to finish a book I was trying to write because I wanted more out of life than a paycheck. Also grateful that I didn't get too despondent over a dream in which I was helping my daughter choose a party dress and she paused for a moment and said, "I don't believe you had the audaciousness to show up in my apartment again. I have no need for you."

Grateful for the ability to keep my eyes on the God of my personal experience today, not on the spiritual dryness that has dwelled in me all week, and definitely not on my current state of affairs. I guess I am finally learning to put into practice the advice that was given to me by the spiritual director of the National Shrine in D.C. when I had entered his office on the spur of the moment a month or two before eviction day—after spending more hours on my knees in the Crypt Church. "Faith is not a feeling," he had answered when I told him that I was afraid because I no longer felt God's presence, much less God's love. "Faith is a commitment."

Grateful for the astuteness to ignore Z'Laitah when she grumbled that she didn't want anyone who was stealing her clothes to speak to her or about her after she heard me tell Sabine that John Lennon was indeed the one who once said that The Beatles were more popular than Jesus. She must have forgotten that she was the one who butted in my conversation last night—just to insist that it was someone from The Rolling Stones—when I had asked Sabine, my Wikipedia at The Shelter, who had made the controversial comment. I sometimes wonder if Z'Laitah's mental illness was triggered from her palpable need to always be the smartest, but that's another issue. Sharon, contrastingly, didn't fare so well, and Z'Laitah very nearly ate her alive. In short, Sharon saw Z'Laitah's boyfriend at the main library this afternoon and told him how blessed he was to have "such a kind mother" because she wrongly assumed, as I did before her, that the handsome young man was Z'Laitah's much beloved chocolate-and-milk son.

A day riddled with frustration and resentment. (a) Monica is in front of the mirror trying out clothes she just found in the donation bin, and all the commotion over such pettiness is driving me nuts. (b) Woke up around 2 a.m., could not go back to sleep, remained lethargic all day, and most likely won't get any sleep tonight since The Shelter is overcrowded again and Ninabelle, who also lost her reserved bed, will be sleeping on the floor in the front room and already she can't shut up. (c) Couldn't go to HOPE to get the stupid voucher because my left foot has been hurting again from all those long walks to TCC, and I ended up spending the afternoon glued to a computer on the first floor of Strozier, reading about the Amish, the Shakers, the Eastern Orthodox Church, et cetera. (d) And guess what members of the White Shameless Club were feasting on while waiting for dinner? A recent television interview in which a certain celebrity was practically urging every American over the age of eighteen to go adopt an African child. Dear God, when will poor black people everywhere realize that what you can give to one, you can surely give to another, and that the only way they'll be able to triumph over their never-ending calamities is to stop extending their begging bowls and turn to you for forgiveness, mercy, and wisdom?

A bearable evening for which I am profoundly grateful. The women in the dining room are watching TV quietly, lo and behold! A sober Sabine is in bed 3, reading. Zhouli is eating again, but has been examining the sole of her shoes with so much intensity that she didn't get out of bed for dinner. Monica and Marvy are playing cards in bed 1. The new Jewish woman in bed 2 is sitting up in bed with her eyes closed and her legs crossed in from of her, as if in meditation, but she's probably another nut. Don't know what the smelly white woman below me in bed 5 is doing, but I can't hear her or smell her and that's good enough. Z'Laitah is working on a new hairstyle, but I can hardly see her since my fence on her side of the bed is now so high that every so often I forget she's even there. The latest occupant of bed 7 hasn't been a problem so far, but I am keeping my fingers crossed since she's so very proud of her eleven years of homelessness. Also on my mind:

(1) Self-hatred and judgment – "Girl, you need to do something about that nappy head of yours," Ninabelle just told Bekkie-Sue, as they entered the big bathroom. They both laughed in agreement. Why are these women so disinclined to judge each other's **LACK OF CHARACTER** forty-something years after the peak of the civil rights movement when they don't think twice about pooh-poohing each other's God-given features? May the Creator of all hair textures have mercy on their myopia.

(2) Mental illness and violence – "You need to watch your back, Z'Laitah was staring straight at you," Pamelia (she's baaack!) told me sotto voce on her way to the 8:15 smoke break. I bombastically replied that I wasn't fearful of anyone, knowing full well that Z'Laitah isn't just anyone. As a matter of fact, she looked as if she was getting ready to punch Aline, a black woman who seemed to be as

culture-shocked as I am her first night here, after Aline touched her arm to signal that there was a puddle of water at the foot of her bunk. (The showers in the big bathroom were leaking again.)

(3) Enemies and truth – That Courtland Milloy, a black columnist from the *Washington Post*, would decide to go to Harpers Ferry National Historical Park in West Virginia to check out what a Ku Klux Klan rally looks like these days, I find hilarious. What I didn't find so funny in Milloy's October 18 column (the paper was on display in the newspaper section on the second floor of TCC library to my delight), was the comment of one KKK member who was quoted as saying that blacks only want to sexually assault white women. (The KKK is clearly in desperate need of new slogans.) I couldn't, however, dismissed the first half of his quote (blacks only exist to entertain white folks) because it was just the other day that I myself was thinking that the black race has far too many clowns earning big money and *illusory prestige* in the entertainment world. And not enough engineers, economists, scientists, and the like.

(4) Ritalin and physical activity – "You're just as loud as he is!" an older woman at the main library grumpily said to a white Shameless who use to stay at The Shelter while the white Shameless chastised her three-year-old. The older woman kept walking, and the white Shameless tearfully told the boy that they're going to have to increase his meds because he wasn't getting any better and she couldn't keep up with his ADHD. And once again I had to wonder whether little boys in this country are so hyper because they're not being physically challenged in a society that

keeps children indoors watching TV, playing video games and eating junk food, to say nothing of a new generation of parents who came to believe that medicating is better than spanking. I also wonder if women are inadvertently creating <u>real</u> chemical imbalances in their brains and the brains of their unborn children by popping so many pills just to keep pain at bay when pain is very much a part of life in a world that demands so much from us yet gives back so little in return. (More than two years after the inauguration of the nation's first *biracial* president—No obnoxiousness intended, but too many blockheads like to pretend that they don't know that Barack Obama is as much white as he is black—I have yet to come to terms with what happened to Hillary Clinton, in spite of the tremendous satisfaction I get from having First Lady Michelle Obama in the White House.)

Did I say that it was a relatively quiet night at The Shelter? Well, lots of water has gone under the bridge since. As it turned out, Marvy suddenly realized that she had better things to do on a Friday night and all hell broke loose when Monica tried to stop her from leaving. Marvy did check out and thank God because I was about to open the emergency door and throw her out myself, and a defeated Monica is now lamenting the death of her virtuousness. She lost her temper many times in recent days, for instance, and she's disappointed with herself for her spiritual backsliding because everybody and everything in our even-handed universe are just fine right where they are. She also lost her temp job because the farmers no longer want the homeless to pick up their vegetables and fruits since most of them proved to be so unreliable, despite her herculean efforts to instill better work habits in them. I am grateful to have met Monica for she exemplifies so well what can happen to a person who misguidedly believes that love alone is enough to make this world a better place.

One of the worst days of the year, if not the worst. I didn't fall asleep until after two only to be awaken by Z'Laitah at 4:28 a.m. because pre-dawn bed making is now a new trend of hers. She, of course, goes right back to sleep on her perfectly made bed while I fume in silence and fight an urge to throw a book at her. Physical exhaustion then turned to anxiety when it dawned on me on my way to STM that October 30, the sixth year anniversary of the day I officially walked away from the World Bank, was just around the corner, and I am still homeless when all I ever wanted since I first got acquainted with God was to experience his love, his mercy and his power right here on earth. . . . An ecstatic Lavermine just walked in (it's 11:04), and she naturally stopped in the dining room to brag about the swell time she had at the FAMU Homecoming Parade this morning. She's also thankful to have gotten permission to stay out late to attend the rest of the festivities, including the homecoming game. (Lavermine has permission to stay out on game nights until midnight during football season.) I bet she would have left The Shelter years ago if being homeless didn't come with so many privileges.

Aggravation du jour: Being told by Monica that she's enchanted to be at The Shelter, that she had never had so many girlfriends, and that the whole experience feels like "a big pajama party."

Consolation du jour: Being told by Sharon that she's ashamed to be at The Shelter because she's "no white trash," and having owned her own business for years, it's not where she expected to be at her age.

Disturbance du jour: Z'Laitah's growing agitation. She's so fidgety that Mr. ShelterDrillSergeant told her "You must not be living right!" when she got spooked after he merely walked past her on his way to the back room. Homelessness hurts, and living with these women isn't helping any.

Error in judgment du jour: Agreeing to meet Sharon at Grace Mission Episcopal Church for their 10:30 a.m. service (only because she told me that they usually serve a great lunch afterward, and they did.) What she did not tell me is that the church is mostly attended by current and former loudmouthed Shelter residents. I also didn't know that the Episcopal Church had incorporated the "Peace be with you" ritual into their service and nearly went into cardiac arrest when Claralynn, a crackhead with an explosive temper who just came back to The Shelter, planted herself in front of me and stuck her hand out, even after I obstinately kept my own hands folded and simply bowed my head to her as a sign of peace. I was as startled as she was when I heard myself say "I don't shake hands" when she refused to go away. Did she really think that I would want to shake her hand just because we're in church when she knows and I know that she'll be back at The Shelter acting like an animal in just a few hours? Besides, those women don't even wash their hands after they use the toilet, and I am pretty sure that she's no exception.

Discovery du jour: That many of the male Shelter guests eat breakfast and lunch at Grace Mission before and after the 10:30 service, then head over to the First Presbyterian Church for more food. Only in America.

Faux pas du jour: Walking from Grace Mission to the main library in the company of Sparky. Not good for my image. The black desperadoes will despise me even more, and The Shameless will surely think I've become one of them.

Disappointment du jour: Assuming that it would be less painful to walk toward The Shelter this evening (end of

Daylight Saving Time). The darkness brought back the memory of being home at 2900 Upshur Street, and listening to "After Hours" with Glenn Hollis on WASH-FM.

12:08 a.m. – Spent the past few minutes talking to Mr. ShelterDirector about Z'Laitah because she really scared me when she threw the big bathroom door open half-hour ago and yelled, "Whoever keeps knocking on the door, grow up!" She was told that it was a Shelter staff who knocked on the door—once—because he wanted to confirm that the showers were locked, but she did not believe it, and went on to rant and wave about hateful people harassing her while she's trying to get some reading done. What did Mr. ShelterDirector have to say? Not much. He knows Z'Laitah is "not well," but there isn't a thing he can do "unless she actually does something." Dear God, do I need to remind you that I am sleeping two feet away from a woman who seems to be on the verge of going postal?

7:37 p.m. – A day of complete lack of clarity and focus. Moreover, the insanity at The Shelter is grating on my nerves so much that I am literally a step away from snapping, and I don't seem to be the only one. Even Lydia Pollyanna isn't being her phony self. (She sulkily told Sharon that she likes to keep her personal life private when Sharon, in another vain effort to be friendly, asked her something like, "Chrisnel told me that you sleep through the night and don't even wake up to pee, what's your secret?") For the record, I did go pick up a voucher from HOPE this afternoon and made the mistake to wear my new Goodwill shoes back to The Shelter, and my poor feet have been in tears since. I must have forgotten that there is usually a good reason why a pair of brand new shoes is donated to a thrift store. Enough unnecessary stress to drive me insane.

9:51 p.m. – "If you don't like what goes on in here, don't come in here," Mr. Jejune just told Pamelia who has already reverted to her old behaviors, in spite of all the vainglorious talk about how much she has changed since she stopped smoking crack. Evidence that Julie was telling the truth when she told me that Pamelia had to leave the two-bedroom home they were sharing with two other women and a kid because she's back on drugs. Have more to say, but I am too exhausted to keep my eyes open. Sort of grateful that Monica *la bavarde* insisted to know how I was doing tonight for talking to her somehow caused the doom I've been feeling all day to be lifted. Even more grateful that I wasn't too bothered when I got misty-eyed while telling her that I feel that God put a curse on me when he told me to go write the novel, nor get upset when she candidly replied that maybe I had simply misunderstood God's message. Where did I hear that before?

Kaycee Boneheaded was a no show the past few nights, but it sounds as if she's been engaging in some serious conversations with the Lord while copulating in her favorite motel room because she's back with a change of heart. In a nutshell, the same Lord who gave her the sapience to stop using foul language ten years ago told her over the weekend to let go of her wish to have The Shelter reimburse her for her fire-damaged clothes (they smelled like smoke) because "that's not what you're here for." Religious foolishness at The Shelter is not what's troubling me right now, however. A conversation I had at the main library with JP this afternoon is. And according to JP, no white waiters (mostly college students) at the casual dining restaurant chain on West Tennessee Street where he works want to do "black tables," and it has nothing to do with racism. He said it took him a while to figure out why they call black people "Canadians," meaning people who don't tip. Most embarrassingly, he said that if a group of more than four black people sit at a table, it's almost a guarantee that they're going to cook up a reason to get something for free. He said he got so tired of the white waiters expecting him to do black tables just because he's black that he refused to do a black table a few days ago. In desperation, they asked a pretty black girl who usually works as a hostess to wait on the three black men who had just arrived. JP said that he kept an eye on the girl from a distance, and she did just fine. The three men originally left the girl $3, less than ten percent of their bill, but upon reflection one of them retraced his steps on their way out, and took back his dollar.

Dear God, you know and I know that I am not trying to preserve any racial stereotype, but African-American pundits (Hello, Professor Michael Eric Dyson) can deny it all they want, something isn't right with my race.

Grateful I woke up with so much calmness in my heart that I didn't care one way or the other when the first thing that came out of Sharon's mouth when I told her that I don't think I'll ever be able to accept that I left my job to do the will of God and ended up in a homeless shelter was: "Can I be honest with you? What you're doing is not working. You need to look for a real job."

Grateful that the nurse was told that Valerie, who was hit by a car a block away from The Shelter, was injured and in surgery, not dead, when she called the hospital this evening. The word is that Valerie was thrown in front of the car because it's the beginning of the month and one of the untouchables assumed that she must be carrying cash, but I am choosing to believe that the purse snatcher was not a monster and that Valerie accidentally fell in front of the car. But who the hell knows what really happened.

Grateful for the backbone to jot down my own comments next to a newspaper article on depression when I came across it at the main library this afternoon. The article was barely three-hundred words, but it seems as if every word was chosen to scare the daylights out of women: "chronic disease . . . remission . . . need aggressive treatment," and if I didn't read the headline, I would have thought that they were talking about cancer. Thank you, God, for having taught me in so many ways that depression is not the shuddersome affliction they claim it to be, and that in many cases it can even be a subtle attempt to bring a troubled soul to You.

Grateful for a pretty good day mostly because I spent my morning at Barnes & Noble skimming though *Running with Scissors* and *The Audacity of Hope,* two books that I would like to read in their entirety at some point. I must say that I am rather proud of myself for not giving a second look to Suzanne Somers's latest book in which she credits bioidentical hormones for being the solution to her menopausal problems, as well as the source of her youthful look at the age of sixty. (Dear Suzanne, I hate to be the one to break the news to you, but unless you want to end up looking like Plastic Surgery Freak Joan Rivers, the wrinkles will ultimately win this war and the sooner you accept it, the less mood-enhancing pills you will need.)

Cannot believe that my cousin Didi left The Shelter a week ago and I didn't even know. I heard that she moved to Baltimore where she has lived before, and I would not be surprised if I see her on the news one of these days, raising hell in front of the Supreme Court.

Cannot believe that Lavermine is in such a lovely mood that she has been calling everybody "darling" and "honey" all evening. In fact, she's standing in front of her locker right this moment, singing another catchy love song. And it's taking all I got not to blurt out that this is a homeless shelter, not *American Idol.*

Cannot believe that Mormon Girl, a pretty blonde whom I thought was an FSU student with housing problems when she first appeared at The Shelter until I heard her speak, admitted that she prefers to hang around black people because they have always been more supportive of her (of her many vices, to be accurate) than her own people, and the black Shameless took it as a felicitation.

Cannot believe that Monica, the queen of love, is so angry tonight that the F-word crossed her loving lips twice while she spoke of her new bunkie who did turn out to be a dingbat. She's also debating whether she should take LeMec back because while he's not very good looking and is so gauche that he can't even dial a phone (and is lousy in bed), he loves her like no other man ever did, and "such pure love shouldn't be taken for granted."

Cannot believe that there was no mention of Valerie's accident in today's *Democrat*, at least none that I could find. (Everything is newsworthy in Tallahassee.) Would never be able to claim residency in a city where reporters of the local paper seem to be asleep at their desks. Or are they protecting The Shelter? The 11 o'clock news did mention that a woman was hit by a car on West Tennessee Street during a robbery, but said nothing about The Shelter either.

5:18 a.m. – Lots of disturbing dreams, which I can't recall except for the one about stealing a croissant from Au Bon Pain and because I thought that I was being followed, I kept running until I found myself on an isolated road, not knowing if I was headed in the right direction. Also dreamt of Z'Laitah. "You hate me because I love you," I told her in the dream. I forgot how much I used to like her. Still admire her intelligence when she's not acting crazy.

10:14 a.m. – Didn't get to TCC until now because I left STM after nine since Lydia Pollyanna didn't come to Mass this morning. Cold out. Breezy. But the sky is such a beautiful shade of blue that it took my breath away. Sparky was walking out of the library as I got in. "You wanna go take our tests for us?" he asked. I smiled and wished him good luck. I just hope that the student he was with doesn't know that he's homeless and conclude that I am, too.

5:28 p.m. – Just arrived at Strozier. Was hoping to get some free food on the Union Green on my way here, but the picnic was clearly limited to a specific group of students and their parents, so I kept walking. Grateful that I did get a free ride from the Seminole Express, though, only because the bus, the campus shuttle, pulled up as I approached the Heritage Grove stop, across the street from Publix, and I noticed that the students didn't have to show their FSU ID to the driver, and I hopped along.

7:47 p.m. – Sabine often jokes that The Shameless are even nuttier during a full moon, and they didn't disappoint. I found myself exchanging words with two women half hour ago because they came to wait for dinner right at the foot of bed 6 and felt provoked when I told them that they couldn't stand there (personal space is another foreign concept at The Shelter.) I wish I could laugh this madness off like Sharon, bedeck it like Monica, ignore it like Sabine, or deny it like Lydia Pollyanna. In truth, I wish I was never born.

Why is Lizzie Licehead standing on the side of bed 6 to wait for the nurse when she could have easily stood on the other side of the room? Of course I had to take a peek at her bloody scalp. Wonder what Louvern would say if she knew that this poor woman was still walking around The Shelter with a head full of lice. Most crucially, I must generate a coughing spell whenever she gets too close because I don't want any of her willow trees to jump on the bunk and make a beeline for my hair even though lice can't jump, or so they say. By the way, both black and white Shameless believe that black people can't get lice and I had to educate one of them on the matter when she insisted that black people never get lice. I got called a know-it-all bitch in return. It looks as if they have never heard of Reformation either since most of them are more than sure that Catholics are not Christians. And guess who's sitting on bed 1 comforting a crying Marvy whom I suspect is more drunk than overwhelmed? Z'Laitah. I reckon that her friendship with Monica is back on. Meanwhile, I am so annoyed by them all that I too want to cry, in spite of a fairly good day mostly spent on a bench next to the Alumni Center (that was before the new president's house was built next door), reading Teresa of Avila's *The Way of Perfection*.

Monica just came out of the big bathroom where she was forced to take a shower because there was a long line of women waiting for the dining room bathroom when she got here. "*Je ne me lave plus là. C'est horrible*," she told me, on her way back to bed. I shook my head, feigning understanding, while I made a mental note to stop keeping the dining room bathroom so clean just to give her an opportunity for more spiritual growth. After all, it was just last night that Monica was telling me that God is in everything, even in the food we eat, the clothes we wear, and the brushes we use to style our hairs and clean our teeth. Surely, God must also reign supreme in a filthy bathroom.

Incredulity du jour: Watching a male Shelter guest shave his head, his face, then clip his fingernails and toenails while sitting at a table at the main library.

Astonishment du jour: Monica finally put her celestial cloak aside to pass a judgment: Lavermine has no consideration for anyone, and is the meanest person she ever met.

Realization du jour: That it's not so much the waiting for God that is consuming me. It's the wondering whether God will provide, and how I am going to start over if he doesn't.

Wish du jour: That I were told ahead of time that my personal road to salvation would be loaded with distractions disguised as false hope, sublime inspirations, majestic but unrealizable visions, in addition to doubt, anxiety and fear.

Hunch du jour: To be wary of my dreams, especially the wishful-thinking kind. I dreamed that I was days away from receiving lots of money (enough to live on for the rest of my life, and to start the charitable foundation of my dreams), and actually believed it upon awakening until reality set in.

Exasperation du jour: Lydia Pollyanna had a more wonderful day than usual because she saw Charlie Crist's "very distinct looking car" on her way to the state library this morning. She also wonders whether Charlie Crist has read the clipping of an article on embryonic stem cell research she recently mailed him with a big handwritten "No!" on the clipping. Do I need to add that she's so excited about the upcoming election that you would think it was her husband running for governor?

Discontentment du jour: Trying to explain to Deanna why my daughter and I are on bad terms after she commented that she forgot that I had a daughter because I rarely speak of her. "She relinquished her financial obligation to me and my brother in 2000 when she voluntarily quit her job to chase her dream of becoming a novelist. Since then, she has lost her car and her home, and has fled the state of Maryland," was how my daughter once described me. But I didn't tell all of that to Deanna and simply said that my daughter resents me for some bad decisions that I made. Who could have foreseen that choosing to be obedient to God would turn out to be something that I would one day categorize as a bad decision just to save face?

Not in a writing mood, but I must force myself to record the following before I forget:

- Marvy didn't come in tonight and Z'Laitah was already asleep when I got here. Guess who spent most of the evening chatting with Monica right on Monica's bed? Her crazy bunkie in bed 2. How can I trust Monica when she's so good at cozying up with people she doesn't like?

- It came to me while I took a shower that while I have no problems being judged for the wrongs that I do, I am presently being judged for things that I didn't do, or at least things that I didn't intend to do: being an irresponsible mother, as well as a con artist who would rather disappear than pay off her debts. I am none of that, God, and you know it.

- Beth Burns was here again this evening, and left with Aline. Julie told me last week that Beth was looking for more women to fill up her Christian home for women (to be later known as Chelsea House), and she seems to be finding them right at The Shelter. I wish Aline the best because she was a good woman. Well, I don't know if she was a good woman, but she was quiet. And in this hell of a place, a quiet woman is a good-enough woman.

- Sabine is still complaining about the woman who came to get her and three other Shelter guests last week to take them to a midday Bible study and some people at the woman's church bristled when they were asked to share their Bibles. I wanted to ask if she would have ungrudgingly shared any of her precious books with the homeless when she was the beautiful and exotic wife of a thriving tycoon, but I do like Sabine and I don't want to antagonize her.

- The new white girl who refers to herself as a "DCF kid," and who already gave birth to her very own DCF baby, thinks that she's pregnant again. I swear the world would be better off if they legalize the most popular recreational drugs, promote the benefits of masturbation, and criminalize sexual encounters between people under the age of twenty-one for it seems to me that sex causes more problems to society than drug addictions. (DCF stands for Department of Children and Families.)

- Pamelia and Andrelene are in the dining room talking about their favorite foods (another hot topic among The Shameless), and about food stamps recertification. The thing is that both women are grossly overweight and are still eating free breakfast, free lunch, free dinner at The Shelter and what would do them some good is not for the state of Florida to increase their food stamp allotments as they're hoping, but to ship them to the third world for a year just to give them a taste of real poverty.

Sitting in front of a computer on the second floor of Strozier with a number of conflicting thoughts running through my mind. I was not experiencing the onset of some deadly disease when I woke up this morning around 4:30 feeling so hot, so nauseated, and with my head spinning so fast that it took me forever to get off the bunk and drag myself to the dining room bathroom where I felt compelled to take a cold shower since Shelter staff had forgotten to lock the showers, I was having my first hot flash. Hard to believe that hot flashes can be so debilitating. Even harder to believe that I was so unprepared considering that it was just yesterday that I was reading an article about menopause in the health and fitness section of the *Democrat*. Dear God, if you are as just as they claim you to be, why didn't you distribute this kind of biological nuisance more equitably? Women already go through so many changes in the course of a lifetime, couldn't you give hot flashes to men?

8:31 a.m. – On the front page of today's *Democrat*: "Call Him Governor Crist." No surprise there. Yet, why do I want to cry? Because the prophecy of that minister (I read his story months ago) who was told in a dream that Charlie Crist was going to be the next governor of Florida even before Charlie Crist decided to run for governor has been fulfilled while my fate still hangs in the balance. I can already see the glee on Lydia Pollyanna's face this evening since Charlie Crist's win is unquestionably her win. Will I have to congratulate her? In the intervening time, I just finished rereading Monday's article on menopause. Since I barely sleep to start with, I won't detect any change in sleeping patterns. Shed quite a bit of pubic hair after the eviction so I think the hairs on my head are here to stay. And if they're not, I guess I will have to start depending on head wraps and wigs until I build up the confidence to start showing my bald head to the world. The loss of libido is a blessing. I am not especially fearful of dry skin, sore breasts or mushy brain. Hell, thanks to you, God, my brain is the sharpest it has ever been.

7:22 p.m. – Spent the past few minutes chatting with Monica, always an interesting experience. I asked what she would want for Christmas if she could have two of her wishes come true. It took her a minute to think it over: a house but not just any house. The house must have a dance room, an art and craft room, a sewing room, and plenty of guest rooms. She also wants a car big enough to carry her bike. Of course, she had to give me an update on how things are going with LeMec. She thinks she made a mistake by taking him back, but he cried so much over their breakup that she had to give him another chance. Things are still not going as smoothly as she expected, but her Sun and Pluto combination is in perfect conjunction with his Mars and Pluto (at least, that's what I thought I heard), an intimation that there is something "potentially awesome" between them. Out of curiosity, I then asked how long her marriages lasted, she sheepishly acknowledged that none of them lasted very long because she has always been "too strong" for the men in her life. Goodness gracious.

8:07 p.m. – Dinner was not worth eating, but what else is new? What was new was that there was no one around to tell Deanna just how wonderful the meal was because Lydia Pollyanna left The Shelter without saying a word to anyone. Did she move to the governor's mansion to help get it ready for Charlie??? (On behalf of Lydia Pollyanna who had left Tallahassee by then, I felt obligated to go shake Governor Crist's hand when I attended the inauguration festivities several weeks later. I never shook hand with a politician before, so I am not sure what I was expecting. All I know is that I felt beset by shame after I held my hand out and said "Congratulations!" and Governor Crist actually took a moment to make eye contact with me and smile a seemingly genuine smile, before he said thank you. I walked away feeling like an impostor, but I at last understood why Lydia Pollyanna is crazy about the guy. He has a good aura. Do I need to add that there was so much free food at the inauguration, and it all tasted so good, that I ate as if there were no tomorrow?)

Grateful that I am more amused and curious by my first hot flash than nervous. "I don't like them," Marguerite emphatically said, twice, when I told her. Can't say that I blame her. Hope I remain amused.

Grateful I am learning to be more selective in what I choose to read in the paper, and even more so on quotes I choose to collect. I have so many books to catch up with that I have no business being such a news junkie.

Grateful that Sharon was moved from the back room to bed 7, yet I still worry about who will be reserved in bed 2 because I've learned the hard way that it only takes one person to change the whole atmosphere in the room.

Grateful for the realization that the typical Asian student who spends a lot of time at Strozier is there to study. But that the typical black student who spends a lot of time at Strozier is there to watch movies, play video games, cruise social networking sites, talk on the phone and, of course, listen to music.

Grateful that I wasn't offended when I went in the dining room after the 9:30 smoke break to ask the group of white Shameless who had congregated there tonight to keep their voices down and Pamelia told me, "You need to leave people the fuck alone and get a job!" My reply to her? "Just because I don't catch the day labor van with you all does not mean that I don't have a job." In restrospect, I should have kept quiet since Pamelia herself doesn't have a job.

Grateful that Mr. Irresistible did believe me when I told him that I missed the last check-in because the clock at the computer I was using at the main library hasn't been reset and I lost track of time since they kept extending my minutes. Still, it remained a nerveracking experience three hours later because I could have easily been on the streets at this moment, looking for a place to sleep, since I don't know where JP lives and don't even have enough minutes on my phone to make a phone call.

Grateful that my sense of worth is stronger than my love of food. One of Lydia Pollyanna's many friends came to me after Mass and asked if I wanted to go out for breakfast. I politely declined because she looked like someone who needed to do a good deed just to make herself feel better. In contrast, Frances invited me over her house for Thanksgiving, but I declined for a different reason. I just could not picture myself asking her to drop me off at The Shelter afterward. Dear God, you must have gotten me confused with someone else because this cannot be my life.

In bed 6 and feeling more unglued than usual after an argument with Monica, which started when she told me that I was too "close-minded" to allow her to teach me how to have "a new state of consciousness." The argument escalated after I replied that it was egotistical of her to assume that her knowledge of spiritual matters was superior than mine because she didn't know what I know, and Lavermine used my words to harangue her moments later. And as you would expect, Monica blamed me for putting words into Lavermine's mouth since she doesn't realize just how much ammunition she gives to The Shameless (and Shelter staff) through her mere association with LeMec. In passing, WCTV was in The Shelter's driveway when I came in shortly before five. I was tempted to tell the pretty Asian-American reporter, off-camera, that if she really wants to know what goes on inside The Shelter she should come and spend a few nights there undercover, but she was too busy interviewing one of the families to pay me any attention in spite of the fact that I was standing inches away from her cameraman, taking notes.

PS: Monica and I did make up, but I saw a side of her that I didn't know existed. "I hate the feeling of impotence," she spat out in the heat of the moment. Poor baby.

Relief du jour: Being told by Valerie's boyfriend that she's feeling much better physically and emotionally, left the hospital a few days ago, was now living with her sister, and didn't plan to come back to The Shelter.

Suspicion du jour: That Sharon is trying to fix me up with Sparky. She not only talks about him all the time (Sparky and her husband are friends), she told me that the three of them were at the nearby McDonald's this morning and my name came up and they wished they had invited me to join them for coffee. She obviously doesn't know me very well.

Shock du jour: Learning that Claralynn is not homeless, but only comes to The Shelter because she's "tired of smoking that stuff every night," and can fight her temptations better when she's not alone. I am actually feeling a tad of respect for her, now that I know that she's at least trying to conquer her personal demons. And speaking of that stuff, I haven't seen JiBonnie in over a week; she's probably back in jail.

Heartbreak du jour: Reading that Haiti is the world's most corrupt nation, according to a recently released survey from an organization that monitors corruption worldwide. If the first independent black republic in the world—and the only group of black people who has ever carried out a successful slave rebellion—has not been able to establish a functional government two-hundred years after their *soi-disant* independence, how will my race be able to regain its dignity in this world, assuming it ever had any?

Vexation du jour: Being told by Sabine that Lydia Pollyanna dumped St. Thomas More for Frenchtown Chapel, the Baptist "church" at the Haven of Rest. Was more perturbed than I thought I would be, although I half-expected her to do just that since her wonderful Pastor Beth was the one who got her out of The Shelter. (Lydia Pollyanna later told me—with a straight face—that she did not reject the Catholic faith by becoming a Baptist because it was perfectly fine to be both Catholic and Baptist since Jesus is the leader of both churches. And it goes without saying that I would love to get Jesus's opinion on the matter.)

Realization du jour: That the failures of the black race shouldn't be measured solely by the poverty factor. It should rather be measured by the mindless TV shows we waste our brains on, the vulgar music we listen to, our tendency to turn everything into a joke as if we could laugh away our troubles, the dropout rates of our students, the high black-on-black crime rates in our neighborhoods, the epidemic of HIV, obesity, drug abuse and devil-may-care pregnancies in our communities, the poorly-written books that we read when we do read, the lack of intellectual and spiritual curiosity in our people, the unabashed lack of respect we have for each other. And these are some of the ailments plaguing black America alone. I wish I could accept my race as is, but I can't.

At STM, even though I don't really want to be here. Can't see you, God. Can't hear you. Can't feel you. Just too much noise in my head. Also in my head:

(1) Love and delusion – I told Monica before I left the hellhole that she needed to go to Alanon because she can't save an addict, and she defiantly replied that she had it all under control and that LeMec was making great progress in all areas of his life, thanks to her. The more I listen to Monica the more I realize that she too is a mirror of who I used to be, who I could still be without your help, God. Though, truthfully, Monica seems to be more in love with the thought of how much LeMec loves her than with LeMec himself.

(2) Love and education – Toussaint L'Ouverture, Napoleon Bonaparte, George Washington, Pol Pot, Idi Amin, Mahatma Gandhi, Sekou Toure, Nelson Mandela, Fidel Castro, Hugo Chávez, Lee Kuan Yew, Paul Kagame were some of the people I found myself thinking about earlier. People whose life story I wish JJ would study for one reason or another while he waits to go to school. And why was I obsessing over JP's intellect on my way to church? Because it's still eating me up that he didn't know about the massacre at the Amish school until I told him about it.

(3) Love and friendship – I finally built the nerve before the beginning of Mass to ask Jo Ellen, the wife of the guy who opens the church every morning, how long they have been married since they seem to have such great harmony between them. "Twenty-six years," she smiled,

adding that she was married to her best friend. I told her that I was happy for her because a good marriage is a gift from God, and I meant it. That was the kind of marriage that I dreamed of, but I guess I should be thankful that I have finally accepted that a good marriage wasn't in the cards for me, at least not in this lifetime. The power to create your own destiny lies in your hands was the main theme at the Nichiren Buddhism class I attended at the main library a few days ago. Sure it is.

Much more on my mind, but the 10 o'clock Mass is about to begin, and I might as well stay put since I was so out of it earlier that I can't even recall the topic of the homily.

So much is happening around me and inside me that it not only makes it hard to focus on God, it also makes it impossible to keep track of it all. Simply put, my life is moving at a faster rate than I can write. A gold mine for the writer in me, but a disaster for the part of me that is desperate for some semblance of solitude and order. Not having a single place where I could go and shut the door behind me is one of the greatest burdens I've ever bore. Had I known where my desire to do the will of God would take me, I would have never taken the call.

Grateful that I've never been in awe with physical beauty, perhaps because some of the ugliest people I've encountered early in life were beautifully packaged. I think what I am trying to say is that I am still disturbed by the article I read this morning about a certain sports-person who hasn't been on top of her game lately, and I can't help thinking that she has lost her focus as an athlete because she's trying so hard to become a beauty queen. Dear God, please let that young woman know that she didn't come into the world to be pretty, and the people whose purpose in life is to be pretty are some of the sorriest people alive, especially when the quest to remain beautiful is even more chimerical than the quest for happiness.

Grateful for an opportunity to reiterate to JP that I would have never walked away from my day job to chase a dream while he was still in high school. I think he understood, but his understanding is not enough. I need to make amends to him for all that he suffered. Also grateful that I was able to speak to him about the latest sex scandals dominating the news (Foley and Haggard). Beyond grateful that his answer was "Guidance is good" when I apologized for my overzealous attempt to drill into him the concept that not every fantasy that popped into his head should be carried out just because he lives in a culture that is bent on self-gratification, irrespective of the consequences. Definitely not grateful that I had to ask him for money to buy a phone card. Dear God, do you have any idea what it feels like to have to beg your own child for money?

Grateful that I've always been blessed with the ability to self-analyze and the willingness to self-correct, even when I didn't have a relationship with God, which makes it even harder for me to understand The Shameless. I haven't seen Betty-Lou at The Shelter in weeks, but there she was sitting at a computer next to me at the main library this afternoon, and flashing me that beautiful smile, while she gushed about being pregnant again, and how she prays daily that she carries the baby full term because her husband wants a large family. And where are they staying? With friends. But her husband was just offered "a very good dry cleaning job" and in the name of Jesus they should be in their own apartment by Christmas. An article I read a week or two ago came to mind as she spoke. From what I recall, the government wanted the states that applied for federal abstinence-education money to also include young adults in their programs and many experts found the government's attempt to intrude in the sex life of young people objectionable. But if the government ends up paying the price when you show up on its doorstep nine months later with a baby that you can't provide for, shouldn't it have the right to put its nose in your sex life?

10:08 a.m. – Goodbye, *Tallahassee Democrat*. Hello again, *Washington Post*. Currently sitting in front of a computer on the second floor of Strozier reading washingtonpost.com (why didn't I think of that earlier?) and was pretty much over the moon until I read the headline about gay marriage in South Africa. Hundreds of black people die of AIDS related diseases in South Africa every day, not to mention the multitude of black women and black girls being raped in that country yearly. Couldn't South Africa aim at being the first country in Africa to create a society black women worldwide could be proud of? Wonder how much money was poured into the coffers of the South African Parliament by the gay rights movement in order for them to pass the bill. (None of this is to say that I have a problem with gay marriages in the States; Africans simply have more pressing priorities. And with regard to the sham trial that took place in South Africa a year prior to the publication of this book, I feel under obligation to add that it would also be nice if South Africa would aim at being the first country in Africa to create a society that doesn't let affluent men get away with murder, a society that Reeva Steenkamp would have been proud of.)

4:04 p.m. – In the magazine section on the first floor of Strozier, and I just finished reading the *Time* article on God vs. Science that Monsignor Kerr spoke about in his homily this morning. Grateful I have no desire to waste my time arguing with anyone about the existence of God, nor do I have any intention to ask anyone to follow my path since the plan God has for me is not necessary the plan that God has for them . . . the rain is already here, moments after I told myself that I should go check in early just to avoid getting caught in it. Oh, well.

9:58 p.m. – A Shelter staff is here at last to turn off the lights and Monica and Marvy are hugging and kissing because Mr. ShelterDirector will be taking Marvy to the airport early tomorrow morning—sans Monica. The *Time* article is still on my mind. Americans want it all, it says: MRIs and miracles. Grateful that my expectations are on miracles, not MRIs. And even if Richard Dawkins were to be right about God being the biggest delusion of all, I would still prefer to be deluded by my mistaken beliefs about you, God, than by man's illusions of truth.

Cannot believe that Lydia Pollyanna who showed up at the "Booked for Lunch" event at the main library at noontime, just like I expected her to do, said nothing when Ben Green, author of *Before His Time: The Untold Story of Harry T. Moore, America's First Civil Rights Martyr*, told the audience—more than once—that Charlie Crist's 370-page report on the Moore Case is "crap."

Cannot believe that Lydia Pollyanna continued to keep quiet when Ben Green, an instructor at Florida State, stated that the *Tallahassee Democrat* is so enamored with Charlie Crist that it opted to completely ignore his side of the story when he, the biographer of Harry Moore, pointed out that Charlie Crist could not have possibly solved the Moore Case because the guy who purportedly confessed to the crime in 1956 died in 1952.

Cannot believe that Lydia Pollyanna remained mute and kept her phony smile in place when Ben Green went on to say that he's very concerned about the accuracy of historical records because he doesn't want the public to keep believing that Charlie Crist did, in fact, solve the Moore Case when the whole investigation of the cold case was made for political gains. Yet the same Lydia Pollyanna had the audacity to come up to me at the end of the lecture and said, "You only know about the Moore case because I told you about it." I impishly smiled in response.

Cannot believe that Claralynn, who has been on a crack-fueled rampage all evening, had the gumption to make it known at dinner time that she "only do white women" because she does not like black women. (Thank God this black woman refused to shake her self-loathing, negrophobic, Uncle Tomish hand when she had her Jesus mask on.) At any rate, the white women at the inglorious table smiled. Some coyly, others boldfacedly, Claralynn being such a stunning example of what is expected from a dumb black woman. The only saving grace is that Claralynn later got into an argument in the back room with Shelter staff, and the police was called because she refused to leave the premises on her own. And what did Monica say when Claralynn, escorted by TPD, walked through the front room on her way out? "I love you, Claralynn. I'll miss you."

Bliss du jour: Noticing that all of the pretty FSU girls who performed at the union at noontime during a homecoming event by the black sororities were wearing their own hairs (no weaves, no wigs, not even any braids).

Decision du jour: To stop being so hard on myself when I can't keep up with the daily writing. Hard to believe that recording my life would turn out to be almost as strenuous as writing *Out of the Trenches*. Dear God, please help me trust that I am not wasting my time. Please.

Disbelief du jour: Reading that Congress has approved over $500 billion for the War on Terror since 2001, yet the military still needs more. How can the decision of one man to go to war cost so much when that money could have been used for nation-building right here in America.

Anxiety du jour: According to the seven-day forecast, it's going to be so cold in Tallahassee next week that it may snow. The libraries will be closed both Thursday and Friday for the Thanksgiving holiday, and I have no intention to go spend my days at the Day Center or at The Chain of Parks. What am I going to do?

Bafflement du jour: Being told by Monica that she didn't say "I'll miss you" to Claralynn last night. All she said was: "I love you, Claralynn. God bless you." She also swore that she never heard Claralynn make odious comments about black women. I wonder how long it will take the experts to classify selective memory as a mental illness.

Hilarity du jour: Sharon and I were talking about pathological liars, and Monica couldn't pass up a chance to share her experience on the subject. In a few words, one of Monica's children became a pathological liar during her first year in college, but Monica was able to help her heal once she realized that the compulsive lying began when Pluto entered the girl's twelfth house.

Regret du jour: Agreeing to go see *Borat* when JP called out of the blue to ask if I wanted to go to the movies with him and Angie. The title of Jimmy Carter's book, *Our Endangered Values: America's Moral Crisis*, repeatedly came to mind as I forced myself to sit through the whole scandalous thing until its stomach-turning ending just to see what all the marvelous movie reviews were about. Judging from the popularity of this movie, one almost has the impression that "Endangered" is too mild of a word to describe what's happening to America's value system lately.

Gratitude du jour: That I didn't get all bent out shape after reading Dan Allender's opinion on people who pin all their hopes on winning the lottery in his book *To Be Told: Know Your Story, Shape Your Future*. Only because winning the lottery has never been a dream of mine, just an easy way I think you, God, will use to provide me with the money that I need to carry out your will since OOTT was rejected by agents alone over one-hundred times. Even more grateful to have been reminded of my "real name" after Dan Allender said that people call us by a certain name, but that God has a different name for us. The relentless setbacks of the past few years have rendered me so weary of the present and so pessimistic about the future that I am more often than not unable to feel the presence of God, much less see his fingerprints in the book of my life. But I am still able to remember my real name because Joséphine was the name I believe God wanted me to have since my late aunt Thérèse dreamed that my mother was pregnant with a girl who should be named Joséphine even before my mother knew she was pregnant. Also grateful to know that Chrisnel is not my "real" middle name, in spite of being the name I officially go by, for it is simply the name I got stuck with after a mistake was made on my birth certificate. I also thank you, God, for the wisdom to stop viewing my entire existence as a mistake just because my name was a mistake and my parents were not exactly thrilled by my birth.

Shelter drama galore:

- Z'Laitah has finally emerged from her latest hibernation, still refuses to speak to most people, including Monica, but has formed an instant friendship with a new fruitcake who recently landed at The Shelter straight from the Caribbean. Actually, the Caribbean fruitcake claims that she has been living in America for almost two years, but has been going from shelter to shelter because she didn't want to live with relatives and their stultifying household rules.

- Spookipoo, my new hellmate in bed 5, is awake and sober this evening and three members of the White Shameless Club were sitting on her bed when I came in, and the meeting of the white Shameless mind is still going on over an hour later because they decided to reconvene after dinner. What's all the hoopla about? Spookipoo and her boyfriend, who are "in desperate need of a change of scenery," finally found "a cool place" to move to after several arduous days of online research: a homeless shelter in Grand Junction, Colorado. And they're leaving as soon as they save enough money since they would like to do some traveling before they settle down.

- "Welcome home!" were the words a high-spirited Sharon used to greet me when I came in this evening, and I had to find a delicate way to ask her to never say those words to me again because The Shelter will never be my home. Sharon later told me that LeMec is always making fun of Monica behind her back, and openly admits that he's only "playing" with her. I wondered if I should warned Monica, but quickly reminded myself that such a spiritually mature woman surely knows what she's doing. Sharon also revealed that she finds it hard to talk to Monica sometimes because she doesn't understand "the different language" that Monica speaks. Did I mention that Monica speaks of chakras almost as often as I speak of the pointlessness of antidepressants?

- A whole lot more to record, but I've been writing all day and my wrist and fingers are sore. Shelter drama actually began at 3:15 a.m. when the fire alarm went off. It was a false alarm and everybody in the front room was back asleep within minutes, but I stayed awake . . . The Caribbean fruitcake is still talking to Z'Laitah, and she's now telling the story of how she was found sleeping in a stranger's car and the nice people in town collected money and placed her in a nice motel for two nights, then the Salvation Army took over and gave her a bus ticket to leave town. The moral of the story: Being homeless forced her to let go of her foolish pride. Do I need to add that I am tempted to put up a sign that says: *I'd rather be a proud fool than a parasitical rolling stone.*

- BigBodyPartVilda was seen with her shirt up and fondling her breasts in The Shelter's backyard, and they can't stop talking about it. Monica said she once saw BigBodyPartVilda "engaging in obscene behaviors" in a fast-food restaurant, and Deanna opined that BigBodyPartVilda behaves that way because she's mentally ill. I beg to differ, but I don't really care. To be honest, I try not to look at her. (I am sharing a cage, um, a room with BigBodyPartVilda in Mental Torture Chamber No. 2 as I rewrite this book in November 2009 after Mr. ShelterDirector decided to do an impromptu "bed switch" a month ago. Shelterqueen was moved back to the front room, of course.) They also can't stop talking about Sabine who is rumored to have passed out on the streets, and is now back in rehab. I hate to say this, but I no longer feel sorry for Sabine. There is a solution to alcoholism and it's called: Alcoholics Anonymous. The program does not work for everyone, that's for sure. But it will work for anyone willing to work the 12 Steps, and that's a guarantee.

Feeling mentally and physically ill after reading another letter from Lulu. Grateful for the $30 she sent, as well as the beautiful art work my Patoutou made just for me, but wish that she didn't tell me that she's now taking a nursing assistant course, given that it's the chief occupation women with our background seem to be drawn to in this country. Of all the people who entered my life these past few years, Lulu has been the only one who has stood by me unwaveringly in word and in deed, and I feel like a fool to have believed for so long that I would be in a position to finance her college education, too, someday. I am not a sex slave in Asia or a war refugee in Africa, but my life hurts more than words could say, and I don't find it worth living.

5:17 a.m. – "What are you studying?" Mr. Aloof just asked me on his way to give one of the women sleeping in the dining room a wake-up call. I stared at him for a moment, not knowing what to say before the truth forced itself out of my mouth, "I am not studying. I am writing." He smiled and said, "Oh," as he walked away. "Oh," I stupidly repeated to myself in frustration. As silly as this may sound, I have more privacy sitting at The Chain of Parks than I have at The Shelter, and would have definitely moved to South Florida and live on the streets if I were a man. And what did I dream about? Of my children eating cookies for breakfast because I didn't have money to feed them. And of Ex-Husband promising to bring us his leftovers after I saw him eating a fancy meal in a four-star restaurant.

10:23 a.m. – Sitting on a bench in the lobby of the College of Medicine where I've been since about 8:30 because it was too cold to walk all the way to TCC after I left St. Thomas More. The only upside is that I had plenty of time to read the long article about Angola that I printed out from nytimes.com yesterday. Yet so much was said (and implied) about the Angolan government's incapability to self-govern in spite of the country being rich in oil and other natural resources (and of China's alarming ascendancy in Africa), that I won't go into details except to say that I am feeling as impotent as Monica must have felt the other night. Going to walk to TCC now since the sun is out and I am meeting JP there at noon. Besides, I need to clear up my head. And a long walk will help, I hope.

5:44 p.m. – Just arrived at the main library and have so much to record that I don't quite know where to begin. (a) JP finally took me to his apartment, and my son lives in one of

Tallahassee's ghettos: people hanging on street corners, music blaring from parked cars, sheets being hung as curtains, no grocery stores nearby, the whole nine yards. (b) Angie acted even more strangely in my presence and my first thought was to paraphrase St. Francis by asking you, God, to help me understand her, though in retrospect, I think I already have a pretty good understanding of her. (c) On our way to his apartment from TCC, JP pointed to an apartment building right behind FSU Stadium and my heart literally sank when he said that it was where ExRoommate lived, basically in my backyard given that I spend more time on FSU campus than I spend anywhere else in Tallahassee. Too discouraged to write another word.

The main topic in the dining room from hell at the moment: Kramer. The black Shameless are having a fit over Michael Richards's use of the N-word, yet Ninabelle was calling Lavermine an old nasty nigger around 5:30 this morning and no one had a problem with it. The main topic on my mind at the moment: Z'Laitah. To sum up, Z'Laitah is not at The Shelter tonight because Z'Laitah has been hospitalized. This woman is just too smart to be mentally ill, God. A brain like hers that is good with science and math could have done so much work for you, much more than I could ever do. Wish that I didn't call her crazy a few weeks ago. Who knew it was possible to feel so bad after being proven right.

PS: Sabine is back from rehab and is behaving *comme si de rien n'était.* "*Bien merci,*" she curtly replied when I asked how she was doing. Next time I won't ask.

Grateful for the courage to have an honest conversation with JP about Angie when he met me at the bus terminal to give me the key to his apartment since he'll be leaving early tomorrow morning to go spend Thanksgiving with her family. "What do you think will happen to my relationship with you if my mere presence makes her so uncomfortable?" I asked. He laughed and said that all young people feel a certain level of uneasines around their friends's parents, and that Angie will over time "chill out" once she gets to know me. I quashed the impulse to reply that it didn't look like Angie wanted to get to know me anytime soon. Also grateful that JP brought "My Boyz" back to mind when he added that I am the only parent his closest friends, Jeremiah, Akai and Keith, felt at ease around because I was always in their faces just like I was in his. God, please help me trust that you will give me the financial means to educate those boys, too, if need be. And please keep them far away from the jails of America whose ravenous mouth is always ready to swallow our black boys and turn them into what society expects them to be. (I honestly did not realize that "My Boyz" are no longer boys until JP told me in the spring of 2010 that Keith, who had joined the Navy, is now a married man with a baby girl on the way.)

Grateful that I've always done my best not to repeat my mother's mistakes, though I didn't always succeed. (Likewise grateful that I wasn't cussed with my father's sins.) "You were fifteen when you had him and you're upset that he has a baby at seventeen?" one black Shameless just said to another while they wait to see the nurse. "I am not upset that he has a baby at seventeen," the boy's mother clarified. "I am upset that he put his name on the birth certificate without giving the baby a DNA test because his baby mama is a slut who even slept with his best friend." Are they serious? What happened to the notion of expecting your children to fare better in life than you did? Even if I had given birth to my children at fifteen, I would have made sure that they know long before puberty that I was not going to sit back and watch them become teenage parents. Even if I had conceived my children with a serial killer, I would have made sure to tell them, daily if necessary, that while evil may run in their bloodline, they do not have to become evil, and that their whole purpose in life may just be to challenge and overcome evil.

Grateful I don't make it a habit to stand in front of a mirror and lament over how much weight I have gained. "I hate fat!" Monica *unlovingly* said to herself a few minutes ago as she assessed her midsection. She ignored me when I commented that she has a very nice figure for a woman her age, but she did start a conversation with another blonde whose biggest problem is that she's now "triple digits." And it took all I got not to tell Miss Triple Digits that she would not have to whine about looking so much older if she would only put on eight more pounds.

Grateful I stood my ground when Sharon pretended to be very disappointed after I told her that I did not want to go to the movies with her and her husband and Sparky over the weekend. I won't be going with them to that restaurant near Lake Ella, or at Annie's on Fourth Avenue (Annie Johnson of Project Annie) for a free Thanksgiving meal either. It may have taken me forty-four years to accept it, but my mother is right: *Qui se ressemble, s'assemble.* The average guest at The Shelter has been to jail a number of times, and I have no desire to be seen with any of them on Tallahassee's streets, Thanksgiving or no Thanksgiving.

Question du jour: It came to me while taking a shower that overcoming my fear of the future may just be a greater gain than winning the jackpot. Am I growing spiritually or simply rationalizing my disappointments and failures?

Sadness du jour: Being told by Monica, who has started to do volunteer work at the Haven of Rest, that Chelsea prematurely gave birth to a healthy baby boy a few days ago, but has gotten so sick since that she may not make it out of the hospital.

Reminder du jour: The shame of being homeless drives me to keep my distance even from people whose affection I have appreciated most of my life. Forced myself to call Joline back since I just about ran out of excuses (JP left me his phone), but our conversation was effortful and dull not because she has changed, but because I have changed.

Exhilaration du jour: Shelterqueen and the Caribbean fruitcake got into an argument and Shelterqueen asked her to get out of The Shelter and go back to her country. To which the Caribbean fruitcake replied: "Me am passenger in Shelter. You there twelve years. You need to go." (Little did I know, then, that I, too, would some day become a source of derision for staying too long at The Shelter.)

Relief du jour: That my old journals are in ExRoommate's apartment, not in a faraway landfill as I feared. I nearly went into heart failure when I could not locate the carry-on at JP's this morning. *What would be the point of going through so much shit if I can't even write a book about it?"* I thought as I dialed up Angie's number, which JP thankfully answered. And, no, I have no plan to write a memoir from memory; memory can't always be trusted.

Flashback du jour: Being told by a guy in OA to let him know when I am done writing OOTT because he knows a few agents who work with "colored writers." "Do I fit your profile of a colored writer?" I wanted to ask, but I told myself that he will soon realize that he was a fool to pigeonhole me when he reads the novel. Will he ever read the novel? (He will not. Because it came to me while editing this book that OOTT was simply a testing ground for *Homeless in Tallahassee*, the original title of this book, and that I no longer have the desire to see it in print. What's more, on a scale of one to ten, I am merely a five as a novelist.)

Gratitude du jour: (a) For a peaceful day in JP's cold and dark apartment. My mind needed a rest. (b) For the fact that I didn't overeat today. Suffice to say that the primary topic at the dining room table was how much food they all ate, and how many gifts they received (mostly used winter jackets and blankets). Most bafflingly, there wasn't a trace of melancholy in the air on a day when most people try so hard to be with their loved ones. (c) That my heart rate didn't even quicken when a drunk followed me for two blocks on my way to JP's this morning (I left The Shelter at 4 a.m., the earliest one can check out, because I was determined not to wake up with The Shameless.) (d) For the ability to listen to the radio again, and thank goodness Star 98 plays the same kind of music as WASH-FM.

2:07 p.m. – Back from taking a walk in JP's neighborhood. About seventy degrees out, yet the window in the living room is still damp, which explains why the apartment is full of mold and smells like a basement. The people who own and manage this building deserve a slap in the face, along with a lawsuit. (The one-bedroom apartment has two windows, which barely let in any natural light, no ventilation of any kind, not even in the kitchen, and no heat.)

7:10 p.m. – Still in shock over the big hug a magnanimous Z'Laitah gave me when I came in around 6:30 while telling me that "all is forgiven." Dear God, because I feel sorry for the woman doesn't mean that I want to be her friend, but that's not the point. The rumor mill went into overdrive the day Z'Laitah went to "the hospital," but I surmised that she had a psychotic episode. Well, to hear Z'Laitah say it, she only suffers from depression and is being told by Monica as we speak that she can be healed through astrology.

8:34 p.m. – Done with the reading of *Teresa of Avila: The Progress of a Soul*, and once again I found myself wondering if being so indifferent to the standards with which the world measures success, whether material or spiritual, is a plus or a minus. I just don't understand the significance of raptures and levitations. Can any of these things find a cure for malaria, or AIDS, or tuberculosis, or the myriads of other diseases that afflict the bona fide indigents of this world? Feed hungry children? Supply clean drinking water? Educate the illiterate? Provide job training—and job opportunities—to the unskilled? Grow trees on eroded lands? Build roads? Heal broken spirits? Restore confidence in God's mercy? That said, I nonetheless thank you, God, for forcing me to take a deeper look at St. Teresa of Avila, a woman who played such an important role in the life of St. John of the Cross, yet to whom I didn't feel a kinship until Dr. Esposito reintroduced her to me. I am also thankful to have been reminded by Teresa of Avila that every blessing comes with its millstone. Wish I was told that in OA and AA, but then again no one would have joined the program if they knew that turning your will over to God could throw your life into such deplorable disarray. I think I finally understand why I was the only person I knew who took the 12 Steps so seriously while most people simply went to meetings and call their sponsors. Looking back, while I loved to boast in meetings that the third step was my favorite, most people readily admitted that they found it difficult to let God take complete control of their lives. Some even interpreted it as a simple decision to move on with the rest of the steps, and I used to listen to them rationalizing their fears of letting go and letting God with grinding teeth. I bet they still have their homes or even bigger ones.

8:53 p.m. – Sharon who is always bragging about her granddaughter's long blond hair just showed me a picture of the girl, and she wasn't exaggerating, her granddaughter is a cutie. On the contrary, my Patoutou has dark hair, dark eyes and dark skin, but she's a cute little girl, too. And once again I wonder whether race and religion are two of the biggest stumbling blocks that one must rise above on the journey back to you, God.

9:19 p.m. – Listening to Monica tell the story of a woman she once saw on TV who hadn't had a meal in nearly a decade, and, sure enough, not to be dependent on food is a goal that Monica herself would like to achieve (astral travel is another). Dear God, I know you know that they would throw stones at me, and understandably so, if I would show up in the developing world and tell hungry men, hungry women, and hungry children that they won't be hungry no more if they just pray a little harder.

Shelter quotes of the day:

He's a good fuck, but he ain't all that. I've had better.

Ma, I need to use the bathroom. [Don't make me hit you, girl.]

Stop talking shit. We all know you would not be able to burst a fucking grape in a fruit fight.

Honey, they don't call me Mrs. Cheddar for nothing. Wine, cheese and pussy only get better with age.

All you got to do is to go sit in the welfare office all day and force them to put you in a hotel, I bullshit you not.

I can't find my wallet. If I find out who stole it, I am going to find you on the street, and I am going to beat your ass.

I am not an alcoholic. I like to drink beers because beers are to Irish what wine is to French. [So, you're Irish now?]

I don't feel sorry for that ho. She's lucky she only got her ass whipped. The little pussy ass bitch should know better. You snitch, you die.

I don't have to shut up. I ain't nobody motherfucking bitch. [That's mighty black of you.] Say one more word, and I will go off on your ass. I promise you.

Now, this is some crazy shit. If she has money to send her Sunday clothes to the cleaners and to eat out every day, what the fuck is she doing here? Is this the best shelter in the world, or what?

So, Laura, what did you and Debra Zemmiller do today? Did you go to the library? [Yes.] Did you stay there all day to play solitaire like you did yesterday? [No, we got bored. So we went to get a few beers, then rode the buses all afternoon.]

You ain't got shit on me, bitch. I am a white woman with a black woman booty, and that's why your old man can't keep his eyes off my ass. [Keep my old man out of your mouth, heifer. Because I will get something for your monkey ass if you don't, trust and believe.]

Listening to these women alone is enough to make me want to scream my head off. The quote about snitches actually came from a pretty brunette who has been going from one shelter to the next since her parents threw her out the day after her eighteenth birthday, and the more I listen to her, the more I sympathize with her parents. On top of that, I came in early for laundry and the following was what the scrawny new blonde who also got her hair braided to please her black boyfriend told Lavermine the moment I joined the line: "She thinks she's royalty . . . there is no high-class and low-class homeless. If you were doing what you were supposed to do, you would not be homeless." To which Lavermine replied, "Girl, you could say that again. You got to have some kind of defect to end up here. You know what I'm saying?" I acted as if I didn't hear them and simply kept my eyes on the article I was reading, as I scrawled down their words. I didn't even get to do laundry because four women had already signed up by the time I made it to the desk. (Interestingly enough, only one Shelter guest ever confronted me over taking notes while she spoke, a former schoolteacher/missionary who now walks around The Shelter fighting evil spirits.)

Cannot believe that Monica didactically told me that I need to do more than get upset about the unfairness of Z'Laitah's situation, and that I need to start visualizing Z'Laitah "bathed in divine lights." Since I don't know what divine lights look like, I replied that it would be much easier for me to visualize a mentally fit Z'Laitah living a productive life and being home with her children. Monica also told me that my own life will quickly improve once I learn to become "proactive with the co-Creator." The co-Creator? She has a lot of nerves, if you ask me.

Cannot believe that being in the presence of one of the most giving persons I've ever met can cause so much discomfort. Sharon has given me so far two friendship cards, two bananas, a candy bar, a pair of brand new socks, a used but in very good condition winter jacket, a yellow rose and a box of crackers. Yet I found myself flinching when she handed me a sweater this evening perhaps because she's always talking about how nice she is, and how much attention she still gets from her husband after thirty years of marriage, and I am sniffing phoniness.

Cannot believe that I was forced to pay 78 cents plus tax for one can of cat food at a convenience store near JP's apartment because I wasn't sure at what time JP and Angie would get home and wanted to leave the cats with some extra food. Though on second thoughts, what I really cannot believe is that a neighborhood filled with black people born and raised in the United States of America is allowing itself to be exploited by immigrants who just got off the boat, so to speak, because of its astounding inability to meet the basic needs of its own residents.

Waiting for lights out with quite a bit on my mind:

(1) Earplugs – It finally dawned on me that coating my inner ears with a touch of Vaseline will help alleviate the maddening itching, and so far so good, but my ears are now aching.

(2) Chelsea – I am glad she's doing better, but do resent Labrina—who now goes to choir practice on Thursday nights yet continues to get "shitfaced" on Fridays and Saturdays—for saying that Chelsea's health only improved after she began to pray for her.

(3) Food Monster – Alive and well since yesterday. Do not feel full no matter how much I eat. A reminder that I am not that much different from Sabine, who was drunk again last night, except that I no longer succumb to the demon within on a daily basis since OA has pretty much "ruined my eating."

(4) Sharon – I am feeling some resentment toward her as well for telling everyone who was willing to listen about how much she cried over *Flicka*, the movie she went to see yesterday. The only time I've seen Sharon cry was when Lydia Pollyanna refused to return her friendship. She definitely didn't cry over Z'Laitah losing her mind, Sabine drinking herself to death, or even Chelsea. But then again, the tendency of some people to care more about animal welfare than the trials and tribulations of their fellow humans has always irked me.

(5) Jesus – Spent about an hour this afternoon, browsing through *A Skeleton in God's Closet*, a 1994 novel in which an archeologist discovered the remains of Jesus during an excavation in Israel. Never heard of the book, but saw it on a table while I waited for a computer at the main library and the title naturally got my attention. Needless to say that I laughed long and hard when one of the characters stated that Christianity created a lot of problems for

itself the moment it turned Jesus into God because there can only be one God. Judaism may have gotten a lot of things wrong (what was the point of the Flood, for instance, when the people who came after Noah were no better than the ones who preceded him?), but they got this one right. While Jesus has probably enjoyed a closer relationship with *our* Father than any other prophet, and is beyond question the world's greatest religious role model, Jesus is not God. I sometimes wish that Jesus had left a handwritten account of his earthly experience, but I would not have believed it even if he did because the all-powerful of this world are simply too sophisticated in the art of historical distortion, especially when there is a need to make their predecessors look nobler than they really were.

"Chrisnel, I like you but sometimes I don't know which part of you to like first," was what the new blonde in bed 2, whose name I cannot spell much less pronounce, told me a minute ago. And because it was the weirdest thing anyone ever said to me, I was still groping for an answer when she added: "All I am saying is just don't get old." Now that I had an inkling of where she was heading, I sucked in a breath and calmly answered that I was well aware that I can be a hard pill to swallow, but that I didn't care about the opinions of others as long as my conscience was clear. Animosity flared from her eyes, but she simply heaved a sigh and looked away. The ignoramus obviously heard me when I had said that I was having some trepidation over the possibility that two newcomers who are currently sleeping on rollaways, may inherit beds 5 and 7 when Spookipoo and Sharon leave on January 1st, and she conjectured that I didn't want the women near me because they were old. So, according to The Shameless, I hate poor people because I don't think that one should use poverty as an excuse to be the ugliest that you can be. I hate white people because I am not impressed by the way they look. I hate black people because I think that the black race is on the brink of moral bankruptcy in light of the fact that too many black people behave as if they do not have a moral code of conduct, in spite of their Jesus obsession. And now I also hate old people because I am not jumping up and down with joy at the prospect of sharing the front room with two more insane women.

PS: Guess who's back after another LCJ vacation? April. And boy is she proud of her latest stay in the big house. She's even thankful for the ten pounds she put on because she was too skinny when she got arrested. She's also thankful that one gets to relax in jail. "Three hots and a cot," she cheered. "And that's all right with me."

11:04 a.m. – At a table on the first floor of Strozier and just finished reading yesterday and today's paper and the following are worth commenting upon. (a) I never heard of racially insensitive parties before, but ghetto fabulous Halloween costume parties in which white students poke fun at people from the 'hood by wearing gold teeth, bling bling, and the like are apparently very popular on some campuses. If young and poor black Americans were more concerned with creating a better future rather than trying to distinguish themselves with silly ornaments, the opinions of the other races would not even matter. (b) Habitat for Humanity has trouble building houses in certain areas because the current residents do not want affordable housing in their neighborhoods. My first reaction was to condemn the snobbish homeowners until I remembered that the main problem with affordable housing is that they are frequently occupied by people with attitudes and behaviors the rest of society cannot afford. (c) NYPD is back in the headlines for the killing of an unarmed black man who had just attended his bachelor's party. It looks like NYPD already forgot the lessons they should have learned from Amadou Diallo and Abner Louima, but I don't want to prejudge the police when I don't have all the facts. (I must confess that I had no problems prejudging the police when JP later told me the following story, which took place in the heart of Washington, DC, the Chocolate City, of all places. In JP's version of events, two officers stopped Vladimir's car for no apparent reason one evening, ignored Vladimir when he asked why he was being pulled over, but sternly advised them to confess whether they had any weed in the car because they will go straight to jail if they don't show honesty from the get-go. There was no weed to be found, but my son and my godson had to sit on their hands on the sidewalk while the car was being searched. What infuriates me the most is that my own son was so frightened that he did not dare to ask the officers for their names and badge numbers lest they hatch up a scheme that would have sent him and his godbrother "straight to jail" since both officers seemed so resolute in their attempt to make an arrest. As a result of this incident and a handful of others that he has either experienced or witnessed, JP is still distrustful of the police years later. So, yes, I very much understand the kind of fear and rage that racist white cops can instill in the hearts of young black men, and that's why I keep talking to my son and the other young people in my life about character building, choices, racial pride, and, above all, about their responsibility to be cognizant of the image that they project, given that their actions have the power to either improve or further erode the world's perception of their race.)

11:50 a.m . – In my purple chairs, and I am so ticked off I can hardly breathe. In brief, I had just taken a seat at a computer on the second floor when this smelly and evil-looking degenerate showed up and plopped himself into a chair right next to me. I just don't understand how all this laissez-faire can be taking place in a university library. What if he goes hide in one of the restrooms and assault a female student? Some people simply have too much freedom in this country. Civil liberty rights run amok?

10:17 p.m. – "I am done. I can't take it anymore. I don't want his black ass no more. I clean my hand off him. He lied to me again. I went through that bullshit with too many motherfuckers already, and I ain't with that shit no more." Those were the lovely words Ninabelle just sputtered after one of the CS workers confirmed that her "husband" didn't check in tonight, again. There must be a reason why love is a four-letter word; it has wrecked the lives of more women than anything else I can think of.

Gratitude du jour: To have located the parish of Blessed Sacrament with its beautiful church and cute little chapel while taking a walk, which is where I ended up spending two hours in prayer and meditation late this afternoon. Also grateful that Lulu added $25 worth of minutes on my phone after I told her that I was merely using the phone as an answering machine when she had called. Still, being a charity case is not something I could ever be truly thankful about.

Perplexity du jour: A few weeks ago, I heard a black woman say that when she went to apply for cash assistance after both she and her husband got laid off, a social worker told her that she will only get help if she states on the application that she was abandoned by her husband and makes sure that he's not home when they come for their visit. Just a moment ago, I heard a white woman say that her 58-year-old mother had to divorce her father after she lost her health insurance just so she could be qualified for Medicaid. Both women think that the government's hidden agenda is to break up poor families. Hmm.

Sadness du jour: Reading the article Valerie D. White, an assistant professor in FAMU's School of Journalism, wrote in this week's *Capitol Outlook* about her student, Nefertiti Williams, whose body was found in the home she shared with four roommates on Thanksgiving Day. By all accounts, twenty-year-old Nefertiti Williams, news editor of the student newspaper, *The Famuan*, had a bright future ahead of her. Equally troubling is the fact that the family of the boy who killed her, a roommate and childhood friend, claims that he, too, was a good kid who never got into trouble before. My heart breaks for both families.

Grievance du jour: Reading an article on the exorbitant price some government employees had to pay after they blew the whistle on some agencies for the way national security issues were being handled after 9/11. While we're on the topic, I still can't get over the story I read the other day about a police chief in Winter Haven, Florida, who was forced to resign after he sent out a memo requesting his officers to stop indulging in food, booze and cigarettes because unfit cops were a liability to the city. In a world that increasingly prefers its realities to be fiction-coated in ways large and small (and where beliefs almost always trump facts), there ought to be a 12-step program for people with a predisposition to tell the truth.

Gaffe du jour: Answering "THANK GOD, NO!" when Sharon asked if JP's girlfriend was white. But why did she infer that Angie was white just because I said that the girl could have been a good match for JP if she wasn't so possessive because she's intelligent, responsible, pretty, and my maternal instinct tells me that she loves him? I went on to elucidate that I had nothing against interracial marriage as long as my son wasn't involved, but I still feel a bit awkward even after she acknowledged that she wasn't crazy about mixed marriages either because she didn't want biracial grandchildren. (This is not to say that Sharon is racist. She just has a preference for blond and blue-eyed grandbabies the same way I have a preference for a black daughter-in-law for the simple reason that I don't want my son to be perceived as one of those pitiful black men who exclusively date white women in their long-in-the-works effort to become who they wish they were but never will be.)

Woke up cocooned in a mantle of serenity and remained there all day until I made it back to the hellhole and found out that Chelsea had died. A memorial service is going to take place at the Haven of Rest on Sunday, but I don't plan to attend since I have no desire to see all the crocodile tears that will likely be shed when most of The Shameless will only be there just for the free food that will surely follow. When I told Sabine how angry I was about Chelsea's untimely death just when she was trying so hard to turn her life around, she said that she too is angry because she prayed really hard for Chelsea's full recovery, and trusted that her prayers would be answered.

One good news: ShamelessParExcellenceMotherOfFour, also known as the patron saint of shamelessness, who once told Shelter staff in a fit of rage (as her children watched) that she wishes that The Shelter burn down with all of them inside and even asked Mr. ShelterDrillSergeant to go suck his you-know-what, left The Shelter tonight, again. I heard that a church is putting them up in a motel while they wait for somebody to give them the key to a house—whatever that means. This woman's baby daddy, Mr. Pothead, actually lives with her, mind you. But he has been diagnosed with a job allergy as well, it seems. If poor women would only take a moment to think about all the misery they inflict on themselves and their children with each pregnancy, they would spend more time on their knees begging God to get them ready for motherhood by strengthening them spiritually, emotionally, intellectually, and financially. And less time with their legs open. (Granted I wasn't thinking of all of that myself when I got pregnant with my children, but I had a strong determination to give them a better childhood than I had, a husband with job security, and a mother willing to help with childcare.)

Cannot believe that I ended up in a war of words with members of the White Shameless Club after Lydia Airhead, formerly known as Lydia Blackvan, yanked the mop out of my hand when I willfully ignored her request to stop mopping. No one had a problem with me cleaning up before dinner until Lydia Airhead decided that she could no longer stand the madness in the dining room, bought herself a portable chair and now parks her lazy behind right in the middle of the room around the time I usually come in and just about forbids me to mop around her because I am disturbing her reading. I told her that she would have grown a few brain cells by now if she didn't waste so much time reading silly love stories, and that alone spurred a barrage of criticisms from the White Shameless Club. Kaycee Sourpuss even said that I was "the most condescending SOB" she has ever met, though I unambiguously sense that she mostly detests me because I just don't pay her the reverence that she clearly expects from black people.

Cannot believe that the young black woman who once told me that she would rather stay at The Shelter than at her grandmother's four-bedroom home two miles away because she wants to be her "own person" (and who is so pious that she reads "nothing but the Word") is pregnant again. Is she worried about how she's going to provide for a new child? Nope. She's just worried about how she's going to break the news to her grandmother. (This woman is barely talking to Granny these days because Granny is pressuring her to move back home to help take care of her three children and she can't do that because it would mean leaving her baby daddy alone at The Shelter since Granddaddy can't stand the sight of him. Yet to hear The Shameless tell it, the deadbeat father of five, who claims that he's been diligently looking for another warehouse job since he got fired in 1999, is only staying with her because half of her monthly check goes to support his drug addiction.)

Cannot believe that Sparky who had gone home to South Florida for the Thanksgiving weekend had the gall to tell me that his parents are so well off they have a vacation home in Italy. (He was in a huff because they refused to fork over a few hundred dollars to help him out until his financial aid kicks in next semester.) I would have been more inclined to believe Sparky if he wasn't still attending a community college four years after he moved to The Shelter. Sparky also invited me out to lunch, by the way, and I told him that I'll think about it. Why did I not say Hell To The No! (the new *expression à la mode* among The Shameless) right away? Because he also told me that he knows how to fix houses, and I may need his help one day.

Cannot believe that I've been so busy reading William Easterly's *The White Man's Burden* that I completely forgot that Tallahassee's Winter Festival, including the lightning ceremony at The Chain of Parks and the Christmas parade, took place this evening until the group of Shameless who had asked permission to stay out late came back around 9 o'clock. My own excitement du jour, however, was to read about the food for education program implemented by the World Bank in the nineties to keep girls in Bangladesh in school. A confirmation that some of my thoughts are not as farfetched as they seem because I came up with the same idea on my own, not knowing that it had already been put into practice in many parts of the world.

Cannot believe that the same Sharon who is so tickled with the fact that her granddaughter inherited her fair skin, blond hair, and blue eyes, rather than her daughter's olive skin, dark hair, and dark eyes, let slip that she grew up "feeling ugly and not good enough." Who would have guessed that the presumably optimal features that she's so proud of were not enough to endow her with self-esteem? (Nor where they able to spare her from the horrendous consequences of drinking and drugging.) I sometimes wonder who I should feel sorry for the most: the black woman with her hair issues, or the white woman with her body image (and hair) issues. If we are given a chance to reflect on our life before we take our last breath, will it even matter what we looked like on the outside?

Was hoping to go to sleep soon after lights out since the TV also goes off with the lights on Sundays when Mr. ShelterDrillSergeant is on duty (his mother, who must be watching over him from heaven since many male Shelter guests tried to beat him up over the years, didn't let him watch TV on Sunday nights), but my mind is still racing:

- Mi-Kum, who still re-applies her makeup every evening after she takes a shower, was jabbering in the dining room long after the 9:30 smoke break. She has been so nice to everyone at The Shelter, always giving them cigarettes and lending them money, yet the ogresses still give her no respect because she's Asian. She even came to talk to me at some point because I, of all people, should be able to understand her anguish. I don't. I am not a friendship seeker. Still, I told her to hang in there and not let THE AMERICAN REJECTS drive her crazy just because Lavermine was walking by.

- April was so intoxicated when she came in that Ninabelle and Labrina had to drag her to bed, yet there she was standing in the front room around 9:25, waiting for smoke break. And before I could see it coming, she was asking me to say a prayer for her husband because he's been having a really hard time in jail since one of the motherfuckers at The Shelter went to visit him and told him about her fling with a Puerto Rican dude. The fact that April seems to like me is a great mystery considering that I would not even call 9-1-1 if she were to get abducted by aliens right in front of my eyes.

- Sabine has been complaining about the clumps of hair on the floor around her bed for weeks, but I didn't realize how bad the problem was until I saw Zhouli use a nail clipper to remove more hair from her head. This woman needs so much more than The Shelter can provide. Rumor has it that she was brought here a year ago by her husband and he did not come back for her. Lizzie Licehead was also dumped at The Shelter years ago by her husband, from what I heard. (Lizzie Licehead still has lice four years later, but her scalp no longer bleeds because the nurses are now required to give her lice treatment on a regular basis.)

- I don't want to believe it, but I did hear Ninabelle, who had a miscarriage several months ago, say that she may be pregnant again. And, of course, no one saw fit to remind her that the man who supposedly got her pregnant, a crackhead with seven children whose whereabouts he doesn't know, can't hold a job for more than a week at a time. (He quit pretending to be a laborer about a year later so he could devote more time to going to jail and breeding more crack babies.) I also heard from Ninabelle's own mouth that he does smack her around now and then, but it's because he gets jealous over all the attention she gets from other men who are always going gaga over her shapely derriere. And according to many of The Shameless, the future father of eight is also a male prostitute who doesn't mind "dropping his pants and getting on all four in a heartbeat." Dear God, do I need to remind you that America does not need one more black baby in foster care?

Barely got three hours of sleep after a rather vivid dream of FirstBadChoice and me being back together, and visiting his mother. Do not understand why I keep dreaming of this man that I haven't seen in twenty-five years when I hardly ever think of him during my waking hours. "We are all vulnerable to be attacked by the forces of evil," R.B. Holmes said in his sermon yesterday. Am I being attacked by evil in my sleep? And speaking of FirstBadChoice's mother, I still regret the call I made to her years ago while doing my Ninth Step. I did not owe that woman an apology for hurting her son's pride when I got married. In fact, she owed me one for not objecting to her only son playing the field while she ruled her own husband with an iron fist. R.B. Holmes also said that "we do reap in proportion to where and how we sow." Dear God, you know and I know that this saying doesn't apply to me for I have shared my home with more people than I can recall over the years. A woman from my mother's church even gave birth to a little girl named Naomie right in my family room on the morning of July 4, 1992 while I was on the phone with 9-1-1. Nope, this you-reap-what-you-sow crap does not apply to me at all. Ironically, it's one of Kaycee Boneheaded's favorite sayings and my chest cramps every time she says it.

1:49 p.m. – Getting ready to leave Governor Square Mall. What did I do all day? Not much. Went to Mass, then walked to Borders where I spent about an hour getting acquainted with some of the books on the best-seller list, and reading the tabloids. (Why do bookstores provide seats for people to come in and read books and magazines that they're trying to sell when they're struggling to remain in business, I have no idea.) I then left Borders and walked to the mall where I spent the past two hours at a table in the food court people-watching, and reading some of the articles I printed out the past few days. Of course, I had to borrow an empty soda cup from a trash can in order to justify my presence at the table for so long . . . "Did you see a ghost?" an abrasive young man just asked, after he caught me staring at his girlfriend. "No," I said, "but I did see too much fake hair." He didn't hear me, luckily.

4:08 p.m. – At a table on the second floor of the main library while I wait for my assigned computer to become available in fifty-five minutes. Somebody got to teach the high school kids who invade this place every afternoon how to behave in libraries. One of the librarians, an older white lady who looks as if she prays daily, even hourly, for retirement day, just told three boys that the library has a one-person-per-computer policy, yet they already regrouped by the time it took me to write the above. A police officer later told me (Hello, Officer Haddon) that some of the teenagers who hang out at the gazebo also keep TPD quite busy. The teenagers, boys and girls, chase the homeless men away from the gazebo after school, then go back and forth between the library and the gazebo. And let's not forget the loud music they listen to—at the library—or the words that come out of their mouths.

8:03 p.m. – Hiding under a sheet and crying tears of rage as a result of silently mouthing "Bitch!" to Labrina after I heard her ask a new Shelter staff to force me to go sit in the dining room because I think I am too good to eat at the table with them. And to my surprise, she actually complained to Mr. Jejune when he later came up, prompting him to walk up to me and asked, "Did you call her a bitch?" And because he has the power to throw me out for calling a prostitute a bitch (I didn't even say the fucking word out loud), I answered, "Why would I call her a bitch when she's a swine?" The Shameless let out a collective gasp as if their virgin ears had never heard anything so offensive. Mr. Jejune really got worked up then, and spent the next twenty minutes (or so it seemed) demanding that I show the utmost respect to all Shelter guests, and I didn't have the guts to remind him that it wasn't too long ago that he had laughed hysterically when

Lavermine called Kaycee Sourpuss a nasty-ass bitch right in front of him. And that he had laughed even louder when another woman referred to her soon-to-be ex-husband as a no-good nigger. (For the record, The Shameless are always quick to recall the hurtful things I said to them, but somehow they always forget the things they said to me. Such as: "Just because you go sit at the library all day does not mean that you're working" when the reality is that writing this book has been more grueling —in every way—than any job I ever had.)

I finally understand why some people don't want your kind in their neighborhoods.

You're a foreigner in your own country. Real Americans do not behave like wild animals.

You can't function in your own society, which is why you're either at The Shelter or in jail.

It's hard to respect others when you don't have any self-respect, but it won't kill you to give it a try.

You don't know who I am or what I do. I don't get drunk with you. I don't get high with you. I don't share motel rooms with you. I don't get locked up with you.

You are an embarrassment to the land of your birth and should be shipped to a special island of your own. Illegal immigrants are more of an asset to America than you'll ever be.

I was somebody before I landed at The Shelter, and I will be somebody again after I leave The Shelter. On the other hand, you are nowhere. You have always been nowhere. And you are on your way to nowhere.

It's well past midnight, but I am too livid to think about sleep. Spent the past few hours ruminating on all of the above. The way I see it, I won't have to speak to these

BITCHES ever again. I'll just post one of my signs. (My vitriolic notes to Shelter staff and Shelter guests have earned me quite a reputation over the years.)

Decision du jour: To stop wasting the few dollars that I have on lottery tickets. I am tired of having my hopes crushed twice a week even when I don't play. Gambling isn't even one of my vices.

Irritation du jour: Trying to find a clean spot to lay out a sheet at the Genevieve Randolph Park because it was practically littered with dog shit. Dear God, please don't let irresponsible dog owners in Tallahassee turn The Chain of Parks into a dog latrine.

Revulsion du jour: Seeing BigBodyPartVilda at the Cherokee Park with her pants down and her hands between her legs. I once heard her joke that she was pretending to be crazy in order to get a check and I believe her because she has always struck me more as a pervert than a nut.

Gratitude du jour: For the courage to be myself at The Shelter, rather than try to metamorphose the abnormal into the normal just to fit in. (In the end, I was the most reviled Shelter female guest, and The Shameless routinely referred to me as "THE SNITCH" because of my tendency to call on Shelter staff whenever the shamelessness gets out of hand. In return, I invented a half-crazed nephew who does not eat anything cold and who will feel quite honored if he has to come to Tallahassee with his crew to avenge his favorite auntie.)

Amusement du jour: My first encounter with Brother Jed. The man seems confident of his ability to bring young people closer to God by traveling from one college campus to the next to preach the Gospel when all he's doing, at least on the campus of Florida State, is providing the students with free entertainment. Though I definitely wasn't amused when I heard a few of the male students ask Brother Jeb to tell more "sex stories," and was more than appalled when one of the most abhorrent ones went on to ask, "Is it okay to take a picture of Satan fucking Jesus in the ass?"

Consternation du jour: $2.3 trillion dollars is what the West spent on foreign aid in Africa the past five decades, according to William Easterly, yet not much has changed. He also addressed the failure of aid agencies to control the AIDS epidemic, though I never understood why the West made it their business to control the spread of HIV in Africa to start with. If Africans are unwilling to slough off some of the self-destructive aspects of their culture—**LIKE EVERY OTHER THRIVING SOCIETY HAD TO DO IN ORDER TO CREATE THE QUALITY OF LIFE THAT THEY ENJOY TODAY IN VIEW OF THE FACT THAT CIVILIZED SOCIETIES ARE CRAFTED, NOT MATERIALIZED OUT OF NOWHERE, OR EMBEDDED IN THE DNA OF AN EXCLUSIVE GROUP OF PEOPLE**—shouldn't they have the prerogative to pay for the consequences of their actions? I do not understand why the West is so eager to save Africans from economic hardship either when they know perfectly well that Africa will always remain a continent of beggars if they don't stop enabling African governments. Africa did exist before all the handouts, didn't it? Besides, everyone with half a brain knows that Western generosity is not nearly as high-minded as it seems. In part because of all the conditions that are attached to foreign aid, but mostly because what really matters to the West, it keeps for itself and only gives away its crumbs. If the Bible was such a gem, Westerners would have kept it under lock and key. (These words, too, came back to bite me after January 12, 2010, but I chose to leave them here.)

"I don't want you to admire me," Z'Laitah just said after I told her how proud I was of her recent efforts to become more cordial. "I want you to like me." Too sick with another cold to elaborate. In the interim, the rich Republican from D.C. (she's also the daughter of a congressman) who is temporarily staying at The Shelter while her dream house is being built in one of Washington's wealthiest suburbs, just walked through the front room yelling, "I need to see more white people," a favorite outcry of hers. "Then get out of The Shelter and go find yourself more," I offered. "Go back to where you came from," she retorted. "Go back to St. Elizabeths. They've been looking for you," I fired back. Sabine's reaction to all of that: "I can't handle so much happiness." If I only had her sense of humor.

Grateful that I was not in The Shelter's driveway when LeMec came to look for me. According to Sharon, Monica told LeMec that she was fed up with his behavior and plans to leave for South Florida soon, and he spent the afternoon pleading his case with her closest Shelter friends with the hope that they will put in a good word for him.

Grateful for the courage to admit that I feel fear today, in spite of all the trust in God's providence that I've been experiencing the past few days. People from the program often said that faith and fear cannot exist in the same person at once. They lied. Or maybe they just didn't know better since many of them also believed that when God wants you to do something, he makes it easy for you.

Grateful for an intellectually stimulating day mostly spent in front of a computer on the second floor of Strozier reading about autocracy, kleptocracy, despotism, proletariat, imperialism, and neocolonialism. Reading *The White Man's Burden* opened up a whole new chapter in my life. It also brought back to the surface issues that I would prefer not to think about, such as the fact that I owe the World Bank Credit Union $15,000 in credit card bills and a home equity loan. Dear God, please remind me that you sometimes destroy us in order for a stronger and smarter version of us to emerge. Please.

Grateful for the perfect timing that allowed me to hear the following story right from the horse's mouth because I would have had trouble believing it otherwise. As said by Lavermine, a man who was about to clean the female restroom at the bus terminal refused to let her use it, but she nevertheless went in, urinated on the floor in retribution, can't stop laughing about it, and the other Shameless are laughing along. I at times wonder if these women who were born and raised in a country where the average woman can more or less carve out a decent living for herself through learning a trade at a vocational school—since a college education is not for everyone, nor does it guarantee gainful employment—were not cursed with abject poverty, ignorance, and contentment as a punishment for turning their vices into virtues.

Grateful to have noticed that the average FSU student on the third floor of Strozier spends less than two minutes on the phone, and the conversation usually ends with: "I'll call you back, I am at the library." Which prompted me to write a note to a girl who was sitting at a nearby table this morning after she made and received more than five calls in less than an hour while she plans a party for a friend. (Will not elaborate on the frustration I later experience at the Samuel H. Coleman Memorial Library, FAMU's main library, but I hope that FAMU students take the hint. And with the best interest of FAMU students in mind, I also hope that FAMU officials enact new school policies that would ban the use of cell phones and MP3 players inside Coleman. And video watching. And online chatting. And singing. And rapping. And socializing. And I am dead serious. And I won't even say a word about "all the indecent booty-shaking," to quote a nice religious lady from The Shelter, that went on at the homecoming parade. And, yes, I am aware that quite a few young men who spend a lot of time at Coleman are not FAMU students. In fact, one of them is sitting right next to me, Facebooking, and laughing out loud, as I write this on August 27, 2010. And I could have sworn that I saw a male Shelter guest at a computer on the 4th floor when I came in, but I told myself that I was seeing things and went to look for another computer, rather than face the fact that the homeless invasion of Coleman Library is well under way.)

Was brutally haunted by all the voices in my head all day:

The voice of fear.

The voice of pride.

The voice of anxiety.

The voice of wishful thinking.

The voice of doubt and despair.

The voice of resentment and anger.

The voice of familial and racial obligation.

The voice of past and present relationships.

The voice of history, religion and the news media.

The voice of guilt and shame (neurotic and earned).

The voice of Shelter's guests' imbecilities and madness.

Dear God, how will I ever be able to recognize Your voice among all the above?

It's happy hour again in Satan's dining room, and Lavermine is now talking about the day she got super high and decided to pluck out her eyebrows. "I was insanely different," she guffawed. "But I was original." Conversely, I am still more than a little peeved two hours after a CS worker who was sitting at the desk at check-in time told me that she saw me walking on West Pensacola Street again, then clumsily added, "Is that what you do all day to keep busy?" As if I were a lunatic of some sort who walks up and down the streets of Tallahassee as my pastime. I could have told her that she most likely sees me when I am either on my way to or from TCC, but I didn't want to give The Shameless any ideas. Monsignor Tugwell said in a homily the other day that we need to learn to replace anger with humility, kindness and patience. And I couldn't help thinking that anger doesn't always deserve the bad rap it gets, that anger can even be useful at times . . . "Darling, according to this chart, you are an extraordinary woman!" Monica, who has been painstakingly studying Z'Laitah's astrological chart, just roared. *Sure she is*, I thought, after Z'Laitah replied that she would prefer to discuss the matter in private. E*xtraordinarily insane*. Okay, I know I am being mean because Z'Laitah has been very nice to me lately. But why do I have this feeling that she's just restraining herself before the big explosion? Cannot stand it, God. Cannot stand it at all. Do you have any idea what if feels like to live with the crazies when I am not crazy? (Dear Dr. Holland, *Weekends at Bellevue* is a good read, but I hope that you don't really believe that we're all mentally ill because the truth of the matter is that while it is a fact that none of us is immune to mental illness, there is a difference between someone who has emotional problems—most of us do—and someone who has a mental illness. A huge one.)

12:42 a.m. – Was awaken shortly after midnight by Sabine wailing "God, please don't take me" over and over. Monica tried to wake her up to no avail, and Z'Laitah commented that it was a pity that Sabine was so tormented in her sleep. I once heard Kaycee Boneheaded say that Sabine has a lot of nightmares because she's afraid to die. Maybe she was telling the truth for a change. But then again, I also heard Kaycee Boneheaded say that Sabine's rich husband visited her at The Shelter not long ago and Sabine felt so much shame that she didn't tell anyone about it, yet Sabine assured me that she hasn't seen her ex-husband in over ten years. On another front, my bottom teeth have been sore for days and were hurting so much that I gave myself a quick dental exam minutes ago. Diagnosis: tooth abscess. Dear God, I know I don't need to tell you that I have no dental insurance and 23 cents to my name.

2:09 a.m. – Spent the past hour reading about Spinoza and Leibniz with the reading light that Deanna gave me. The Bible's God is either a vindictive bully who created women as a scapegoat to be held responsible for all the weaknesses of men and to, of course, bear men's babies. Men's baby boys, to be precise. Or an impassive observer who talks a lot of crap about love when compelling evidence of his great love for humanity can't be found anywhere. The god of the philosophers is so complex that he is incomprehensible to a large extent, unless one has a Ph.D. in abstract thinking. Still, I am delighted to have been reacquainted with Baruch de Spinoza through *The Courtier and the Heretic: Leibniz, Spinoza, and the Fate of God in the Modern World* for the more I read about Spinoza, the more normal I feel, in spite of all his extraneous talks about essence and substance, attributes and modes. A glaring example of how too much thinking can lead even the best of minds to a whole lot of absurd thoughts.

8:09 p.m. – Another argument just broke out in the big bathroom. Kaycee Sourpuss let the N-word slip out of her xenophobic mouth again because somebody "sprayed" one of the toilet seats with urine and she characteristically assumed that "it must be the work of a nigger." I can't stand Kaycee Sourpuss myself and also wish that somebody would "slap the dogshit out of her," but when will black people in America start demanding from each other the same level of respect that they demand from white people? A conversation I had some time ago with a young man at Union Station in D.C. just came to mind. "They use it to make us feel bad, but we use it as a term of endearment," I remember him saying when I had asked if he knew the history behind the N-word after I had heard him use it repeatedly while speaking to his friends. He went on to spell out for me the difference between "nigger" and "nigga," and I stood there thinking that the black race was even more screwed up than I thought if black people in the United States of America cannot use the brains that God gave them to come up with their own original term of endearment to address each other. (Dear Dr. Laura, shouldn't you know by now that in today's America one cannot engage in any "debate" about black culture, if one is not black. About homosexuality, if one is not gay. About the State of Israel, if one is not Jewish. About the *Ten Stupid Things Women Do to Mess UpTheir Lives*, if one is not a woman? Having said that, I must add that your response to "Jade," was way over the top, but why do intelligent 21st century women still rely on others to help solve problems that only persist because of their unwillingness to take a stand in their own lives?)

Puzzlement du jour – Kaycee Boneheaded and Pamelia are in the big bathroom talking about their long list of health issues and how they know for sure that it's the devil trying to persecute them but he's wasting his time because they were both children of God who were determined to keep on living in Jesus's name. And once again I can't believe just how skilled these spiritually comatose women are in the art of hiding behind Jesus. Do they not realize that they would not have to deal with so many obesity-related illnesses (and waste so much of taxpayers's money) if they would only ask their Creator for the desire and the strength to tame the devil within?

Ordeal du jour: Being told by Mr. ShelterDrillSergeant to get out of the dining room if I can't sit properly at the table like everyone else. (I had placed a chair by the entrance of the shithole since his new rule is that you won't be served dinner if you're not sitting down.) I did walk out, but I was so angry that I was tempted to snatch a plate of food just to throw it at him. (This quagmire came to an end when Mr. ShelterDirector decided to let The Shameless eat outside if they so wish, and thank goodness Shelter staff didn't care whether I sat at one of the picnic tables or not. Well, one did. But I put him back in his place with a note.)

Enragement du jour: "You don't have to tell me, I know you are." And that was the unforgettable (and unpardonable) answer that the new wino from Chicago gave to Lavermine after the baldheaded monster broadcasted that people who really care about her know that she's "all bark and no bite." Miss Wino must have forgotten that Lavermine was making fun of her pimples daily, as well as her uncanny aptitude for ass-kissing, until she decided to become friend with the evildoer out of pure gutlessness.

Indignation du jour: Being snappishly told by Mr. Nasty Librarian (he knows who he is) to not worry about it "because it's free" when I asked him why doesn't the main library set up its printers to print double-sided. I don't have a habit of crying racism in every negative encounter with a white person, but there was just something about his demeanor that makes me wonder if his reply would have been different if I were a white woman. After all, I know he knows that there is no such thing as free paper.

Amusement du jour: Reading online that a tooth abscess is one of the most painful things a human being can go through and that left untreated the infection can spread to other parts of the body, the brain prominently, and be fatal. I had to laugh because not only I am still alive, I think the little surgery I performed on myself in the bathroom and repeated twice afterward must have been successful since the swelling is gone and the soreness has receded.

Awkwardness du jour: Stripping off before Mass in a futile attempt to avert another hot flash. My sweater and turtleneck got so hot you would think they just came out of the dryer. Still curious, but no longer amused. (I now take my layers off in the parking lot during the winter months, and am so cold by the time I enter the church that I don't have to worry about hot flashes.)

Hunch du jour: That I am, in all probability, getting exactly what I deserve from life since I don't believe in free grace, free salvation, free freedom, or free anything. Put another way, I am, I hope, earning my place at your table, Dear God. And I trust that you will give me the wisdom to make the most of my money miracle when you decide to grant it.

Stupefaction du jour: Listening to a board member of The Shelter say to *la vieille chouette* that he's overjoyed to see her because she has "such a beautiful and bubbly spirit." Lavermine has lost some of her Shelter sovereignty, but she indisputably remains a Shelter darling.

Finally awake only because I spent the past hour with my head on a table on the first floor of TCC library, napping. Still tired, but at least my brain is working again:

(1) Agonizing expectations – Just spotted a book titled *How Expectancies Shape Experience* on a book cart, and I don't need to read any of the case studies to accept as true the concept that people, in effect, tend to experience what they do expect to experience in practically every area of life. Yet I can't help thinking that the same cannot be said for me because my expectations literally turned my life into a living hell.

(2) Daughterly guilt – Called Mama on my way here. Her headache of the last few days has subsided, but I still worry. She said she did go to her cardiologist

and he looked at her as if she was going to die and was surprised that nobody came with her. She also asked if I had spoken to the kids recently because she called them over a week ago and her calls were not returned. I need to stop blaming myself for the failures of my children.

(3) Learned tactfulness – I left The Shelter around 6:15 and walked straight to TCC because I didn't feel like going to Mass, and Sparky was already waiting in front of the library when I arrived at 7:24. He said he planned to spend the next few hours in one of the private study rooms on the second floor to get ready for his last two finals. And I acted as if I didn't know that he got banned from The Shelter, is now sleeping in the woods near TCC, and keeping his belongings in his locker at the TCC gym.

(4) Pseudo reconciliation – Z'Laitah rushed to the dining room bathroom again this morning just to stop me from using it. Monica did me no favor when she put me back in touch with that woman by telling her how bad I felt when she went to the nuthouse. And speaking of Monica, Sharon told me last night that she's nursing some hard feelings toward her for talking about love yet behaving selfishly. A generous soul like Sharon most likely thinks that everyone else is selfish, but she has a point. For example, Monica once told me that I could use her phone for as long as I wanted, yet looked apoplectic when I later met her at the main library and told her I'll bring the phone back in one hour. She didn't say it, but it was clear that she was afraid that I was going to leave town with her "rare and expensive phone, which very few people can afford."

(5) Involuntary fasting – I've been so hungry that I am seriously thinking about applying for food stamps, notwithstanding my determination to never go that

route again. (I could go to The Shelter for lunch when I am not on TCC campus, but would rather stay hungry than see that hideous backyard and its execrable occupants in the middle of the day.) How will I be able to explain to a case worker that I left my good job at the World Bank, to quote my mother, in order to go do the will of God, and God did not provide? Hard to believe that I, whose motto used to be I KNOW GOD CAN AND WILL, have lost the assurance that my despair, my fears, my humiliations, my losses, my disappointments, my shame, my perseverance, my obedience even matter to God. Wish I were like the average believer, inclined to pin my hopes on a better life in heaven, and perfectly satisfied with a God who allegedly made his presence known thousands of years ago, yet has no problem doing a disappearing act in the here and now when millions of people go hungry daily and don't have the choice to go apply for food stamps.

(The hunger problem was solved when it occurred to me that if I stay at First Presbyterian Church until 1 p.m. on Sundays, they will, more often than not, let me take as many pastries as I want on my way out. My heartfelt thanks to Karen Celander, an ECHO volunteer who helps serve lunch once a month, for her empathy, and to the folks from Christ Presbyterian Church for their generous spirit. Still, by the end of 2010, I was so sick of eating pastries that I wanted to weep at their mere sight. I quit attending the 7 a.m. Mass around the same time since I had told some people there—with great confidence—that I didn't plan to be in Tallahassee on January 1, 2011. I had stopped showing my homeless-forever face on FSU campus, too, by then.)

7:46 a.m. – Just arrived at Strozier and guess who strolled in right behind me? Ninabelle and Darla. I hate to put it this way, but it will not come as a surprise if a shooting occurs in this library one day over a drug deal gone bad. After all, it was just a few days ago that Ninabelle was asking everybody to stay out of her business because Bekkie-Sue said that she saw her come out of a crack house in Frenchtown. The Shelter has a Day Center, a fairly big back yard, and a "rear pavilion." Those people have no business imposing themselves on this campus the way they do.

7:33 p.m. – "Your life is going to be hard," Mr. Irresistible said to me moments ago after he asked why I was skipping dinner and I answered that I prefer to go to bed hungry rather than being forced to sit at a table with people I didn't like. "You need to learn how to live with others, do you think I like my coworkers?" he added matter-of-factly. "I know how to pay for the consequences of my actions," I replied mostly out of spite since the only reason I was able to skip dinner is because Sharon used her food stamp card to buy me about $20 worth of groceries.

8:04 p.m. – Well, this is it. Monica rented a car and will be taking LeMec with her. She was scheduled to leave next week, but LeMec is suddenly so sick of The Shelter that he can't bear to spend one more day here. Z'Laitah is currently sitting on Monica's bed, saying goodbye, and Sharon and I just agreed that the charade will be over after the holidays once Monica realizes that LeMec just needed another vacation away from The Shelter. By the way, Deanna told me that LeMec "has a history of pimping women," and that even Mr. ShelterDirector warned Monica, but Monica would not listen.

8:50 p.m. – "If you don't like it here, you can leave from the same door you came in," Mr. Jejune just told me after he heard me say that it was irresponsible of The Shelter to let lice crawl all over the sink and the floor of the big bathroom, thanks to a new white Shameless who had mirthfully brushed them off her hair, given that the bathroom is located so close to the sleeping area. And what is Mr. Jejune doing as I write this? He's in the dining room laughing about how dirty women are because "the men don't have shit crawling on them." Dear God, please help me keep in mind that when life serves up lemons, writers don't make lemonade. They write books.

Wide awake at 3:36 a.m. because of another World Bank dream, the worst I've had so far. In short, I dreamed that I was trying to get permission from a security guard to enter the A building to visit Lily Wang (Lily retired from the bank long before I left, if I recall correctly, and we were both "support staff" at the M building on K Street, not at the A building . . . actually, I was just a "permanent bank temp," but that's a different story.) In any event, not only the security guard refused to call Lily to get her approval, he accused me of being a fraud and went to get a "higher-level staff" I later worked with in the A building who in essence told me that she had always heard that there were lots of lazy people in America, but that I was the first one she actually met. It's going to be a crying day.

Grateful I kept a poker face when a morose Z'Laitah turned to me moments before lights out and said something like: "You know, Chrisnel, I've been second-guessing everything lately and I want to be me again." Thank goodness she paused long enough to give me time to grab pen and paper before adding, "I am usually right on target about what my instinct tells me. I might have been cold, I might have been rude, but I was myself. Being so mindful about what other people think and feel is incapacitating." She went on to say that she was tired of bending over backwards to understand others because it was "a kind of hypocrisy" that she was "maneuvering" herself into since the reality is that she doesn't trust people, never has and never will, doesn't care if she establishes a rapport with them, and will no longer allow herself "to be governed by their opinions." She's also mad at Chelsea because they had met during one of her "episodes" (I did not ask her to elaborate), and Chelsea refused to understand that she was having a hard time and she was now feeling guilty for being pissed off at a dead woman. "The me before had some problems," she concluded in a self-aggrandizing way. "But nothing like now. I have a set of stringent principles that I adhere to in order to survive in this world, and my way is how I am going to do things from now on." Monica must be sobbing right about now. She failed again.

Grateful to have stumbled on the outstanding essay Randall Robinson wrote about Haiti back in January 2004: "Honor Haiti, Honor Ourselves; Forget Haiti, Forget Ourselves." I admire Randall Robinson's intelligence. I applaud his boldness. And I am flattered by his earnest concern for the Haitian people. But like most black leaders, Randall Robinson is too soft on sins. The sins of his race, that is. Influential foreign governments are thwarting the Haitian people's effort to create their own brand of democracy, he wrote. While there may be some truth—and perhaps a lot of truth—in his allegation, how much longer will poor and uneducated black people continue to blame white men for their stunted evolution? Or to keep viewing them as the panacea to their problems? (That's not saying that I do harbor a deep-seated resentment toward white men. If truth be told, I am very much impressed by the way many of them use the brains that God gave them. I just find it upsetting to watch black people deifying white people the same way I find it upsetting to watch women deifying men and religious folks deifying God's messengers.)

Grateful for the presentiment that I will have to let go of my long-standing fixation with seeking the truth once I am done writing the memoir because my life will be more bearable if I simply learn to go along with all the bullshit. Maybe some happiness will even flow my way if I cement the decision by giving up my "dangerous beliefs" about God through becoming a good Christian woman (Hello, Reverend Yozefu-Balikuddembe Ssemakula, better known at STM as Father Joseph.) Also grateful for the presentiment that I will have to edit the memoir myself, then self-publish it, if I want to maintain control over its subject matter, its format, its front cover, its back cover, and last but not least, its spine. And, no, I won't be overly discomfited if more than a few mistakes turn up in the book because I never claimed to be a professional editor, or an English teacher. Hell, English isn't even my second language. And in the strangest of ironies, I don't even read or write my first language.

Flashback du jour: Being told by ExHusband a year or two ago after I gave him some unwanted spiritual advice in another failed attempt to turn him into Father of the Year: "Sure, I should definitely turn my life over to God. Look at the great job he's doing with yours." (He did apologize, but the comment still stings in light of the fact that God has yet to prove him wrong.)

Disgruntlement du jour: "I ain't lying to you, girl, there would have been a riot in that town if it was my brother they had messed with," the latest guest from Georgia just said to Kaycee Boneheaded. What is she talking about? I don't know and I don't care, but it saddens me that black people have yet to take that word out of their vocabulary (and their common consciousness), given that their neighborhoods have always been the biggest victim of their own rioting.

Hilarity du jour: "*Salope!*" Sabine sneered after an unsightly, unschooled, unmarried and unemployed white Shameless who went into labor with her last child in another homeless shelter a year ago told us that she was pregnant. When the woman asked me to translate, I told her: "She said congratulations!" The *salope* smiled from ear to ear. But then again she looks like the type who would have smiled even if she understood French. These women simply have no character, plain and simple.

Disturbance du jour: Seeing Nicolitta and her latest lover, a skinny brunette who also looks like a crackhead, in the midst of a loud argument in front of the main library. Last I heard, Nicolitta had left Tallahassee to go back to her family in New Jersey when her relationship ended with the black rascal she began to date after she and Darla broke up. Dear God, please let this emotionally ill girl know that you didn't give her a vagina just so she could use it as a dumping-ground out of loneliness or lust.

Wonderment du jour: Ninabelle and Lavermine have been so nice to each other lately that Ninabelle started to call the malefactor "Miss Lavermine." Guess who was calling Lavermine an old bag and a nasty piece of work when I came in this evening? All told, The Shameless praise one another one minute, tear each other down the next, make up a day or two later, only to start the whole dog-eat-dog pattern all over again. It's enough to make you wonder if those women are even aware that they can learn to express their frustration and anger without having to resort to razor-sharp tactics that border on the archaic.

Cri de coeur du jour: I finally found some free time to read the articles on depressive children and faith-based prison programs that were published in the Nov. 20 – Dec. 3, 2006 issue of "*State*," FSU's faculty and staff bulletin. I will not waste time commenting on elementary-school children filling out questionnaires on depression except to say that it makes me sick that the mental health experts are making such a killing diagnosing young people with mental illnesses (and that was before I even heard of "preschool depression.") And because I still believe in a God whose power can be seen on earth by anyone who genuinely seeks him out, I felt even worse after I read that some people were pushing for the need to have more evidence-based programs in prison because there was little proof that faith-based programs actually reduce the rates of recidivism. Dear God, if I only knew why you were keeping yourself so well-hidden?

The following conversation took place between a worker on FSU campus and myself on my way back to the hellhole this afternoon:

>Cheer up! It can't be that bad.
>
>Why do you say that?
>
>Because you don't look like you want to go.
>
>I don't want to go.
>
>Keep praying. He will work it out. He always does.

I guess I am beginning to wear my misery in Tallahassee the same way I wore it in New York City. Dear God, do you have any idea how disappointed I am in you?

"Hallelujah! Thank you, Jesus. I do praise you, Lord! Jesus, Jesus, Jesus. Hallelujah! Thank you for providing for me again, Lord." Those words are actually being said by a woman in the back room, but I can hear her as distinctly as if she were two feet away. Black women at The Shelter are such a perfect illustration of how off-putting it is to be a loud woman that I've redoubled my efforts to learn to lower my voice while speaking because I, too, am a loud black woman. And what is she so thankful for? From what I gathered, she got tired of her braids and cut them off, but didn't know what she was going to do with her hair until she gets them redone at the end of the month, but a fellow Shameless made her day by giving her . . . she just walked past me, on her way to the dining room to show off her new hairstyle. Dear Jesus, since this good-looking but very dark-skinned woman seems to be a big fan of yours, please do me a favor by letting her know just how ridiculous she looks in that blonde wig. While we're on the subject, I heard Z'Laitah say this morning that the reason why she wears fake hair is because men do not like women with short hair. I made no comments because I didn't want her to think that I was eavesdropping, but, Dear God, women don't like men with small penises either, then why isn't penis augmentation as fashionable as hair extensions and breast implants?

Feel so worn out by all the chaos around me that I want to cry more than I want to write, but I need to write to calm my nerves down, if nothing else.

- My towel didn't come back with the laundry because the CS worker who got the clothes out of the dryer thought that it belonged to The Shelter, and by the time I realized it, she had already passed it on to another Shelter guest. And now I have to buy a new towel because I am not about to start sharing towels with those people, too.

- Armed with a can of bathroom cleaner, a very quiet Zhouli has been cleaning her mattress all week, but she must be satisfied with her work at last because she's sleeping on the bare mattress tonight. (Zhouli virtually begged TPD to take her to jail a year or so later after she was asked to leave The Shelter for acting crazy and she had nowhere to go. She was eventually deported, according to Mr. ShelterDirector.)

- My ears are so sore from wearing earplugs that I was tempted to go line up with The Shameless for some Tylenol PM. To top it all off, I woke up with several red itchy dots over my stomach and am now wondering if the damn bed is infested with bedbugs. (They made their grand arrival five years later. A nightmare in and of itself. And it didn't take long to realize that the battle of the bedbugs was not mine to win because the pesky creatures were more clever than I ever could be.)

- Shelterqueen was standing in front of her locker singing and humming at 5:07 this morning and I had to say something. In retaliation, she's been talking about dumb-ass foreigners who are blue in their hearts and don't belong in America all evening, and images of a can of red paint being dumped on the white-as-snow bedspread that one of her friends, "a powerful lawmaker who works on Capitol Hill," just gave her for Christmas has been dancing in my head nonstop.

- Prostitute-turned-prophetess Labrina, Ninabelle, Bekkie-Sue, and Kaycee Boneheaded just finished presiding over another Bible study. Father Lord always sends an omen to Labrina whenever the police is on their way to arrest her or any close relatives, the Holy Ghost told Ninabelle in a dream that she will be a married woman by her next birthday, Bekkie-Sue stopped smoking weed five days ago, and not one cuss word has come out of Kaycee Boneheaded's sacrosanct mouth since she found Jesus twelve years ago. Switching gears, she's now telling the fascinating story of an African scientist who had invented a cure for AIDS back in the late '80s, but kept it to himself because the greedy white scientists wanted him to give it away to them for free.

- Mr. Grouch did not serve me dinner tonight because I was still in the bathroom when he did his head count. Since I had no idea that dinner was going to be served five minutes early, I went downstairs to complain and was given a plate, but I am still seething. Do Shelter staff really think that they can penalize me for the slightest infraction when Lavermine is terrifying people day in, day out and they don't care? I know I keep saying this, but I'll say it again: I just cannot believe that my obedience to God got me into this mess. The worst is that I have no idea how to get myself out of it. "Go get a job!" most people say. As if a job will solve my financial problems. As if a job will heal my broken heart. As if a job will restore my dignity in my eyes and the eyes of my loved ones. As if a job will provide me with a testimony of God's redeeming love, mercy and power to bring to the land of my birth.

Cannot believe that I couldn't find anything about Léon Dimanche online (JP introduced me to YouTube.) I didn't expect to find all his songs, but you would think that such classics as *Bon Voyage, Nostalgie, Va-t'en* or *Adieu* would be on the Net. I bet the Frank Sinatra of Haiti would have been known internationally if he was born, say, on French soil. (Many of his songs can now be found on the Web with music videos that are so stupefyingly mediocre that they make my skin crawl.)

Cannot believe that The Shelter is buzzing with excitement tonight because The Shameless have been receiving "presents" all day. Who knew that people born and raised in the richest country in the world could be satisfied with so little? Dear God, do you have any idea how hard it is for me to say thank you to all those people handing out soaps, washcloths, deodorants, hand sanitizers, lip gloss, dental floss, and so on, when the only person I want to receive a present from is you? Meanwhile, if I receive one more pair of cheap white socks I may just start screaming.

Cannot believe that when I told JP, who got injured while playing basketball with his coworkers, that all he needs to do is to stay off his feet for a few days, he cagily replied that Angie thinks he should go to the hospital and that even Angie's mom who used to work in the medical field said that he can become crippled from two strained ankles if he doesn't see a doctor. It felt as if he was questioning not only my maternal wisdom but my love, and that hurts so much since he always trusted my judgment before. And why is Angie's mother giving medical advice to my multicultural American-born son when she knows so little about him that she told her daughter to be extra careful with JP on the basis of his Haitian lineage?

Cannot believe that there was an article on the front page of today's *Democrat* asking the community for help because The Shelter is in desperate need of donations. The president of The Shelter's board of directors was quoted as saying that there was an increase in homelessness all over the country, which brought back to mind an article I recently read about all the problems Las Vegas is facing in its efforts to curb its homeless population. Wonder if the number of homeless rights advocates would shrink if they were required to live incognito in a homeless shelter for thirty days before they get hired. (Sorry, Jake. I know this book is probably going to undermine the hard work you're been doing on behalf of The Shelter, but . . . but I told the truth. And believe it or not, I used to have *almost* as much compassion for the homeless as you do until I landed at The Shelter.)

Cannot believe that I found myself hugging Lavermine, even though no gun was pointed to my head, after she pleaded with me to come down the bunk because she was having a bad day and felt that I am the only person at The Shelter who can truly understand how an intelligent woman like her ended up homeless. (She's not intelligent, but brainless she's not.) The long and short of the story is that I stifled my repugnance and embraced *El Diablo,* the exceptionally fitting nickname that was given to her a year later by Anna R., a worth-mentioning songwriter who also became a target of Lavermine soon after she and her three adorable children set foot inside The Shelter. I even exhibited a pretense of kindliness when she confessed that she was overwhelmed with shame because she had let alcohol and drugs take over her life when the reality is that I don't even understand how any right-thinking black person would even entertain the thought of experimenting with illegal drugs after seeing the havoc drug addiction has wreaked in black communities.

Acknowledgment du jour: Never imagine that the following thought would cross my mind, let alone register in my consciousness, but I can't deny that while Z'Laitah still has her moments and is definitely an impetuous and self-seeking woman by nature, she has been acting relatively normal since her hospital stay. I wish I could give you the credit, God, but it's not you. It's the pills.

Decision du jour: Using the dollar JP gave me for bus fare to buy another Florida Lotto ticket not because I finally had the dream I've been waiting for—the dream in which God says to me: "Joséphine, you can go buy that winning ticket now. Today is your deliverance day." But because I am hurting and my children are hurting and ten million dollars are up for grabs . . . well, maybe $2.5 after the I.R.S. and all the sharks take their cuts, but that's not the point.

Breaking news du jour: Being told by Monica (I used JP's phone to call her) that she and LeMec are now living in Fort Myers with a couple they met on the road. She got a job as a translator, and is in the process of encouraging LeMec to go look for work. He misses his old friends dearly, but she's helping him cope with the change the best she could. It goes without saying that I spent a good amount of time gossiping with Sharon on all of the above, and we're both looking forward to the sequel. (Monica, the Gypsy girl, biked away from LeMec less than a month later.)

Satisfaction du jour: JP admitting that if he had listened to me he would not have to worry about the whopping emergency room bill that is undoubtedly on its way. And in spite of what The Shameless have to say about TMH, I am very grateful for the timely, efficient, and friendly service that they provided to my son, in spite of his lack of health insurance. (Shelter guests have a very complex relationship with TMH. Many of them swear that the service there is shockingly inadequate, yet the ambulance is at The Shelter so often that the 9-1-1 folks might as well keep one on standby in The Shelter's driveway.)

Sadness du jour: Learning that ExRoommate was kind enough to drop JP off at the hospital, but could not pick him up because she was busy baking cupcakes. A big argument I had with ExRoommate years ago in the kitchen of 2900 Upshur Street instantly rushed back to mind. Briefly put, I was struggling to become abstinent in OA, and she was determined to bake a cake. The cake batter ended up on the kitchen floor, and we didn't speak for days. Dear God, please help this daughter of mine understand that food addiction is the leading intergenerational disease/coping mechanism/ bad habit—depending on who you ask—in our family, and that it will ultimately destroy her if she doesn't learn to put a bridle on it.

Exasperation du jour: Another article about The Shelter in today's paper. Dear *Tallahassee Democrat*, it does not take a rocket scientist to deduce that if every able-bodied Shelter residents were charged a few dollars a night (they have money for cigarettes, alcohol, drugs, sex, cell phones, fast food, and God knows what else, don't they?), or required to share half of their food stamps with The Shelter, or assigned to do daily chores, or disciplined whenever they display animalistic behavior, most of them would not have stayed long enough to turn the place into a bastion of shamelessness. I heard Mr. Jejune once said that The Shelter should be renamed "The Leon County Mental Institution," but "The Epicenter of Savageness in the Heart of Tallahassee" would be a more appropriate name. (The Haven of Rest, unlike The Shelter, does have a code of conduct for both residents and visitors, and they don't hesitate to ask you to leave the premises if you violate it.)

Reality check du jour: Angie calling JP every five minutes while he was at the emergency room until I picked up the phone and told her in my nicest and most conciliatory voice that he'll call her back once we leave the hospital. She then wanted a minute-by-minute account of the experience, and I had to put my foot down to stop him from getting on a Greyhound bus to go join her for Christmas. Hard to believe that the girl managed to steal my son from me in such a short amount of time, but she did. (Four years later, I still have a hard time accepting that I am no longer the No. 1 woman in my son's life, even though Angie stopped intruding on my alone time with JP long ago and even asked me to come along when they were about to leave Tallahassee in the summer of 2009. Dear God, please help me accept the harsh realities of motherhood since it looks like *The Girl Who Stole My Son* is going to grow up to be my son's life partner and the mother of his children.)

A very painful day during which being homeless lay heavily on my mind every single minute. Literally got sick at the sight of the usual Shelter guests who camp out at McDonald's every morning when I went there on my way to Bethel to wish a Merry Christmas to Sharon since she got permission to stay out tonight and I don't plan to get in until ten tomorrow night. Got even more annoyed during the next few hours as I listened to Rev. Holmes and Monsignor Tugwell's dazzling sermons on the miracle of the virgin birth as if Mary was the first (mythical) virgin on earth who has ever given birth. Annoyance gave way to in extremis despair after checking the lottery results when I got to the main library. And despair gave way to anger after reading another article on the gender pay gap that still persists in this day and age, despite so many women being their sole head of household. (If women are serious about equal pay, why don't they stop buying shoes and clothes for ninety days and see what happens?) Incidentally, tonight's Bible study just ended. Kaycee Boneheaded has been anointed by God just like Elijah, and is thinking about becoming an evangelist. (Being an evangelist, for what it's worth, is the long-term goal of roughly one out of two black Shameless.) And who is she talking about at this moment in time? The very blessed Juanita Bynum who has been so useful to millions of black women all over the country and I can't help thinking that if Juanita Bynum is the prophetess of No More Sheets, I must then be the prophetess of No More Weaves. (If being a weaveless black woman is good enough for the first African-American first lady, it should be good enough for most, if not all, black women. And God bless Robin Roberts for the courage to ditch her wig, as the world watched, while undergoing breast cancer treatment. And for the confidence to keep her hair short as she continues to reach greater professional heights.)

Grateful that the rain did lighten up on my way to JP's this morning because I later heard on the news that Tallahassee hasn't seen so much rain on Christmas Day since 1897. Grateful for a wonderful day in JP's company, even though all we had for dinner was ham and cheese sandwiches. Grateful he understood why I could not bring myself to wish him a Merry Christmas. (The way I see it, there was nothing merry about our Christmas.) Also grateful for an opportunity to have another candid conversation with him about women's anatomy after he showed me several pictures of him and Angie taken over the summer. To come to the point, I took one good look at Angie in an itsy bitsy bikini and told him that he needs to be aware of the possibility that her belly may never look the same again once she gets pregnant because even if she starts doing sit-ups right after the placenta comes out and lose all her baby weight within 72 hours like the average celebrity mommy (the ones who did not carry fake "baby bumps," that is), a few recalcitrant muscles never regain their original firmness and even if they do, a layer of loose skin is likely to stay behind. JP responded to all of that by saying that I am one of those people who can only be found in movies, and that he plans to milk my character to the max when he someday writes a script that is loosely based on his life. And who does he plan to have play me? Not Kimberly Elize. Not Angela Bassett. Not Viola Davis. But "Joan" from "Girlfriends" because I am as peculiar as the character, he says.

Grateful that I've finally learned to put greater emphasis on what people do as opposed to what they say. I just don't understand why James Brown, a man who was arguably the epitome of all that is wrong with black America, could have ever been a spokesperson for black pride when it was blindingly clear that he, too, suffered from the Michael Jackson syndrome—minus the skin bleaching, the white children, and some other stuff . . . JP thought I was joking when I told him that poor black people around the globe should refrain from dancing and listening to music for a whole year and use the time to assess their standing in the world, devise new behavior modification techniques, and create a different reality for themselves, but I was not. I love music, too, have great respect for accomplished musicians, and am fully aware of the therapeutic value of most musical compositions, but too much singing and dancing, and too little thinking about the link between bad choices and social-economical status, have created adversities of astronomical proportion for the black race, and can't be good for its soul. (I sincerely hope that Bob Herbert and Leonard Pitts, two of my favorite columnists, won't hold an eternal grudge against me for this one. Though after reading Mr. Herbert's August

20, 2010 column "Too Long Ignored" in which he called black America's apathy toward the cancers that have been allowed to metastasize in their communities a "screaming shame," I daresay that he should cut me some slack.)

Grateful that Patoutou's young mind has yet to be corrupted by all the foolish expectations the world places on this one day, and she sounded as pleasant as usual when she answered "Not yet" after I asked if Santa had brought her something. (Lulu's husband, who will soon transform himself into a churchgoing devil whose only hobby is to maintain a reign of terror in his own home, is laid off again.) Patoutou did go on to say that Santa promised to bring her a belated gift, but I still feel like a failure of a godmother.

Not grateful that I am already worrying about where I am going to spend the day tomorrow since the libraries will remain closed and I am not about to show my face at JP's again because Angie is due back home, and I don't want to impose. (JP later told me that Angie takes umbrage at the fact that I only visit when she's not there, but because I am acutely aware of how little it would take for me to turn into a "monster in law," I'll rather her complain about not seeing me than about seeing too much of me.)

Sitting on the usual bench at Tallahassee Mall because I couldn't think of anywhere else to go after I left St.Thomas More. On my mind this morning:

> (1) Poverty and immune system – The red dots over my body did stop itching and disappeared altogether, but my head and throat hurt all night and yellow mucus was what came out when I coughed this morning. Was a bit nervous until I remembered that I survived months of coughing up yellow and green stuff as a child, and will most likely survive now.

(2) Writing and perception – A security guard just walked by and he not only smiled, he waved. I guess I should be thankful for the veneer of respectability that writing gives me. Otherwise, I would simply be one more homeless woman, loitering around. Still, I can't help wondering how long it will take him to figure me out and to treat me accordingly. I could never adapt to this lifestyle, and do not understand how The Shameless can be so carefree.

(3) Winter break and idleness – I can't wait for the spring semester to begin for not having a set schedule to follow is downright excruciating. I can always go sit in my purple chairs at Strozier (I sit on one and put my feet on another just like a real student), but the mere thought of being under the same roof with people from The Shelter when the students are not around makes my chest cramp. (Strozier was forced to change its policies after a gruesome incident took place on its fourth floor in the fall of 2008. A "guest card" is now issued to visitors, which must be used to enter and exit the library, children under the age of fourteen must be accompanied by an adult, and the homeless invasion came to an end once and for all after they made it impossible to access their computers without a FSUID and password.)

(4) Lying and mating – And guess who was standing in the driveway when I walked out of the kitchen at 6:22? A well-dressed, well-rested, and almost handsome Sparky. He said that spending nearly two weeks in his parents's mansion (I am exaggerating, but not by much) felt so good that he only came back to Tallahassee because he can't afford to miss this semester since he's due to graduate in the spring and is starting a job at the courthouse next week. He obviously forgot that he had told me that

his parents's main residence is in South Carolina, not Ohio, that he's graduating next fall, and that he started the courthouse job weeks ago. (Sparky did eventually graduate, left The Shelter a month or two later, and did not come back. And by the summer of 2010, many Shelter residents were taking classes at TCC by and large because all you had to do to get a "free check" every semester, they say, is to maintain a 2.0 GPA.)

(5) Character education and self-control – Saw Andrelene and her new boyfriend (old boyfriend is back in jail) near the Haven of Rest on my way to Mass and was very much taken aback when she told me that she was banned from The Shelter a few days ago because she was having some personal problems and came in "a bit tipsy" (she, too, turned out to be a practicing alcoholic) and attempted to choke Lavermine after Lavermine ridiculed her for being drunk. I did not realize how imperative it is to teach children self-control at an early age until I met these women. This isn't to say that I don't feel like choking the she-devil myself some days. To be clear, Lavermine can drive somebody crazy in any number of ways, without saying a word. She smirks. She chuckles. She grunts. She grimaces. She rolls her eyes. Or she simply shakes her head and giggles whenever she sees you. She also makes it a point to go fart next to people she doesn't like. What's more, the line between her enemies and her friends is so blur that I've heard her say on more than one occasion that Kaycee Boneheaded is not a friend of hers.

(By January 31, 2010, I was so sick of Lavermine, who was by that time cracking jokes about the earthquake in Haiti, that I sent an email to Mr. ShelterDirector in which I daringly asked whether he was being blackmailed by

Lavermine. By March 1, 2010, I was so disgusted that I shot off another email to Mr. ShelterDirector—and to TaMaryn Waters, a *Tallahassee Democrat* reporter who had just done a pity piece on homelessness in which a very grateful Lavermine was quoted. Lavermine's picture was not in the paper, but she was one of the characters in Ms. Waters's melodramatic montage that premiered on tallahassee.com on Sunday, February 28, 2010. As it turns out, the evil beast either got her disability check and/or her "settlement money," and left The Shelter on April 30, 2010. The topic at the dining table that evening: "The wicked witch is gone. Thank you Jesus." One woman even threatened to commit suicide if Lavermine comes back. As for me, I was so demoralized by four years of Shelter living that her departure didn't provide any stress relief. In fact, I still expected her to come back "home" a week later, especially after Mr. ShelterDirector told me out of the blue on May 3 that Lavermine is depressed because she misses The Shelter. I was furious, but I can't say that I was surprised when she came for her first visit on May 12, and even stayed for dinner—gumbo from Planet Gumbo. She began to do "volunteer work" two days later, but that, too, didn't surprise me because I knew by then that The Shelter is a place that rewards people for being the worst that they can be. Yet at the same time, I am also very much aware that I would not have had the motivation, the self-confidence, the single-mindedness, nor the time, to write this book without my torturous experience at The Shelter. A confirmation that God does indeed behave in "strange and unexpected ways at times," to quote Father Joseph.)

Cannot believe that I got so distraught after I finished reading *The End of Faith* that I went to dictionary.com to confirm the meaning of the word "faith." Monsignor Tugwell once said in a homily that Christians must come together and shine their lights into the darkness of atheism and I disagree because I don't believe that there is anything "dark" about atheism. It doesn't take a "dark" person to question the existence of God in a world that is more saturated with sorrow than grace, just an intelligent and courageous one. Faith is not enough. At least, not anymore. Simply stated, God's actions speak much louder than God's words. And at this point in time, the world needs God's actions more than it needs God's "Word." (And I desperately hope that you do agree with me on all the above, Dear God, because my life is going to be ruined beyond repair if you don't.)

Cannot believe that world-class Freudian projectionist B'Laitah, who is in a lovely mood tonight because her lover boy who has been making quite a bit of money selling plasma bought her a new pair of running shoes, told me in all seriousness that I'll be a liability to the people I want to help because of my elitist attitude, which is an indicator of the self-hatred I work so hard to conceal. "Your behavior toward people is not compatible with your belief system," is how she put it. And when I asked her to give me an example, she looked me square in the face and said that I am always talking about God while I look down my nose at people, and that wasn't godly behavior. I told her that my dream was to help needy women in search of a better life for themselves and their children, not pleasure seekers taking advantage of the system while they insist on behaving like animals. And I thank you, God, for the sagacity to hear this woman out, yet not to listen.

Cannot believe that JP, who was at the main library downloading more songs when he should have been home resting his ankles, said that I sounded like an old racist white man after I told a teenage boy, whose pants were hanging so low he could barely walk, to tighten his belt because I didn't want to see his underwear. So, there I was having to explain to my own son that while racist people criticize black people in order to prove their points about our innate inferiority, I criticize black people in the hope that they will become conscious of how they are contributing to their own suffering. (We should not expect the police to stop doing what they do, if we're not willing to stop doing what we do. And our students will never excel in school—regardless of how high-performing the teachers—if the value of an education is not promoted at home where the kind of character building that matters the most in life begins. Maybe Congress should consider passing a law that requires the parents of failing students to attend parenting class.)

Gratitude du jour: That my mother still functions fairly well mentally and physically on the eve of her 79th birthday, in spite of her various health problems, and that she has such a strong support from her Seventh-day Adventist Church—a humbling reminder of the social importance of religion. (My mother keeps changing for the better as she got older, and even sent me money—voluntarily—a handful of times this year alone. On a related note, ExHusband flew to Haiti shortly after the earthquake, came back a "changed man," and has been making some efforts to be a better parent to at least one of his oranges: our daughter. And speaking of ExRoommate, she has gone from overweight to obese in recent times but still denies that she has a food addiction, has attended more colleges than Tea Party First Lady Sarah Palin, changed her major more times than she can recall, and is still nowhere near receiving her bachelor's degree. And I just hope that she soon comes to the realization that being smarter than average doesn't amount to much without the adoption of the healthy daily habits that can conceivably turn an ordinary life into an extraordinary one since the only people she has any respect for are those who seemingly live extraordinary lives.)

Sadness du jour: Not answering the phone when Joline called because I can't bring myself to speak to anyone lately, with the exception of JP, Lulu and Patoutou. (By January 2012, my spirit was so broken that I didn't even want to speak to Patoutou. I had also made up my mind that, in order to hold on to the little bit of sanity that I had left, I will be gone from The Shelter long before the end of the year even if that means becoming a prostitute since a couple of old geezers who religiously cruise the streets of Tallahassee in the early morning hours seem to find me very attractive. I still don't know where I found the emotional wherewithal to survive the impasse when I was more than sure that a cruel God had played a joke on me and that it was up to me to regain control of my life, but my abiding gratitude goes to RAW, a k a Mr. Professor, for coming into my life a few months later, even though "forever" was never an option for us since he's almost as destitute as I am in the aftermath of a drama-filled divorce and a loss of full-time employment. For introducing me to persimmons, NPR, and the fishing world. For giving me a small radio that turned out to be a vital stress buster in the struggle to stave off insanity. For taking the word "breathtaking" to a whole new level. And for being such a chilling reminder that love is indeed a four-letter word.)

Frustration du jour: Reading that homicide is up in Houston courtesy of hurricane Katrina evacuees, and down in New Orleans because half of the population is gone. While poverty does indeed beget all kind of vices, poverty alone is no longer an acceptable excuse for the kind of sinfulness that is allowed to breed and fester in the communities of a group of people who advertise their Jesusness so unbridledly. Since Jesse Jackson and Al Sharpton clearly have an affinity for marches, I suggest that they capitalize on their God-given talent by pioneering an era of racial self-questioning, mind reprogramming, character reshaping and image rebuilding through consciousness-raising marches, one bad neighborhood at a time, then launch a full-fledged Moral Fitness Crusade by 2020. (Maybe they'll even be an inspiration to Haitians in the process. After all, how can "a new Haiti" be built—with, hopefully, a new capital city far away from earthquake-prone Port-au-Prince—when Haitian officials don't seem to realize that the absence of trustworthy leadership not only scare investors away, but also make them look power-hungry and incompetent, to say nothing of callous and greedy. And when the average Haitian has nothing but scorn for the land that their ancestors died for. A land that, I believe, can regain much of its original beauty and worth by 2040—Prior to becoming *la risée des Caraïbes et de la communauté internationale,* Haiti used to be known as La *Perle des Antilles*—if dirt poor Haitians are willing to stop their descent into deeper levels of hell through renouncing some of their self-defeating beliefs and behaviors, developing more productive mental habits, and creating a healthier and more respectable culture. In plain English, why should God show mercy on Haiti when so many Haitians are ashamed of one of God's greatest creations—themselves. And showing no respect to their compatriots. And relying on other human beings to deliver them from hell on earth. And wasting precious time and energy venerating—how shall I put this—valueless and diabolical idols. Call me what you like, but there is no doubt in my mind that experiences also trail expectancies as far as poverty and everlasting misery are concerned.)

Shelter quotes of the day:

"I ate so much I feel as if I am going to have a heart attack," a self-satisfied Shelterqueen cried out on her way downstairs to go get a razor since she had forgotten to get one at check-in time and can't afford to step out of The Shelter with unshaved legs because her man can't stand hairy women. "Let's hope that it's a fatal one," I thoughtlessly mumbled to myself. A very stupid thing to say given that death is the last thing that I would wish on that woman. As a matter of fact, I wish Lavermine eternal life. In hell. Right here on earth.

"Girl, I am serious. If I ain't, you better believe I is going to try again," Ninabelle, who is in a state of high excitement over her doctor's appointment next week, later said to a drunk Bekkie-Sue who just lost another job because her unreasonable boss expected her to be on time every day. And it took all I got not to blurt out that she should at least learn to speak proper English before giving birth to another child because while Ebonics may be The Shelter's lingua franca, she won't get very far in mainstream America if it's all she can speak.

"I can't wait for her to go. *Elle me tape sur les nerfs. Je ne peux plus la supporter. C'est une autre folle,*" Sabine told me in response to Kaycee Boneheaded's announcement that her son wants her to go stay with him and his girlfriend to help care for her two-week-old grandchild. Sabine and Kaycee Boneheaded used to get along just fine until Kaycee Boneheaded spent a few nights in bed 1. I guess the saying that you don't really know someone until you live with them also applies to Shelter life. (Sabine got a subsidized apartment and left The Shelter in 2008 and has been sober since, as far as I know. Labrina moved in with her nephew in a nearby town after one last trip to jail. And according to Ninabelle who turned out to be Labrina's third cousin, Labrina now has a new occupation that she's very proud of, babysitting her grandnieces and her grandson, and is even thinking about going back to school since earning a college degree has always been a dream of hers. Marvy came back to Tallahassee months later, and died from alcoholism shortly thereafter.)

"She's very depressed and just needs to take more meds. Just ignore her." What Shelter staff reportedly told a frantic Sharon when she went downstairs to complain after Z'Laitah walked up to her moments after lights out and proceeded to belittle her for reasons that didn't make sense to anyone listening. Feel so stupid to have believed even for a minute that such a self-absorbed woman, with no desire to be a better human being, could be changed by antidepressants. And it makes my blood boil that depression is such a convenient explanation for every cultural, spiritual, and environmental malady under the sun. (That being the case, it shouldn't come as a surprise that reading the preface of Irving Kirsch's *The Emperor's New Drugs: Exploring the Antidepressant Myth* turned out to be the best antidepressant pill I could have taken on the morning of July 24, 2010, especially since my eyes unexpectedly welled up with tears an hour earlier when I had asked Brother Paul, the gentleman who took over the Frenchtown Breakfast in the Park after our Lord Jesus Christ called Pastor Eric to other ministry opportunities, whether he would have followed his own advice and "joyfully" carry his cross if God's will for him was to be homeless.)

Grateful that the food monster has been staying in its cage lately, especially after my mother told me that a close relative of ours is about to undergo angioplasty to unblock a clogged artery. Do I expect the food monster to remain in its cage forever? No. But I trust that you, God, will continue to give me the strength to not give him too much attention when he escapes again. Also grateful for the certainty that you can and will regulate my hormones the same way you're teaching me how to regulate my emotions. (I haven't had a hot flash since, knock on wood. But I still have night sweats every now and then, especially after I was moved to bed 24 and found myself sharing a windowless room that is about fifteen feet long and eight feet wide with seven other women, many of them of unsound mind, though, thankfully, Lydia B., known in certain circles as Roxaaaanne!!!, is smart. And sane. And well-behaved.)

Grateful to Don Piper for giving me a glimpse of what can happen when God decides to mold a soul though a physical breakdown. Though if I were given a chance to spend ninety minutes in the vicinity of heaven (he didn't actually pass through the pearly gates), I think I would have made better use of my time because I would have been more determined to have a talk with the Creator rather than with dead relatives. Also grateful that Mr. Piper readily admits that he's still skeptical of other people's near-death experience, which means, I hope, that he won't be too upset with me for my own skepticism. And since I love flowers more than I love gold, the streets of my heaven will assuredly be paved with forsythias, daffodils, tulips, peonies and azaleas in the spring. Zinnias, marigolds, petunias, periwinkles, impatiens, cannas, caladiums, coleus, dahlias, daisies, begonias, geraniums, portulacas, celosias, hollyhocks, black-eyed Susans, coneflowers, hydrangeas, and Oriental lilies in the summer. Yellow chrysanthemums in the fall. And royal blue pansies in the winter.

Grateful that my feelings were not hurt when I told Z'Laitah that it's hard to accept that I am going to start a new year in a homeless shelter as a result of my choice to remain obedient to God in good times and bad times and she dryly replied, "You made a mistake, that's all. Lots of people make mistakes based on their spiritual beliefs." She also said that I am still mourning the loss of my home because I had gained a lot of validation from being a homeowner and my identity was tied up to the house. And I didn't bother to tell her that I was always more proud of being the owner of the best looking flower garden in my neighborhood than I was of being a homeowner. (I still see Z'Laitah at the main library from time to time, but she was indefinitely banned from The Shelter for physical assault in the first half of 2009 after a series of thirty-day bans for similar offenses. I was never one of her victims, but she did tell me once that she considers me to be "THE SCUM OF THE EARTH," and my feelings are still hurt since the opinions of deranged Shelter folks mean so much to me.)

Grateful that I am not afflicted with empty-headedness like most women at The Shelter. "Dang, there must be something in the water. Everybody is dropping dead these days," the new heavily-tattoed blonde with multiple nose rings, eyelashes long enough to make Tammy Faye Bakker blush, and a small number of missing front teeth exclaimed when she entered the dining room late last night and I told her that Elizabeth Vargas had just announced that Saddam Hussein is dead. "With respect to Saddam," Z'Laitah began when I asked her opinion on the execution this evening, but quickly rephrased herself by saying, "In regard to Saddam," after a sober Spookipoo growled, "That man does not deserve any respect!" Kaycee Sourpuss who was waiting to see the nurse simply shook her head and groaned, "Unfuckingbelievable!" and I couldn't have said it better myself. (Kaycee Sourpuss was "put out" two years later after one last confrontation with Shelter staff over her deep-seated inability to keep her racist thoughts to herself, and chose to leave Tallahassee for good since she was receiving her disability payments by then and didn't really have to be at The Shelter. The irony that the state of Florida has made the dreams of many of The Shameless come true while I am still waiting on God nearly a decade after eviction day is not lost on me, either.)

3:30 a.m. – Never thought I would say this while I am still at The Shelter, but I am glad to be awake. It took me forever to fall asleep and when I did, it was one nightmare after another. I dreamed that I was facing jail time and the possibility of losing custody of my children, that it was the week before finals and I suddenly remembered about a class I had signed up for but never attended, that one of The Shameless found my journal and share its nitty-gritty with Mr. ShelterDirector, that *la vermine* drove me so crazy

I beat her in the face with a shoe right in the dining room, that I had forgotten to drive a car because I hadn't driven in so long, that my daughter was on the other side of a ditch and I couldn't get to her. Who could have imagined that my dreams alone would compel me to have somewhat of an appreciation for my insomnia?

8:04 p.m. – A quiet evening since many of The Shameless couldn't stomach the thought of spending New Year's Eve in a homeless shelter and thank God because I am about to burst wide open with stress. One of the worst days of my life, no doubt. Don't know if I am more petrified over being followed by FSUPD this morning as I walked from STM to Bethel, or by TPD this evening as I walked from Blessed Sacrament to The Shelter, or by finding out that Daneecia, too, is crazy, in spite of appearing to be perfectly sane all this time. This has got to be a long, horrific dream from which I am going to wake up at any time because it cannot be my life. (For the record, I thought of flagging TPD down just to query if Walking While Black was now a crime in Tallahassee, but I forced myself to practice "restraint of tongue," on account of my homeless status.)

10:06 p.m. – Can't stop obsessing about Daneecia. And how did the most frightening conversation I've ever had with another human being in my entire life begin? I saw the woman at Bethel, to my horror, since The Shameless don't usually go to that church, and next thing I know, she's receiving a blessing at the altar and R.B. Holmes is telling her that he would love to hear more about her line of work. Burning with curiosity, I naturally felt obliged to grill her the first chance I got, and she was more than happy to apprise me of her mystical powers. To sum things up, Daneecia has been called by God to be a Homeland Security expert, a Secret Service agent, an overseer, and an intervener. She's also an unidentified forerunner for the next president, and is thinking about joining the presidential race herself if she can raise the necessary funds.

11:23 p.m. – Back in bed 6 after spending the last fifteen minutes in the stairwell, talking to Sharon. She said not to worry about FSUPD because they can't make an arrest if they haven't first issued a trespass warrant, but stressed the importance of carrying at least one dollar with me at all times because I can be arrested by TPD for vagrancy if I am not carrying any money and a valid ID. (My Maryland driver's license expired last January.) And as far as Daneecia goes, Sharon thought that the whole affair was too funny for words, even after I told her that Daneecia left her husband because she's convinced that the F.B.I. has hired their nine-year-old twins to spy on her. I stared at her in disbelief, too panic-stricken to disclose that I was now *seriously* questioning the mental fitness of every single person at The Shelter, including hers and mine.

And *the never-ending nightmare went on, far away from the streets of Tallahassee. The good news, some might say, is that the spiteful woman who wrote this book was replaced by a much gentler version of herself by the time she landed at the Santa Barbara Rescue Mission in January 2015. So much so that she, of all people, was asked to become a "Volunteer Homeless Guest Monitor" when the time had come for "St. Sarah," the mother of all housemothers, to go back to her fellowship. The ego-deflation process is a mind-altering endeavor, that's for sure.*

9 781634 981965